WOMANHOOD MEDIA:

Current Resources About Women

by

Helen Wheeler

The Scarecrow Press, Inc.
Metuchen, N.J.   1972

Library of Congress Cataloging in Publication Data

Wheeler, Helen Rippier.
  Womanhood media.

  1. Woman--Bibliography. I. Title.
Z7961.W48   016.30141'2   72-7396
ISBN 0-8018-0549-9

CONTENTS

AUTHOR'S NOTE

"Womanhood Media" will be outdated almost as it comes off the press. Although the book collection is detailed and selective, the attempt at comprehensiveness in listing other media, especially audiovisual, must remain just that ... an attempt, with no implied recommendations. The author would appreciate receiving updated information.

INTRODUCTION

The seventh-grade social studies teacher was away
for the day representing the administration at a meeting.
He'd left instructions to divide the class into committees.
I followed the routine, the furniture-moving, the choosing
who would join what committee, etc., and gave them their
final instructions: "After you've established your committee,
elect a chairman." Except that I said, "... elect a chairman or chairwoman, as the case may be." Gales of
laughter.

Another day, this time an elementary school, and I
was subbing for the librarian. A fourth-grade girl blew in
during her free period. Although a "non-reader," she was
a library assistant and enjoyed being there. She determined
that I too would allow her to linger (no one missed her). I
watched her struggle with crayons and paper, and gave her
the Scotch tape she requested. Soon the other kids were
laughing at her: she had taped a crude sign on the front of
"my" desk, in the manner of the regular librarian's, with
my surname prefixed by "MS." Didn't she know how to
spell MRS.? ... maybe she's a MISS ... she's got a ring
though.... I jumped in with something about "If you'd had
a man substitute, what would you put, 'Mister-married' or
'Mister-not-married'?" And up popped Ms. Downtrodden:
"And there isn't any word for girls either--my brother got
an invitation to a birthday party that called him 'Master'!"

If progress is to be made in achieving equality for
men and women, it will be made for the most part by women themselves, for ours is a male-dominated society, and
as such, self-perpetuating. Rage and so-called humanism
are two approaches advocated by some to eliminating sexism
generally and its byproduct/symptom, discrimination in employment, education and government. Unfortunately, flam-
boyant demonstrations are exploited by the male press to
the detriment of the total Movement, including persons working systematically (although not necessarily within the system) at clearly-defined, constructive goals. At the other
extreme are the naive women who advocate goodwill on all

sides for what seems to them to be a PR problem.

        The trend in 1972 is to "put down" Women's Libera-
tion--the male media load the term, select incidents for a
"news coverage" that satirizes, and exploit guests from the
Movement.   They are able to utilize techniques which if applied as blatantly and discriminantly to other groups would
result in governmental or public stricture.   The men are
beginning to run scared; their good thing is threatened.
They have always assumed a superiority which gives them
the right to take over the sidewalk (try Madison Avenue at
mid-day).   Now they are consciously shoving, attempting
things they can get away with because of brute force, more
spending money, a male police, unity, or control of the
mass media and of women.   And it is doubly rewarding to
shove around a female of another race.   Men are especially
threatened by the over-30 woman who is good-looking, self-
sufficient and not humble.   Men are reacting to Women's
Liberation everywhere, as individuals and as groups, and
aligned with them are women victimized into chattering on
about preferring the status quo.   The standard windup of
the Media Male-Duped Dame conversation has become
the righteous declaration, "However, women certainly should
get equal pay for the same job. " But they can't get the
same job--one aspect of the overall inequity of a double-
standard, patriarchal society's disuse and misuse of women.

        Environment and parents' religion and politics shape
our lives, attitudes and self-perception.   Self-knowledge in
combination with intelligence, sensitivity, information and
courage are combined in few individuals, but mature people
who are aware of the inequality which exists between the
sexes have shaken off some of the inevitable indoctrination
to which everyone is subject from the moment of birth.
This book should help to answer some of the questions of
the woman who has just begun to think for herself.   It should
be useful to the participant in and coordinator of varied
types of women's studies programs. * And it provides the
basis for building a book collection supportive of contemporary developments, as well as access to the other media.

---

*A New York Times survey (Suzie Dreyfoos "New college
trend: women studies" Jan. 7, 1971:37) reported 60 colleges and universities offering such courses at the beginning
of 1971, and the demand is growing.   Women's Studies do
not take only the form of courses--they can consist of such

To effect real change, women need a variety of techniques and devices, as well as improved communication, which favor documentation and data over emotion and personal anecdotes. They need to get the attention of other women as well as healthy men. The franchise did not produce radical improvement in woman's condition because it was not accompanied by real social change. In addition to exercising her right to vote, she needs more women candidates for whom she can vote. Products and services associated with advertising that ridicules women and with industries that discriminate against women employees are numerous. Solid refusal to buy the guff peddled by advertising agencies and politicians is a possibility, but in order to exploit the Ballot and the Boycott, the third "B"--the Brain--will have to be used more fully, in introspection, reading, study, reflection, research and documentation.

[*cont.] things as extension meetings, workshops, skills classes, inter-departmental coordinated coursework, and other provisions meeting local needs. See also Chronicle of Higher Education, Nov. 11/30, 1970; and U.S. Women's Bureau Pamphlet no. 10, "Continuing education programs and services for women, 1971."

Part I

A WOMEN'S LIBERATION AWARENESS INVENTORY

The main purpose of the Awareness Inventory which follows is not to test knowledge of such things as the history of the woman's suffrage movement, legislation affecting women, or names in the news. Rather, it should function to evaluate attitude and openmindedness. An effort has been made to set out only factual information, however--there is no room for subjectivity in matters of civil rights or law enforcement, for example.

The Answer Key answers each question and documents the information with sources outside the Movement insofar as possible. References to readings in which topics can be pursued are interspersed; complete information about the books referred to appears in Part III, "A Basic Book Collection." For convenience, the titles in the Basic Book Collection have been serially numbered; these numbers are utilized in the Key in citing some of the sources of data and information. For each question, Key information is generally presented in the following order: (1) the correct answer, (2) documentation of the source of that answer when necessary, and (3) occasional commentary.

1. The Women's Christian Temperance Union played a part in the history of women's rights because it was organized (check the one most appropriate answer:)
    as a kind of early Alcoholics
        Anonymous   all of these
    by and for legally helpless women   none of these
    when drinking was a greater social
        problem than it is now

2. "The law cannot do the major part of the job of winning equality for women. Women must do it for themselves. They must become revolutionaries." This is from the writings of

Susan B. Anthony   Mary Daly
Shirley Chisholm   Abraham Lincoln

3. The cause of female rights and the end of slavery were
linked in the U.S.A.   Why?

4. The official inauguration of the women's movement in
the U.S. as well as the beginning of the international women's movement was the publication in 1792 of Mary Wollstonecraft's "Vindication of the Rights of Women."
        TRUE   FALSE

5. With the advent of the Civil War, women's rights activities in the U.S. virtually halted.
        TRUE   FALSE

6. Historically, American women's clubs were brought into
being by the Industrial Revolution.   They generally served
two purposes: (1) self-education, and (2) . . .
        betterment of social conditions   book reviews
        provision of a meeting-place for
        women not affiliated with churches

7. The only issue on which American women have voted
as a separate group was the Equal Rights Amendment.
        TRUE   FALSE

8. During the American colonial period, women could vote.
        TRUE   FALSE

9. The territory of _____ was the first to give American
women the vote, in 1869.
        Colorado
        Virginia   Wyoming

10.   Elizabeth Duncan Koontz was elected president of the
National Organization for Women in 1970.
        TRUE   FALSE

11.   The "Norwegian Beauvoir" is
        Margaret Bonnevie   Birgitta Linner
        Anna-Greta Leijon

12.   The first U.S. Congresswoman was
        Shirley Chisholm   Jeanette Rankin
        Martha Wright Griffith

13.   The English suffragette who inspired 19th-century
American women to spur on their activities was
      Susan B. Anthony   Lucy Stone
      Emmeline Pankhurst

14.   Jane Addams and Lillian D. Wald were both actively
involved in
      settlement houses   all of these
      social work   none of these
      women's rights

15.   Perhaps the outstanding orator of the early American
women's movement, "a real spellbinder," was
      "Aunt Nancy"   Lucy Stone
      Elizabeth Cady Stanton

16.   "I hope that in future years many women may know the
pride, as I shall know it on the ninth of June, of receiving
an honourary degree from your distinguished university.   I
beg ... that I may be the last woman so honoured, to be
required to swallow from the very cup of this honour, the
gall of this humiliation."   In 1937 a poet was honored by
New York University, only to discover that the banquet at
the Waldorf for male recipients wasn't included! She was
      Emily Dickinson   Virginia Woolf
      Edna St. Vincent Millay

17.   The goal of the Women's March for Equality in August
1970 was
      abortion-on-demand   all of these
      equality employment opportunity   none of these
      free 24-hour day-care centers

18.   The Chinese technique, "speak pains to recall pains,"
is somewhat analogous to rap sessions, or consciousness-
raising, which small groups of radical women began to form
in the 1960's.   Revolutionary feminism utilizes this technique,
and calls it
      a bitch session   group therapy
      a hen party

19.   Founded in 1966, the single largest group within the
Movement (18,000+ members) is
      Aphra   League of Women
      National Organization of   Voters
        Women (NOW)   none of these

20. Acronyms are popular and convenient. For what do the
following stand?
      OWL   WEAL
      SCUM   WITCH

21a. "Shitwork" is the term radical Feminists often use
to refer to . . . .

21b. Liberated women now use the words <u>fuck</u> and <u>screw</u>
to convey
      rape   all of these
      sexual intercourse   none of these
      social intercourse

22. When he asks, "What do you think of Women's Lib?"
he reveals
      his ignorance   all of these
      that he doesn't read   none of these
      that he's scared

23. Use of "Miss" and "Mrs." is discriminatory.
      TRUE   FALSE

24. "The lamb chop is mightier than the karate chop" is
the slogan of
      Bruce Tegner and Alice McGrath,   Men's Lib
         authors of "Self-defense for   The Pussycats
         girls..."

25. Rape is a political crime.
      TRUE   FALSE

26a. Many techniques of self-defense take too long to learn
and cannot be remembered or used without continuing, on-
going practice.
      TRUE   FALSE

26b. Even if the time were available for teaching advanced
techniques of self-defense to girls and women, it would be
neither practical nor desirable.
      TRUE   FALSE

26c. Attacks made on females, whether serious or annoying,
are made in the expectation that no defense will be offered.
      TRUE   FALSE

27.   The two most common mistakes which are made by women who try to defend themselves against a stronger assailant are
      beating with fists against a man's chest
      hitting with the elbow
      pulling back on the assailant's little finger
      trying to squirm or struggle out of a body-grab

28.   The single most important defense for a woman is the
      elbow   side of the hand "chop"
      kick

29.   The Women's March for Equality, Feminists' activities, Women's Liberation, Women's Studies programs, etc. are said by some to detract from that which should have a greater priority, i.e., ending the war in Vietnam.   How would you answer them, assuming that you feel that human equality, i.e., the women's equality movement, is the more important of the two?

30.   The New York Times education editor is _____.

31.   In considering the overall averages for academic ex-cellence, the category of _____ colleges rates the lowest in the nation.
      coeducational   women's
      men's

32.   One specific area where women college and university students have made progress in convincing administrations that they are not children and that they deserve equal treat-ment with male students is
      in loco parentis   parietals
      open-houses

33.   A carefully disguised study of discrimination in college admissions in 240 American universities showed that white applicants were accepted more frequently than black, and that males received preference over females.   In both cases, the data did not quite reach .05 level of significance, how-ever.   An unpredicted and statistically significant result of the study was a sex-by-ability interaction.   What does this mean, and why is it significant?

34.   More U.S. girls than boys have been graduated from high school every year since the Civil War.
      TRUE   FALSE

35.   More women received Ph. D. 's in 1930 than ever before and ever since.
      TRUE   FALSE

36a.   Since 1920, when the Women's Bureau was founded,
many changes in the woman worker have taken place.   THEN
she was most likely to work in _____; TODAY, in _____.
      a factory ... an office   an office ... a factory
      a factory ... a factory

36b.   THEN she was most likely to be _____; TODAY,
_____.
      married ... single   single ... married
      single ... single

36c.   THEN she was typically in her late twenties; TODAY,
in her late _____.
      twenties   forties
      thirties

36d.   Approximately half of all women 18-64 years of age
are in TODAY's labor force; in 1920, approximately _____
were.
      one-quarter   three-quarters
      one-half

36e.   In 1920, the life expectancy of a baby girl was in
her mid-_____'s; TODAY it is in her mid-_____'s.
      60 ... 80   40 ... 80
      50 ... 70

37.   The average income of full-time women workers is
      approximately 60% of men's
      approximately 75% of men's
      almost the same as men's

38.   Most women workers are clericals; most clericals
are women.   However, the average income in 1970 for
women clerical workers was $5,551, while men's was
approximately _____.
      $750 more $3,000 more
      $1,500 more

39.   The Women's Bureau is a part of the U. S. Department of
      Health, Education and Welfare   Justice
      Labor

40. Women account for ____% of those found in tests to
have an aptitude for engineering, yet they supply only a
small percentage of the nation's engineers.
       10%   35%
       25%   40%

41. "Everyone understands the injustice of paying one person less than another for the same work, but there has not
been sufficient concern over the nationwide practice of rele-
gating women to _____."
       dead-end jobs   all of these
       low-paying jobs   none of these
       part-time jobs

42. 19th-century woman's alternatives to marriage generally were governessing, factory work and _____.

43. Approximately _____ of the companies recruiting at
Northwestern University in recent years considered female
graduates for business and industry.
       two-thirds   three-quarters
       90% [inasmuch as discrimination-by-sex is against
       Illinois law]

44. The International Ladies' Garment Workers' Union
membership is made up of a black female and Puerto Rican
female majority. Its leadership is predominantly
       black and Puerto Rican female   white male
       black and Puerto Rican male

45. The year 1962 saw an all-time high for women in
the U.S. Congress, when there were
       20   30   40

46a. The MAJORITY of states have laws limiting the
maximum number of hours a woman can work.
       TRUE   FALSE

46b. The MAJORITY of states have laws ruling that
women cannot have certain jobs which men can have.
       TRUE   FALSE

47. Women make up ____% of the national labor force,
of whom more than _____ work out of economic necessity.
       25% ... one-third   38% ... one-half
       38% ... one-quarter

48.   It has been said that when a male college graduate
applies for a job, he is given an aptitude test, and that when
a female college graduate applies, she is given
    a physical examination   nothing
    a typing test   the Pill

49.   To expedite the Senate's action making "the historic break-
through for women"--female Senate pages--possible, the provi-
sion stipulates
    the appointing Senator must assume full responsibility for
        the safety of his female page in travel to and from the
        Capitol and at her place of residence
    the females' salaries will not be as much as their male
        counterparts' ($7, 380)
    they will not be on the streets of Washington after dark
    they will not enter the Men's Room (to summon spon-
        sors for roll calls, etc.--standard page practice.)

50.   In 18th- and 19th-century London, clerks were men
and women.
    TRUE   FALSE

51.   Across the board, in offices and factories, women
earn an average of $_____ a year less than men for
performing exactly the same work.
    $1, 000 $3, 000
    $2, 000

52.   Newspapers, employers and employment agencies "get
around" the prohibition against sex-discriminatory Help
Wanted ads in the classified section by _____.

53.   In terms of getting the LOWEST percent of what men
get for exactly the same job, the MOST discriminated-against
group of female employees (earning 42. 8% of what their "fellow" workers receive) are
    clerks   saleswomen
    managers and proprietors

54.   In 1968 about one million persons were employed as
professional engineers, of whom _____ were women.
    less than 1%   more than 9%
    more than 5% but less than 9%

55.   Women have probably gained LESS status in _____
than in most other professions in recent years.
    education   medicine
    librarianship   the ministry (theology)

56.   Men outnumber women in the executive, managerial,
top governmental and top scientific positions in Soviet Russia.
     TRUE   FALSE

57.   Most medical schools claim that they hesitate to accept
women because of the fear that they will have children and
drop out before completing their education.   This fear is
largely unfounded: it has been shown that ___% don't marry
until after medical school.
        53%   none of these, i. e. most never
        70%   marry

58a.   There are approximately _____ women physicians
in the U. S. A.
        21, 000   100, 500   205, 000

58b.   U. S. Dept. of Labor statistics for 1968 show that
___% of all physicians are women.
        6- 7%   26-27%   46-47%

59.   Medical schools often discriminate against women applicants, accepting only those
        who are far superior to the average male applicant
        who indicate that they plan to teach and/or research
        whose qualifications are about the same as male
           applicants but who do not request financial assistance

60.   Proportionately, there are more women physicists in
Italy than in America.
     TRUE   FALSE

61.   A concerted effort to recruit women into policy-making
and leadership positions as _____ is being made by _____ .
        faculty ... community junior colleges   all of these
        head librarians ... public libraries   none of these
        foreign service officers ... United States
           Information Agency (USIA)

62.   "It is unheard-of, uncivilised barbarism, that any
woman should still be forced to bear such monstrous torture
.... It is simply absurd that with our modern science painless childbirth does not exist as a matter of course....
What unholy patience, or lack of intelligence, have women
in general that they should for one moment endure this out-
rageous massacre of themselves? ... I tremble with in-
dignation even today when I think of what I endured, and of
what many women victims endure through the unspeakable

egotism and blindness of men of science who permit such
atrocities when they can be remedied," is from the autobiography of

> Isadora Duncan   Queen Victoria
> Margaret Sanger

63.   Girls and women are discriminated against as students
while in school and as employees later in the education
system.   How many specific ways in which this discrimination mitigates against the woman who is an employee of
education can you identify?

64.   The number of women on college faculties and staffs
is about _____ of the total.

> one-fifth   53%
> one-half   two-thirds

65.   Academically competent women are forced out of college teaching by overt discrimination.   A less-obvious means
used is

> belief that qualified women don't exist   all of these
> lack of day-care facilities   none of these
> nepotism

66.   There were _____ women on the faculty of the University of California at Berkeley in 1910 as there were in
1968.

> about the same number of   twice as many
> about half the number of

67.   A survey conducted by the American Society for Personnel Administration and the Bureau of National Affairs
(Bulletin of March 5, 1970) showed that, of companies con-
ducting on-campus job-recruitment interviews, 97% go to
co-ed institutions, 63% go to men's schools, and ____ go
to women's colleges.

> 12%   30%   66%

68.   When employers are confronted with the question of
why they pay women less, their answers are (check 2 or
more)

> 1.   tradition--society and management tend to discrim-
>   inate against women in the employment market.
> 2.   lack of skills--management feels that women have
>   not developed the skills to compete with men.
> 3.   choice--management says women choose to accept
>   jobs that pay less.

4. choice--management says women seek short-term employment rather than careers.

5. lack of mobility--management says women do not have the mobility of men.

6. turnover--management says women have a higher turnover rate than men.

69. At a conference sponsored by the Urban Research Corporation of Chicago in cooperation with IBM, Polaroid, Bank of America, and Sears, Roebuck, the subject of equal pay and promotion for women was discussed at the final session. The speaker--the (male) manager of the Human Relations Division of Polaroid--stating that industry "reacts to stimuli"--went on to say that "The only fear stimulus I can see for the women's movement is the possibility of _____."

consumer boycotts   all of these
government enforcement   none of these
women's unions

70. "Any intelligent woman who reads the marriage contract, and then goes into it, deserves all the consequences," was written by

Isadora Duncan   Zsa Zsa Gabor
George Eliot   Kate Millett

71. Maintenance of a separate domicile by a married woman, even with an intact marriage, is not permitted in many states. She can, however, have good and sufficient reason for needing to maintain a separate domicile--for instance, _____.

72. In proving paternity, the burden of proof is always on the mother.

TRUE   FALSE

73. An unmarried mother has few rights at all; one exception is _____.

74. Females can marry, with parental consent, at age 12 in some states.

TRUE   FALSE

75. Puerto Rico recognizes common law marriage.

TRUE   FALSE

76. According to a Gallup Survey quoted in Family Circle

magazine, husbands two-to-one want their wives to be wage-earners.
TRUE   FALSE

77.   Into which of the following categories do most of the divorced mothers you know fit (assuming that they are typical of such women: several school-age children, no independent income, and little or no savings?)--
   no alimony "awarded" and partial support for the children, with no guarantee of payment
   no alimony "awarded" and full support for the children regularly paid
   alimony "awarded" and full support for the children; the mother enabled financially, if not in other ways, to care for their children.

78.   At the end of World War II, women war-workers were queried by Elmo Roper.   Approximately two out of three wanted to continue working in permanent jobs.
   TRUE   FALSE

79.   The only grounds for divorce existing in ALL states is
   adultery   mental cruelty
   attempt on the life of spouse or endangering life of spouse

80.   Henry Foster, New York University law professor, estimates that ___% of alimony gets paid.
   25%   50%   75%

81.   Lawrence R. Teitlin, professor of industrial psychology at the City University of New York, points out that the percentage of divorces is small at the
   bottom of industry among factory-workers
   middle socio-economic point among white-collar workers
   top of industry among executives

82.   Women can be made to pay alimony in MANY states.
   TRUE   FALSE

83.   Medically, abortion is defined as the termination of pregnancy within the first ___ weeks of gestation.
   12   20   24   28

84.   "D and C" stands for
   diaphragm as contraception   douche and cleanse
   dilation and curettage

85a. The death-rate from childbirth and complications of pregnancy is about ___ times as great as the death-rate from clinically-performed abortions.

   3   5   10

85b. Childbirth under the best circumstances is more dangerous than a competently-performed abortion.

    TRUE   FALSE

86. Fetus is used to refer to
    offspring of the womb from the end of the third month
       of pregnancy in 'man' kind until birth
    spontaneous expulsion from the womb before viable
    the human organism in the first three months after
       conception

87. In the U.S.A., the majority of illegal abortions are performed on unmarried women.

    TRUE   FALSE

88. A woman of limited financial resources, over 21 years of age, resident of your community, someone you know moderately well, informs you that she is certain she (1) is pregnant and (2) needs an abortion. She wants to know WHERE TO GO. She is not interested in your opinion of her situation at this stage of the Game. Her physician is willing to "help" her only to the extent of confirming her pregnancy and indicating that she is six-eight weeks along. And she has "had it" with her clergyman too. The only hospital in your community is not secular. How would you advise her? Be specific.

89. The U.S.A. spends _____ money on allergy research _____ the whole Western world spends on contraceptive research.

    three times as much ... as   less ... than
    about as much ... as

90. Leading methods of contraception are listed below. Indicate their relative effectiveness by assigning numbers from 1 to 8.

  ___ chemical barrier   ___ intrauterine de-
  ___ condom   vice (IUD)
  ___ diaphragm or cervical   ___ pill
       cap with jelly   ___ rhythm
  ___ douche   ___ withdrawal

91.   A cheap, safe, reliable and simple method of birth-
control is
    abstinence   vasectomy
    hysterectomy

92.   "If government knew how, I should like to see it check,
not multiply, the population. When it reaches its true law of
action, every man that is born will be hailed as essential,"
was written by
    Ralph Waldo Emerson   Margaret Higgins Sanger
    Oliver Wendell Holmes   Brigham Young

93.   The U.S.A. is the only industrialized nation in the
world which does not provide public child-care services.
    TRUE   FALSE

94.   Two main concerns voiced by most people and groups
attending the White House Conference on Children in 1970
were
    (1) _____ .   (2) _____ .

95.   _____ American mothers with children under six
years of age are employed.
    1. 3 million   4. 2 million
    approximately 500, 000

96.   Some young mothers are now demanding that day-care
centers be created, not just because they want or have to
be free to work, but because _____ .

97.   Why suddenly do more and more young mothers find
housework "stultifying?"

98a.   Opponents of the day-care center concept argue that:
    it would be o.k. for children of welfare mothers, so
        they can get out and do some work
    mothers want to be fancy-free
    parents won't spend enough time with their children
        guiding their morals, stimulating their thoughts, pro-
        viding them with security, etc., if day-care centers
        are available
    all of these   none of these

98b.   Opponents of day-care centers believe that:
    parents regard the center as a place to raise children
    these parents are not willing to cope with the responsi-
        bilities of having children

women are just bored, want to get out of the house and
their real responsibilities and obligations
all of these   none of these

99. A widow (or one divorced or separated, or with an
incapacitated husband) can deduct up to $_____ a year for
care of her child while she is employed.
    0                                    $1250 (i.e., 50 weeks x $25)
    $600   unrestricted if validated

100. One of the most powerful consumer groups in Japan
is that of the housewives.
    TRUE   FALSE

101. To "comparison shop," without cost, the best value
among sleeping bags now on the market, turn to
    Consumer Reports   Bess Myerson Grant
    "Readers' Guide to Periodical Literature"

102. Before offering items to the public, cosmetics manufacturers are required to
    conduct safety tests   all of these
    file the formulas with the Food   none of these
      & Drug Administration
    print the ingredients of products
      on labels

103. The traditional pattern in the U.S.A. has been to
permit but not require women to serve on juries and in
the military.
    TRUE   FALSE

104a. The Equal Rights Amendment was before the U.S.
Congress for more than 45 years.
    TRUE   FALSE

104b. Passage of the Equal Rights Amendment to the U.S.
Constitution was supported by all of the following:
    B'nai B'rith Women   Presidents Eisenhower,
    several state legislatures   Kennedy, Johnson, and
    Teamsters Union   Nixon
    National Assoc. of Colored   St. Joan's Alliance of
      Women   Catholic Women
    TRUE   FALSE

105. Set up under the Civil Rights Act of 1964, and charged
with investigating complaints of discrimination and seeking to

conciliate them, was the
    Equal Employment Opportunity Commission
    National Organization for Women
    Women's Equity Action League

106. Title VII of the Civil Rights Act of 1964 prohibits
some, but not all, employers from hiring, firing or in other
ways discriminating against any individual for which of the
following reasons? (Check one or more)
    age   religion
    color   sex
    national origin   all of these
    race   none of these

107. "Discrimination against women is incompatible with
human dignity and with the welfare of the family and of
society.... The full and complete development of a country,
the welfare of the world and the cause of peace require the
maximum participation of women as well as men in all
fields" is from
    John F. Kennedy's inaugural address
    the Planned Parenthood International Manifesto
    the UN Declaration on the Elimination of Discrimination
        Against Women (1967)
    the U.S. Dept. of Labor's Women's Bureau's Handbook
        (1969)

108. "The number of women in politics has never been
large, but now it is getting even smaller. Women are a
majority of the population, but they are treated like a
minority group. The prejudice against them is so wide-
spread that, paradoxically, most persons do not yet realize
it exists. Indeed, most women do not realize it ..." is
from
    A White House Diary, by Lady Bird Johnson
    My Life with Martin Luther King, Jr., by Coretta
        Scott King
    Unbought and Unbossed, by the Hon. Shirley Chisholm

109a. One of your U.S. Senators is _____.
    b. One of your U.S. Congress(wo)men is _____.
    c. The female U.S. Senator is _____.

110. All of the following Congressmen supported passage
of the Equal Rights Amendment.
    Birch Bayh   Hiram Fong
    Emanuel Cellar
    TRUE   FALSE

111. Androgynous
    is a term used in botany: "bearing both staminate and
        pistillate flowers in the same inflorescence or cluster"
    means hermaphroditic   is all of these
    means both male and female in one is none of these

112. Sexual desire for those of the same sex; sexual relations between individuals of the same sex.   This statement
defines
    androgyny   all of these
    homosexuality   none of these
    hermaphroditism

113. A lesbian is
    a native or inhabitant of the   all of these
        island of Lesbos   none of these
    a homosexual woman
    eligible for membership in The
        Daughters of Bilitis

114. The Mattachine Society's membership is predominantly
    homosexual   "straight"
    lesbian

115. "Gay," "fairy" and "queen" are examples of slang,
all referring to a/an
    homosexual   all of these
    lesbian   none of these
    adult male homosexual

116. University of California scientists estimate that from
    _____ million adult, single males are homosexuals.
    1 to 2   3 to 4   5 to 6

117. Homosexuality (sexual relationships between consenting adults) is legal throughout
    Canada   all of these
    Mexico   none of these
    U.S.A.

118a. _____ form the majority of those suffering primary
and secondary cases of syphilis reported (1970) by the New
York City Board of Health.
    males aged 15-25   welfare families
    prostitutes and call girls   young people

118b. One out of _____ New York City sexually-active

women now (1971) has gonorrhea.
10   50   100

119. "The Disciples of Sappho, Updated," referred to in
Judy Klemesrud's <u>New York Times</u> (VI: March 28, 1971)
article, are
  lesbians   unwed mothers
  members of communal all-women-and-children families
  poets who use Sapphic verse (stanza of three 5-stress
   lines followed by a short line)

120. Some people group the activities/concerns of "Gay
Liberation" with those of "Women's Liberation." <u>Aside from
your personal opinion</u> of or reaction to this connection, on
exactly what bases is it made?

121. According to David R. Reuben, M.D., most girls become prostitutes
  because they like it   to support the dope habit
  having grown up in an environment in which prostitution
   was "normal"

122. Prostitution in the U.S.A. is legal
  in one state   nowhere
  in a few states

123. Ann and her father are both seriously injured in a
highway collision. Ann is taken by ambulance to one hospital; her father to another. When Ann is wheeled into the
operating room, the surgeon, shocked, says, " I cannot
operate on this girl. She's my daughter." Who is the
surgeon?

124. HE said: Before all else you are a wife and mother.
SHE said: That I no longer believe. I believe that before
all else I am a human being, just as much as you are--or
at least that I should try to become one. HE was _____;
SHE was _____.

125. Most women who become matriarchs do so because
  of the status the role carries   they are deviant
  the role is forced on them

126. What is the <u>point</u> of all this talk about the vaginal
orgasm?

127. What is the "nuclear family?"
    communal living   family of mankind
    sociologists' term referring to today's family isolated
        unto itself

128. A traditional story of unknown authorship, ostensibly
with an historical basis, but serving usually to explain some
phenomenon of nature, the origin of man, or the customs,
institutions, religions rites, etc., of a people is a
    legend   proverb
    myth   tradition

129. In psychology, to devise superficially plausible ex-
planations or excuses for one's acts, beliefs, desires, etc.,
usually without being aware that these are not the real
motives, is to
    free associate   rationalize
    justify

130. Sex-typing and confinement of females in roles involve mythology and rationalization. Can you give examples
of such myths?

131a. Women drivers have a lower accident-rate than men.
    TRUE   FALSE

131b. It has been shown that more road and automobile
accidents are caused by women than by men.
    TRUE   FALSE

132. An analysis of the civil ceremony and marriage
licensing law reveals that, in general,
    love and affection are not requirements of legal marriage
    you have to have sexual intercourse in order to have a
        valid marriage
    rape is legal in marriage
    all of these   none of these

133. "Washerwoman's hands" are a symptom of
    cholera   "shitwork"
    overwork

134. "The Feminine Mystique" refers specifically to
    "a strange discrepancy between the reality of our lives
        as women and the image to which we were trying to
        conform..."

the fact that "the passive woman who does nothing is
    very destructive"
the stereotype of the passive woman as "feminine"

135.   Women are the only oppressed group that have lived
divided from one another and in intimacy with their masters.
    TRUE   FALSE

136.   A new magazine by, for and about feminists is
    Aphra   Essence
    Body and Soul   all of these
    Elle   none of these

137.   Fear, ignorance, naivete and indoctrination contribute
to the mass media's being able to portray the Women's
Liberation Movement negatively.   For example, most Americans have accepted the picture of the bra-burning feminist.
Can you identify other examples of inaccurate reportage and/
or built-in assumptions about the Movement?

138.   Mod Donna is
    an oratorio   symbolic
    a servant girl married to a   all of these
        vet named Charlie   none of these

139.   The term "feminine hygiene" is
    collectively, sanitary napkins, tampons and related
        paraphernalia
    frequently misused in the print media to imply contra-
        ception
    the branch of hygiene dealing with sexual behavior as it
        relates to the welfare of both individual and community

140.   Techniques employed by commercial television net-
works to placate feminists include _____ .

141.   Bella Abzug conducted a difficult campaign for a West
Side Manhattan Congressional seat, culminating in the November 1970 election.   The mass media covered it nationally,
however, playing up such things as her hats and forthright
walk.   What other--possibly more relevant--facts did they
convey to you, a member of the public, about Ms. Abzug
the candidate?   For example, her
    approximate age ___   political party ___
    occupation ___   marital status ___
    religion, if any ___   did Ms. Abzug win? ___

142. "This Exploits Women" and "This Ad Insults Women"
are stickers some people use. Name one product/service/
advertisement you have noticed on TV or in public transpor-
tation which exploits women.

143. In 1830, Louis Antoine Godey started _____. Why
do some people regard this as an unfortunate "first?"

144. "The Doctor" is "dedicated to the brotherhood of
healing," says the
        announcer on the TV soap-opera of that title
        collection-agency utilized by many physicians
        preamble to the A. M. A. "PR" brochure
        statement of ability-to-pay required by many physicians
           of their private-practice patients

145. What 1956 best-selling biographical work discriminated
against women?
        American Freedom and Catholic Power, by Paul Blans-
           hard (Beacon)
        Family of Man, by Edward Steichen (Simon & Schuster)
        Lyndon Johnson Story, by Booth Mooney (Farrar)
        Profiles in Courage, by John F. Kennedy (Harper)

146. "Write the Peace Corps--they have a thousand ways to
say 'I love you' without getting caught!" says entertainer
_____ on his public service message to the nation.
        Shelly Berman   Soupy Sales
        Bill Cosby

147. A handful of _____ dominate the TV writing field
        advertising men   middle-aged men
        middle-aged men   and women
                                          young men

148. "Women's Lib" is
        a negative term   all of these
        an organization   none of these
        the counterpart to "Black Lib"

149. Feminists object to "Sesame Street" because it
        is male-oriented   all of these
        patronizes   none of these
        portrays stupid people as laughable, e.g., Buddy and
           Jim
        receives much of its financial support from taxes

150. Masochism is
      often confused with misogynism
      the getting of (sexual) pleasure from being dominated,
         mistreated or hurt
      thought to have been originated by Count Donatien de
         Sade, 1740-1814, whose writings describe various
         sexual aberrations
      all of these   none of these

151. Sadism is
      named after Count Donatien de Sade, 1740-1814, whose
         writings describe various sexual aberrations
      often confused with masochism
      the getting of (sexual) pleasure from dominating, mis-
         treating or hurting one's partner
      all of these   none of these

152. Of the 17th Assembly District Democratic Club, this
notable American politician wrote, "The party and raffle
formed the year's big fund-raising event. They were run by
the women of the club ... [which] I could see, if they
couldn't, was exploiting the women. It lived on the pro-
ceeds." From the autobiography of
      Emanuel Celler   Norman Mailer
      Shirley Chisholm   Margaret Chase Smith

153. When asked to name the nicest thing he'd done for
his wife, one celebrity on the "He Said, She Said" TV show
replied "two sons" (Jack Klugman); another "married her"
(Greg Mulavey). These are examples of
      chauvinism   machismo
      male chauvinism   misogyny
      narcissism

154. When a man says to a woman, "You need some
      loving," he means _____.
When a man says to a woman, "You're crazy," he means

_____.
When a man says to a woman, "What's the matter with
      you?" he means _____.
When a man says of a woman, "She needs to see a head-
      shrinker," he means _____.
When a man says of a woman, "She's well-adjusted," he
      means _____.
When a man says of a woman, "If it wasn't for the kids,
      I'd get a divorce," he means _____.

When a man says of a woman, "She's a ball-breaker," he
  means _____.
When a man says of a woman, "She lost the baby," he
  means _____.
When a man says, "My son," he means _____.
When a man says, "That's just human nature," he means

_____.
When a man says, "the girl," he refers to _____.

155. "In Madame Curie I can see no more than a brilliant
exception. Even if there were more women scientists of
like caliber they would serve no argument against the fundamental weakness of the feminine organization," was said by
      Albert Einstein   Jean-Jacques Rousseau
      Enrico Fermi

156. "Woman's reign is a reign of gentleness, tact, and
kindness; her commands are caresses, her threats are
tears. She should reign in the home as a minister reigns
in the state, by contriving to be ordered to do what she
wants," was said by
      Albert Einstein   Gore Vidal
      Jean-Jacques Rousseau   George Washington

157. There are many responsible men in the legal profession and in the legislatures who believe that women should
have longer sentences than men or are willing to countenance
such laws. Of seven judges in the Pennsylvania Superior
Court, only one felt the law requiring or permitting longer
sentences for women than for men for the same offense was
unconstitutional.
      TRUE   FALSE

158. A person, especially a man, who hates women is a
      masochist   sadist
      misogynist

159. Men active in the early struggle for women's rights
in the U.S.A. included all but one of the following:
      Frederick Douglass   William Lloyd Garrison
      Robert Frost   Wendell Phillips

160. A form of social organization in which the father or
eldest male is recognized as head of the family or tribe,
descent and kinship being traced through the male line, is
      chauvinism   patriarchy
      machismo

161.   Maleness at its most arrogant, militaristic, patriotic,
sexist; most in evidence in Latin America, where conditions
are especially conducive, but universal:
    chauvinism   patriarchy
    machismo

162.   "It's just possible that all men are male chauvinists
on some level. It just may be that the Lysistrata idea is
the only way to get any sanity across." What does this
statement from <u>Time</u> (August 31, 1970:16) mean?
    membership in Lysistrata is advocated by its founders
        as the only way to unity
    that there is a reactionary trend toward ancient societal
        structure, Greek law, etc.
    that women may have to go on a sex-strike in order to
        achieve world peace generally and equality in particular
    all of these   none of these

163.   The federal Office of Minority Business Enterprise
(OMBE) offers programs of assistance for minority businessmen and women.
    TRUE   FALSE

164.   "Literature cannot be the business of a woman's life,
and it ought not to be. The more she is engaged in her
proper duties, the less leisure she will have for it even as
an accomplishment and recreation," was written by poet
    Robert Frost
    Milton   Southey

165.   Women are especially threatening to men, i.e., more
than men of other races, religions, nationalities, etc., are,
because _____.

166.   "There is no occupation concerned with the management of social affairs which belongs either to woman or to
man, as such. Natural gifts are to be found here and
there in both creatures alike; and every occupation is open
to both, so far as their natures are concerned," was written
by philosopher
    Aristotle   Sartre
    Plato

167.   Some people contend that there will be little real
change towards sexual equality until

hell freezes over | women boycott
many women recognize that they | women unite
   lead contingency lives | all of these
the colossal male ego changes | none of these

168. Leonard Michael Broderick is a prosperous cattle
raiser and wholesale meat dealer of Canberra, Australia.
His wife, after taking a fertility drug in hope that she would
be able to deliver normally after having had to have two
Caesarian sections, gave birth to nonuplets. Only the first-
born, a girl, was born in satisfactory condition. His comment:

all I wanted out of this was a son | no comment
all that matters is that my wife | we can always
  is well | adopt children

169. How many female "juniors" or "the thirds" can you
name?

170. "How many roads must a man walk down before they
call him a man?" is an example of a song refrain which is
part of our contemporary vocabulary with its emphasis on
<u>manhood.</u> Can you name other examples from everyday
phraseology?

171. Airlines defend their discriminatory policies by claim-
ing that sex is a bonafide qualification for a stewardess, who
may be fired when she marries or attains age 32. Another,
specific economic advantage of such policies for the airlines
is _____ .

172. The theory of the political, economic and social
equality of the sexes is called
    caste   slavery
    feminism

173. A rigid class distinction based on birth, wealth, etc.,
operating as a social system or principle is
    caste   slavery
    feminism

174. "The only position for women in SNCC is prone," is
attributed to
    Stokeley Carmichael   Pauli Murray
    Eldridge Cleaver

175. "Women? I guess they ought to exercise Pussy

Power, " is attributed to
    Stokeley Carmichael   Angela Davis
    Eldridge Cleaver

176. "On the one hand, he believed that women are just as intelligent and capable as men and that they should hold positions of authority and influence. But when it came to his own situation ... he was very definite that he would expect whoever he married to be home waiting for him" are the words of the widow of
    John F. Kennedy   Robert Kennedy
    Martin Luther King, Jr.   Malcolm X

177. "Measured in incontestable dollars and cents, which is worse--race prejudice or anti-feminism? White women are at an economic disadvantage even compared to black men, and black women are nowhere on the earnings scale," was written by
    Shirley Chisholm   Pat Nixon
    Pauli Murray   Harriet Tubman

178. Match the following quotations:
    Man without woman is head
      without body; woman with-
      out man is body without
      head. _____

    A woman is but an animal,
      and an animal not of the
      highest order. _____

    When a woman has scholarly
      inclinations there is very
      likely something wrong with
      her single nature. _____

1. Edmund Burke, 1729-1797
2. German proverb
3. Friedrich Nietzsche, 1844-1900

179. In the decade 1960-70, the number of black families headed by only a mother jumped 50%.
    TRUE   FALSE

180. The history of the contemporary black civil rights movement is generally considered to have begun in the U.S. in 1955, when _____ [name a specific event].

181. He pronounced woman to be "an imperfect man, " an "incidental" being
    Saint Thomas   Simon de Beauvoir
    Sigmund Freud

182. Contemporary American church-women's organizations
are for the most part oriented to
    abortion-law repeal
    civil rights for women, especially within the church
        hierarchy
    money-raising and church-housekeeping

183. On January 25, 1970 the Vatican refused to grant ac-
creditation to a German diplomat, Elisabeth Muller, because
    she represented East Germany   all of these
    she was a woman   none of these
    she was not a Roman Catholic

184. "Blessed art Thou, O lord ... Who has not made me
a gentile ... a slave ... a woman" is
    attributed to Martin Luther
    from the Hindu Code of Manu V
    the daily Orthodox Jewish prayer for a male

185. "In childhood a female must be dependent on her
father; in youth, on her husband; her lord dead, on her sons;
a woman must never seek independence" is
    attributed to Martin Luther
    from the Hindu Code of Manu
    from the writings of Pope John XXIII

186. "Woman as a person enjoys a dignity equal with men,
but she was given different tasks by God and by Nature which
perfect and complete the work entrusted to men, " is
    attributed to Martin Luther   by Saint Paul
    from the writings of Pope John XXIII

187. "God created Adam master and lord of living creatures,
but Eve spoiled it all, " is
    attributed to Martin Luther   from Saint Paul
    from the writings of Pope John XXIII

188. "Let the woman learn in silence with all subjection
.... I suffer not a woman to teach nor to usurp authority
over the man, but to be in silence, " was said by
    Hari Krishna   Saint Paul
    Muhammad Ali

189. What one cause for divorce did Jesus Christ recognize?
    abandonment by the husband   fornication by the
    adultery by either partner   wife

190. "You may go over the world, and you will find that
every form of religion which was breathed upon this earth
has degraded woman. There is not one which has not made
her subject to man.... What power is it that makes the
Hindoo woman burn herself on the funeral pyre of her husband? Her religion..." is from an 1885 speech by
    Mohandas K. Gandhi   Elizabeth Cady Stanton
    John Stuart Mill   Harriet Beecher Stowe

191. Why do nuns who have made the shift into mufti often
retain some form of distinctive head gear?

192. "God does not claim that He is Hindu, that He is
Christian, or that He is Moslem.... He is interested in
our love for Him.... Simply by following the example of
namacarya Srila Haridasa Thaku, anyone can gain the
greatest benefit of developing love for God," reflects the
beliefs of
    Scientology   the Hare Krishna move-
    Tagore   ment

193. "The church has served to legitimize a patriarchal
culture," said Dr. Mary Daly, a theologian at Jesuit-run
Boston College. "It's time to rework the basic myths and
symbols of theology in light of the new awareness of how
women have been exploited." The feminist attack on
Christian orthodoxy focuses on three areas: the masculine
Godhead, ethical hypocrisy, and religious symbols. Can
you give an example of each?

194. "How sad it is to be a woman! Nothing on earth is
held so cheap," wrote the poet _____, influenced by
_____.
    Fu Hsuan ... Confucius   Solomon ... Yahweh
    Giovanni Boccaccio ... The Decameron

195. "Woman is the source of all evil; her love is to be
dreaded more than the hatred of men; the poor young men
who seek women in matrimony are like fish who go out to
meet the hook," is from the wisdom of
    Aristotle   Socrates
    Plato

196. A frequently recurring concept in organized religion
is that woman--particularly as a sexual being--is associated
with sin and evil. In _____ and _____ particularly,
this has been a central idea. (Check two.)

Buddhism   Christianity
Confucianism   the Moslem religion
Shintoism

197.   Only a man undefiled by woman's sexual allurements
is fit to perform the highest religious functions; thus, the
insistence on _____.
    celibate priesthood   eunuchs
    homosexuality   male and female
    purdah   clergy

198.   "The female is a female by virtue of a certain lack
of qualities; we should regard the female nature as afflicted
with a natural defectiveness, " was said by
    Aristotle   Socrates
    Plato

199.   Where is the nearest (to where you live or work)
public library?

200.   You have a friend who asks about this Women's Liberation "thing. " What can she do to explore her possible
role?
    consciously try to know herself better--identify the
       forces which have shaped her points-of-view over
       the years
    exercise her citizenship--vote, ascertain her representa-
       tives' voting histories and contact them, serve on
       juries
    join the local chapter of an organization such as N. O. W.
    read, watch/listen to TV, with an "open mind"
    all of these

AWARENESS INVENTORY ANSWER KEY

1. by and for legally helpless women.

2. Shirley Chisholm (<u>263</u>, p. 166). <u>Note: 263 refers to the book title in the Basic Book Collection; 166 refers to the page in that book.</u>

3. Women began fighting for the right of females to speak publicly for Abolition; this was the "consciousness-raising" factor--the earlier feminists did not see the family as a decadent institution, but they discovered that they were not allowed to be seriously dedicated to public issues.

4. FALSE. The official inauguration of the women's movement in the U.S.A. as well as the beginning of the international women's movement was the Seneca Falls (New York) Convention, July 19 and 20, 1848. The "Declaration..." is reprinted in <u>105</u>.

5. TRUE. As usual, they pitched in to end the war the men had brought about.

6. betterment of social conditions. "A Woman of Fifty," by Rheta Childe Dorr, describes clubs as instruments of social reform in <u>91</u>.

7. FALSE. The only issue on which American women have voted as a separate group has been temperance.

8. TRUE. The right to vote was then based on ownership of property; women were gradually disenfranchised by laws prohibiting their voting: Virginia in 1699; New York in 1777; Massachusetts in 1780; New Hampshire in 1784; New Jersey in 1807.

9. Wyoming. Pioneers in the west, accustomed to women who could run a homestead, were more easily persuaded than eastern men that women were not frail or feeble-minded.

10. FALSE. Elizabeth Duncan Koontz became director of
the Women's Bureau of the Department of Labor in 1969;
NOW's national president in 1970 was Aileen Hernandez.

11. Margaret Bonnevie (74, p. 33).

12. Jeanette Rankin (World Almanac & Book of Facts,
1971, p. 820).

13. Emmeline Pankhurst.

14. all of these. Addams founded both the Women's International League for Peace and Freedom and, in Chicago's
slums, Hull House, the first social settlement house in
America (1899). Wald was associated with New York City's
Henry Street Settlement. Both are still in existence. See
"An Early College Girl," reprinted from Jane Addams'
autobiography, Twenty Years at Hull House, in 91.

15. Lucy Stone.

16. Edna St. Vincent Millay (Letters of Edna St. Vincent
Millay by Norma Millay Ellis, Harper, 1954).

*   *   *

If you haven't fared too well with these questions, or if you
would like to know more about this line of questioning, the
following readings from The Basic Book Collection are
recommended:

Adams, M.	The Right to be People.
Beard, M.	Woman as Force in History
Beauvoir, S.	The Second Sex.
Brittain, V.	Lady into Woman.
Brown, D.	The Gentle Tamers.
Burnett, C.	Five for Freedom.
Farrar, R.	A Wondrous Moment Then.
Flexner, E.	Century of Struggle.
Hale, S.	Women's Record.
Kraditor, A.	The Ideas of the Woman Suffrage Movement.
Kraditor, A.	Up from the Pedestal.
Lerner, G.	Grimke Sisters from South Carolina.
Rover, C.	Punch Book of Women's Rights.
Scott, A.	The American Woman.

Stanton, E.   History of Woman Suffrage.
Wollstonecraft, M.   A Vindication of the Rights of
                     Women.

      *   *   *

17. all of these. Read Judy Klemesrud's "Coming Wednes-
day, a Herstory-Making Event" New York Times VI:6f,
August 23, 1970 and "It Was a Great Day for the Women on
the March," IV:4, August 30, 1970.

18. a bitch session. Group therapy and hen-party are
terms men use when women get together, especially in a
bitch session or cell group.

19. none of these. It's the National Organization for
women--a big difference. NOW includes men in its membership, e.g., Warren Farrell, founder of a men's consciousness-raising group; James Clapp, active abortion reformer
(see McCalls:52f, July 1970, "Five passionate feminists");
and Lawrence Lader, author of 206.

20. OWL = Older Women's Liberation; WEAL = Women's
Equity Action League; SCUM = Society for Cutting Up Men;
and WITCH = Women's Independent Taxpayers, Consumers
& Homemakers (one example).

21a. housework. "Shitwork" has been defined as "work
that is relegated to women in our sexist society" by the
Women's Liberation Center of New York in a mid-February
1971 mailing. Typing, filing are also included. "The
Politics of Housework" by Pat Mainardi is an interesting
commentary, reprinted in Loren Baritz's The American
Left, among other places (Basic books, 1971). Basically
it is work that women do because men won't, and thus,
chores that women have been conditioned to accept. All
the rest is "rhetoric," e.g., men's rationalization that
women can't/shouldn't do other more (psychologically,
financially) rewarding jobs ("they'll get married, pregnant
...").

21b. none of these. Liberated women now use the words
fuck and screw to convey a depersonalized version of sexual
intercourse involving the physical use of a woman by a man
who cares nothing about her, i.e. a male concept of sex.

22. all of these probably. Just asking the question indicates

an assumption of a pro/con situation--what's to discuss?
Like asking what you think of health, life....

23. TRUE. No one asks a man to accompany his use of
"Mr." with an indication of his marital status. When Rep.
Jonathan Bingham (D/N.Y.) suggested that women refer
to themselves as "Ms." (pronounced "miz"), the response
was more than 90% favorable. Some secretary's handbooks
have suggested it for some time. If "Ms." ever becomes
generally accepted, it shouldn't outrage traditionalists. We
will simply be returning to the custom of Shakespeare's
times, when "mistress"--the root of both of our current
abbreviations--was the polite salutation for all women.
(McCalls:41, March 1971).

24. Pussycats. See "Backlash against Women's Lib" by
Betty Rollin in Look:15f, March 9, 1971. The Pussycats
are a cutie-poo anti-Lib group; Tegner and McGrath discourage karate too.

25. FALSE. Paul Lauter and Florence Howe, "Conspiracy
of the Young," Chapter 10, The Female Majority, p. 291.
Though rape is increasingly commonplace (up 14% between
1967 and 1968,) it is not a political crime, although it is
the most often reported crime of violence against persons,
according to the FBI.

26a, b, and c. TRUE (220).

27. Beating with fists against a man's chest, which is a
useless target; and trying to squirm or struggle out of a
body grab.

28. the kick. "At least 90% of the attacks which might be
made involve a reaching or grabbing action ... it would be
silly for a girl to depend on her fists for self-defense. Not
only is her reach shorter than a man's, but punching de-
pends on power and a woman cannot hope to oppose the
power of a man's fist with a counter-punch using less
power. In order to come within punching distance of a man's
face, you would have to place yourself in the most vulner-
able position possible" (220).

29. Ecological disruption, imperialism, racism, wars--all
the negative aspects of capitalism--have been the results of
patriarchal, male-dominated society. And do you really
think they would pitch in tomorrow and work for equality

of the sexes were the War to end today?

*   *   *

Related Readings, Questions 17-29

Cudlipp, E.	Understanding Women's Liberation.
Firestone, S.	The Dialectic of Sex.
Greer, G.	The Female Eunuch.
Leijon, A.	Swedish Women--Swedish Men.
Morgan, R.	Sisterhood is Powerful.
Tegner, B.	Self-Defense for Girls.
Thompson, M.	Voices of the New Feminism.

*   *   *

30. Fred M. Hechinger. See Section 4 of the Sunday New York Times.

31. women's (98, p. 117).

32. parietals (98, p. 125). Sexual freedom is not the main issue--adult status is. In loco parentis places the college in the position of regulating outside-of-classroom private lives of students--colleges establish rules regarding such things as curfews, keys, clothing, conduct, etc.

33. Males were markedly preferred over females at low-ability levels, but this difference disappeared at the higher levels. Since there are more students, both male and female, at the lowest of our ability levels, it is clear that overall women are discriminated against in college admissions. Elaine Walster, et al., "The Effect of Race and Sex on College Admission," Institute for Research on Poverty, University of Wisconsin, Madison.

34. TRUE (34, p. 26). See also: "The Woman Ph.D." by Rita James Simon, et al. in Social Problems:221-36, Fall 1967; and "The Educational Establishment: Wasted Women" by Doris Pullen in 98.

35. TRUE (see answer no. 34).

36. a. a factory ... an office   d. one-quarter
     b. single ... married   e. 50 ... 70
     c. thirties
     ("Profile of the Woman Worker..." May 1970, the Women's Bureau).

37. approximately 60% of men's (New York Times VI:12,
16, April 26, 1970 = 60%; "Fact Sheet on the Earnings Gap,"
Dec. 1971 = 59% in 1970).

38. $3,066 more. "Fact Sheet on the Earnings Gap," Dec.
1971 rev.) On the average, a woman needs a college degree
to earn more than a man with an 8th-grade education.

39. Labor.

40. 40% (U.S. News:44-6, Sept. 8, 1969).

41. all of these. From a statement before Commerce and
Labor Committee of the Ohio House of Representatives, presented by Dorothy Haener, Int. Rep. of United Auto Workers.
(Employers protest that women want part-time jobs; it is
doubtful that they want low-paying jobs which are dead-ends.)

42. prostitution.

43. two-thirds. (Frank S. Endicott, "Trends in Employment of College and University Graduates in Business and
Industry," Northwestern University 24th annual report, Dec.
1969; 25th annual report, Dec. 1970; 63% of 208.)

44. white male.

45. 20. They frequently were elected or appointed to seats
vacated by the death of men, usually spouse.

46a. TRUE. 36 states have such laws, although the state
attorney general has ruled them illegal in 6.

46b. TRUE. 25 states have such laws, ranging from not
being allowed to mix alcoholic beverages to specifically being
excluded from the position of director of a Department of
Mines. ("Women's Legal Rights in All 50 States," Carmen
Miguel, researcher. McCalls':90-5, Feb. 1971.) Wives in
California and Nevada must get court approval to run businesses.

47. 38% ... one-half (Flora Crater, The Woman Activist,
May 5, 1971). In 1946 women held 45% of all professional/
technical positions; in 1969, only 37%. Median earnings of
women have dropped from 64% of men's in 1957 to 58% in
1968. The unemployment rates of women are consistently
higher than those of men.

48. a typing test.

49. the appointing Senator must assume full responsibility
for the safety of his female page in travel to and from the
Capitol and at her place of residence. All the others came
up, however. (New York Times:26, May 14, 1971.)

50. TRUE. "And when the typewriter was first introduced,
men said it was too complex a machine for women to handle.
But when they discovered that typing was drudgery and women
could be induced to do the work for less money, the men
graciously dropped the Smith-Corona in our laps." (Susan
Brownmiller's "$=power=masculinity," The MBA:18f, March
1971; also in Bell Telephone magazine.)

51. $3,000. (Susan Brownmiller op. cit.). And the gap is
widening according to the Dept. of Commerce. Average salary,
female B.A. (B.S.): $6,694; male, $11,795.

52. by utilizing separate sections of the newspaper for
some categories of workers, e.g., Sunday New York Times'
Section 4 "The Week in Review" for some personnel in education, libraries and health, and especially Section 3, "Business and Finance," wherein male pronouns and allusions
abound. Even the regular Classified Section 9 continues
some discrimination, e.g., Sept. 27, 1970: HELP WANTED
--MALE/FEMALE "Administrative Assistant. This is
addressed to the man who would be attracted by ...."

53. saleswomen (1970) ("Fact Sheet on the Earnings Gap,"
Dec. 1971 rev., U.S. Women's Bureau, page 2).

54. Less than 1% ("Why Not Be an Engineer?" Women's
Bureau Leaflet 41 [rev 1971]). Although women are employed in many types of jobs, an examination of women in
the professions is especially revealing because generally
speaking there is less opportunity for a woman employed in
a profession to be restricted/relegated to shitwork (although
she is likely to get the less desirable jobs and tasks in that
profession, of course); the professions involve both the education and employment fields; presumably the woman who
perseveres through years of negative vocational/personal
counseling, educational requirements, internship, licensing,
etc., within an overwhelmingly male population is in a better
position to have insights into sexism and is more likely to
provide leadership for change than the woman who works
with women or away from people at chores not stimulating

her mind; and women lawyers and physicians are desperately needed to work in such Women's Liberation activities as abortion and abortion law repeal.

55.   the ministry (Columbia Owl:9f, April 28, 1971: "Women: the 'Silent Majority' in the Eyes of the Church," by Emily Hewitt).   The sentiment against women in the ordained ministry runs deep.   An authoritative study of the Protestant ministry states flatly, "Any female minister must overcome tremendous prejudice.   The church is the most conservative of all institutions in this regard.   Women have gained far more status in most other professions than in ministry."

56.   TRUE (27, p. 179-180).   Although by and large there is no discrimination as between men and women with respect to the occupations they may enter, there are professions, such as teaching and medicine, where women outnumber men; most of the direct patient care is done by women. What is also true--and this may represent a lag in the process of equalization--is that men outnumber women in the executive positions.   In 1959 there was only one woman in the presidium of the Supreme Soviet, which numbered 15 members.   (Footnote: Mme. Furtseva was removed in 1961, the year after she became Minister of Culture.)

57.   70% (Time:31, Jan. 11, 1971).   And 87% of those who do marry while in medical school delay having children until completely trained.   The main concern of prospective women M.D.'s is an end to discrimination in the admission process; they would also like more flexible scheduling while in school.

58a.   21,000 ("Medical School Alumnae, 1967" (c)1968, American Medical Association, p. 6-8; Time:31, Jan. 11, 1971).   7% of U.S.A.'s 300,000 M.D.'s = 21,000.

58b.   6-7% (Women's Bureau, "Underutilization of Women Workers" [rev. 1971] p. 10).

59.   who are far superior to the average male applicant. "Let's Put Women in Their Place Like, for Instance, City Hall" by Dr. Jean Mayer.   McCalls:74-8, Feb. 1971).

60.   TRUE ("A Singular Woman" by Barbara Falconer. McCalls:43, Feb. 1971).

61. none of these. The National Faculty Association of
Community and Junior Colleges (an affiliate of the National
Education Association and the American Association of Junior
Colleges) lists positions specifying males; for example, from
its "Junior & Community College Position Vacancies for
1970-71," p. 5: Chesapeake College (Wye Mills, Md.)
listed "1 Counseling (man), 1 Librarian (man), 1 Physical
Education (Men's)." The "Summer 1971 Guide to In-Service
Courses & Programs for Junior and Community College
Faculty and Staff" (American Assoc. of Junior Colleges,
prepared by Jose de la Isla and distributed gratis) listed
a "summer workshop for new junior college presidents and
their wives" at the University of California at Los Angeles;
Frederick C. Kintzer, director, indicated in May that it
was completely booked, with tentative plans for another one
in summer 1972.

    "Career Opportunities in USIA" (reprinted as Appendix
1, page 293f of John W. Henderson's United States Information Agency, Praeger, 1969) provides the following recruit-
ment information for prospective foreign service officers:
"What kind of officer does USIA need for its Foreign Service? The Agency answers the question this way ... [an
analysis follows using he, his, him exclusively, and continues ...] A demonstrated ability to live and work in
strange lands among strange people, often without the com-
forts of life that we take for granted. This, incidentally,
applies to the officer's wife as well.... USIA is an equal
opportunity employer. Candidates are appointed solely on
the basis of merit, initially to Class 7 or Class 8, de-
pending on qualifications, age, and experience. Candidates
must be chosen without regard to race, creed, or color."

    Men are about twice as likely as women to be chief
librarians: in a study of 26 cities serving a population of
500,000 or more, there were only three women directors
of public libraries; only four of the 74 largest college and
university libraries have women directors; 12% of women
librarians are chief librarians, but 22% of the men are.
Men librarians earn about $1,500 more per year than
women, even when the educational qualifications are the
same. Men who are not chief librarian tend to earn
more than women who are. Of the 55 graduate library
schools accredited by the American Library Association
(ALA), 9 are headed by women; one of these is "acting."
(Sources: SRRT Task Force on the Status of Women in
Librarianship no. 1, August 1970; American Libraries,
November 1972.) American Libraries, the "journal" of the
ALA, in describing the placement center to be operated at the

annual ALA conference by The National Registry for Librarians and the Texas State Employment Service, drew the reader's attention to the fact that "The policy of the U.S. Employment Service prohibits the acceptance of a job order which bears discriminatory specifications in respect to race, creed, color, or national origin" (May 1971, p. 517).

62. Isadora Duncan (266, p. 195-6).

63. Some examples: Women teachers do not hold supervisory or administrative positions relative to their number employed in the school system. Women are subject to arbitrary termination of their jobs upon becoming pregnant in many systems. Textbooks and other learning materials used in many schools portray the stereotype roles of females as docile and subservient and males as strong and aggressive, which results in harmful limiting and conditioning of students during very influential periods of their lives. The vocational and academic counseling provided for girls is often narrowed to jobs for which women are traditionally suited, rather than expanded to career opportunities for both sexes, openly, equally and fairly. Funds for girls' athletics, intramural and interscholastic, are not allocated equally with boys', and in some systems, rules prohibit girls from participating in interscholastic athletic teams with boys. Guidance counselors are not trained with special emphasis on needs and professional opportunities for girls outside the traditional patterns.

Education-as-an-employer demonstrates well the discrimination against women in all types of work. It is of special interest because: education supposedly is a public domain for the most part, nonprofit, beyond commercial exploitation; it is able to groom and produce the employee that it later misuses, i.e., education of females reinforces, channels; all institutions and sectors of our society are represented within the field of education--disciplines, professions, subject-interests, unions--professional as well as non-professional--including service to and employment of all ages, sexes, religions, races; it is a hierarchy-patriarchy (and as such, supports and participates in such things as war); it has traditionally been male-dominated, with women doing the shitwork--men get more money, status, power, decision-making, authority (over women and children), are able to cross lines in jobs; women get less money, are functionaries, clericals, custodians, para-professionals, sealed into one-job categories; and above all, because education should be serving as a model for those who are being

educated, especially the young whose last chance it is to
"relearn" their role.

64.   One-fifth (New York Times IV:9, March 4, 1971).
Figures released in April 1971 by the Dept. of Labor showed
that the number of women on college faculties and staffs is
still only about one-fifth of the total.   And the small percentage of women on faculties and professional staffs of U.S.
colleges has barely changed in 60 years.   Women's rights
groups have filed hundreds of discrimination charges against
various schools.   Only about 10% of our college teachers
are women, and this figure may drop.   This has come about
as colleges for women became coeducational, as home
economics departments became departments of nutrition,
and even in teacher-training programs.   At the Harvard
School of Education, where 65% of the students are women,
there are 12 women on a faculty of 185, and all of the administrators are men.   (Jean Mayer's "Let's Put Women in
Their Place Like, for Instance, City Hall, " McCalls:74-8,
Feb. 1971.)   Barnard and Wellesley are the only two major
women's colleges with a majority of women on their faculties.

65.   all of these.

66.   twice as many ("A Singular Woman, " Laura Nader,
points to a study made by some Berkeley women described
in February 1971 McCalls:43 by Barbara Falconer).

67.   30% (The MBA:28, March 1971).   "Nearly 60% of the
corporate respondents to the ASPA/BNA survey indicated
that they ... still disqualify women on the basis of sex for
jobs running from claims adjustor to airline pilot. "   How
Big Business regards the little woman's place is apparent
in the note attached to the credit-card holder's monthly
statement encouraging him to "Introduce your wife to two-
card convenience.   She's busy--she's involved--she's today's
wife-on-the-go.   Her calendar may well be as full as yours--
with meetings to attend--people to see socially--quite a bit
of shopping--and the over-all responsibilities of running a
household" [American Express].

68.   1, 2, 3, 4, 5, and 6. (The MBA:28, 9, March 1971).
Turnover characteristics for both groups are remarkably
similar--approximately 61% of both groups are still with
their first employers and 28% with their second, in a research reported in "The Young Executive; A Behavioral
Profile" (1970).

69. government enforcement. New York Times Woman's
Page [six], May 15, 1971: Enid Nemy's "Getting Women
Better Jobs." Dr. Henry Morgan: "When you talk about
equal employment of blacks today, you don't have Amos and
Andy jokes. You still have jokes on the women's issue.
Society hasn't taken the issue seriously." One of the motiva-
tions in the black issue was "an element of fear ... a
residual of fear ... a fear of violence. It isn't altruism.
The only fear stimulus I can see for the women's movement
is the possibility of government enforcement. How can I
take that seriously when I see a male government? The
threat is not very great."

                    *   *   *

Related Readings, Questions 30-69

Astin, H.	The Woman Doctorate.
Baker, E.	Technology and Woman's Work.
Bernard, J.	Academic Women.
Bird, C.	Born Female [References made to 1968 ed.].
Chicago University.	Women in the University of Chicago.
Epstein, C.	Woman's Place.
Lopate, C.	Women in Medicine.
M. I. T. Symposium...	Women in the Scientific Profes- sions.
U.S. Dept. of Labor Women's Bureau.	1969 Handbook on Women Workers.

                    *   *   *

70. Isadora Duncan (266, p. 187).

71. Eligibility for public office; to entitle her to serve on
juries; for reasons of probating a will; to vote; etc. etc.

72. TRUE.

73. Custody of the child unless the father acknowledges the
relationship and/or marries the mother.

74. TRUE (125, p. 17). Kansas, Massachusetts, New
Jersey, Pennsylvania, Rhode Island, and South Carolina.

75. FALSE (125, p. 4). Puerto Rico and 24 states do
not recognize common law marriage.

76. TRUE. The husband who wants his wife to be a wage-earner generally has several built-in provisos: he indeed welcomes the extra wages his "working wife" brings in-- assumes that she will get a job which offers no conflict with his ego, status, salary, or rank; she will be in a "sexless" environment and/or resist all temptations to extra-curricular activities; she will take on the employment as an activity strictly secondary to her primary home responsibilities --all chores will continue to be carried out, meals, sex, kids, housework. As Ed McMahon says about a rice dish, "You know, when a man works hard, he likes to come home to a good hearty meal...." The husband of the employed wife who is "different" is easily identified: his main concern is not that his wife be a wage-earner, but that she be a satisfied, fulfilled person.

77. _____.

78. TRUE (34, p. 42). The efforts of the Suffragettes finally provided American women with the vote in 1920. Radical social change was never achieved, however. Women as usual could be counted on to pitch in and answer their country-men's call; World War II found them in war-plants and other jobs as well as in the Services. Despite their desire to remain on the job, they were returned to their "normal" places washing dishes and typing to make way and provide peace-time support for men.

79. Adultery (125, p. 75). Refusal by wife to move to new residence (Tennessee) and wife's lack of chastity (Kentucky, Virginia) are grounds for divorce in some states.

80. 50% (127, p. 25).

81. at the top of industry among executives (127, p. 136). Professor Teitlin claims that executives often choose a mistress rather than a divorce. In business circles, divorce may be frowned upon, but infidelity is less so. While the percentage of divorces at the top of industry is smaller than in society as a whole, the amount of marital unhappiness would seem to be greater.

82. TRUE. Carmen Miguel's "Women's Legal Rights in All 50 States" McCalls:90-5, Feb. 1971. In 17 states, i.e., more than one-third, women can be made to pay alimony.

83. 20 (New York Times VI:10f, April 11, 1971): "A

Report on the Abortion Capital of the Country" by Susan Ed-
miston; Columbia Forum:18f, Winter 1970 "The Truth about
Abortion in New York" by Robert E. Hall, M.D.). "An
abortion, for example, is medically defined as the inter-
ruption of pregnancy during the first 20 weeks, for a fetus
born after this time may survive" [Dr. Hall]. New York
law permitting abortion within 24 weeks was a political
compromise: since there is greater chance of survival
after 28 weeks, they split the difference!

84. dilation and curettage.

85a. 10.

85b. TRUE. Four times as dangerous, according to Gar-
rett Hardin, lecture, April 1964. A therapeutic hospital
abortion, performed in the first 12 weeks of pregnancy, has
a mortality rate of less than 1/100,000. Contraception via
the pill has a mortality rate of 2-3/100,000 users per year.
Childbirth itself carries a mortality rate of 20/100,000.
Every contraceptive method, no matter how faithfully prac-
ticed, has an inherent failure rate, ranging from 1% per
year for the pill to 30% or more per year for the rhythm.
("Abortion Laws Should Be Repealed" testimony by Joan
Lamb Ullyot, M.D., before the Judiciary Committee of the
California State Assembly, October 22, 1970), a one-sheet
summary distributed by the Society for Humane Abortion,
San Francisco.)

86. Offspring of the womb from the end of the 3rd month
of pregnancy...

87. FALSE (202, p. 101). "In the U.S. ... at least
60% of illegal abortions are performed on married women
..." [Dr. Edmund W. Overstreet, University of California
School of Medicine].

88. Although abortion for any reason if performed by a
physician is legal in Alaska, New York, Washington and
Hawaii, progress is being made in eliminating laws relating
to abortion and making knowledge of sources of safe abortions
available. Some possible answers to your sister's question
are: The Clergy Consultation Service, Parents' Aid Society,
and Women's Medical Center. For information about these
and others, see Part V, "Directory of Sources." Contact
should also be made with the local women's center and
liberation group(s). See also 211.

89. Three times as much money on allergy research as the
whole Western world spends on contraceptive research. (Report by Patricia Williams on the Commission on Human Relations' meetings held in New York City, Sept. 21-5, 1970.
New York Chapter N. O. W. Newsletter:12-13, Nov. 1970.)

90. 6 - 4 - 3 - 8 - 2 - 1 - 7 - 5 (1 pill, 2 IUD, 3 diaphragm with jelly, 4 condom, 5 withdrawal, 6 chemical barrier, 7 rhythm, 8 douche). (See 202.)

91. vasectomy. ("For Men Only: Foolproof Birth Control"
by Ernest Dunbar in Look:45, March 9, 1971). Arthur Godfrey publicizes that he has had a vasectomy to encourage
other men to be voluntarily sterilized by means of this
operation; also Dr. Paul Ehrlich of Stanford University
(Consumer Reports:384, June 1971) and sportscaster Jim
Bouton. The "difficulty" with this technique is the male's
concern with his manhood, i. e. , he may mistakenly assume
it will effect his potency. For further information, contact
The Association for Voluntary Sterilization (14 West 40th
Street, New York, N. Y. 10018, or, The Association for
Vasectomy at the same address).

92. Ralph Waldo Emerson, 1803-1882. Conduct of life,
Chapter 7 (Every woman too!).

                    *   *   *

Related Readings, Questions 70-92
        Callahan, P.   Law of Separation and Divorce.
        Duncan, I.   My Life.
        Group for Advancement of Psychiatry.   The Right to
                             Abortion.
        Havemann, E.   Birth Control.
        Lader, L.   Abortion.
        Phelan, L.   The Abortion Handbook for Respon-
                             sible Women.
        Pilpel, H.   Your Marriage and the Law (rev.)
        Schulder, D.   Abortion Testimony.
        Wertenbaker, L.   The Afternoon Women.

                    *   *   *

93. TRUE (81, p. 44).

94. day-care centers and a child-advocate (New York
Times IV, Dec. 12, 1970).

95. 4.2 million (Flora Crater in The Woman Activist,
May 5, 1971). It is estimated this figure will increase
32% by 1985. Local governments should provide in their
budgets funds to support public child-care facilities for
children of all income-levels; high schools should offer
vocational training in early child care; coordinating committees on the local level of public and private organizations
involved in early child care should be set up.

96. They believe that the experiences the centers can provide are good for their children. (Bruno Bettelheim, "Why
Working Mothers Have Happier Children," Ladies' Home
Journal:24f, June 1970). The child who has always had his
mother at his beck and call may never learn the give and
take that makes life with others possible. For this movement to succeed, we need to adopt an entirely new attitude
about what is best for mothers and children. So long as
the employed mother feels that no matter how good working
may be for her, it it still bad for her child, little good will
come of it for either of them.

97. We are living in a time of transition and this includes
family life. Though girls may still want to have a husband
and children, they want many other things too. For years a
girl is encouraged to enlarge her mind, usually in coeducational classes. Then she must switch from studying or
working to being a wife and mother. After years of apparent equality, it is made clear to her that males are really
"more equal" and she may well resent this. Our educational system, while supposedly preparing girls for an equal
occupational life, advocates the values of a now-antiquated
form of marital life. A more rational attitude about what
is best for the child and for the mother in our modern world
will make it possible for work to be a normal part of
woman's life, and so that employed mothers can be just
that, employers will make the necessary arrangements--a
shorter working-day for mothers, flexible hours, and day-
care.

98a. all of these. They also claim children will be ne-
glected or at best subjected to mass custodial care; of course
it is true that day-care centers must be carefully adminis-
tered.

98b. all of these. They also point out that Hitler used day-
care centers as an effective means of breaking down the
family structure!

99. $600.   ("One working mother versus the I. R. S. , " by
Lisa Hammel, New York Times:36, May 30, 1971).   "Mar-
tinis are tax deductible....   Why not milk?" asked the
demonstration poster.

100.   TRUE.   Laura Nader says "American women haven't
taken advantage of their buying clout.   One of the most
powerful consumer groups in Japan is the housewives' consumer group.   Women in this country could really wheel
around some of the companies whose products they use"
(McCalls:43, Feb. 1971).

101.   Consumer Reports.   At the public or community college library.   June 1971 issue of Consumer Reports, for
example, has a feature on sleeping bags; others on black
and white television sets, room air-conditioners, dental
irrigators, and voluntary sterilization.   If you didn't know
the exact issue, Readers' Guide could lead you to it and to
other product information.

102.   none of these.   Today's Health:17, June 1971:   "Cosmetics manufacturers are not compelled to print the in-
gredients of products on labels, file the formulas with the
FDA, or conduct any sort of safety tests before offering
items to the public.   If an allergist seeks information that
would help him in treatment, the firm is not required to
furnish it. "

103.   TRUE (34, p. 204).   A typical male outcry at the
time the Equal Rights Amendment finally came out of
Committee was an expression of the assumption that women
would be unwilling to be drafted, serve in the armed forces,
etc.   If anything, women in service are eager for opportunity to do more--to realize their potential beyond the
clerical jobs to which they are routinely assigned.   Women
representing more than 40, 000 serving in the Army, Navy,
Marines and Air Force, and doing mainly clerical work,
came out with public statements on sexism in the military
in 1970 (NOW Acts: 10, July 1970).   In World War II,
350, 000 women enlisted in the armed forces (see 118, p.
228 and chapter 10).
        Jury service has become a negative duty for many
Americans, who are accustomed to regarding it as an unfortunate drawing-of-lots that picks on them, and there is
often no stigma attached to trying to get out of serving.
Women called for jury duty are sometimes "counselled" by
a discouraging male judge regarding such things as a case
being lengthy, late, of an embarrassing nature for them

etc. In some states, e.g., Louisiana, a woman can not
automatically serve on a local state jury.

104a. TRUE.

104b. TRUE (The Woman Activist, August 4, 1971).

105. The Equal Employment Opportunity Commission,
which, in any event, does not provide for teachers, employees who are members of staffs of less than 25 persons, or who are in state, municipal or civil service.

106. Race, color, religion, national origin, sex. All except
age. Among those not covered were employees of local, state,
and Federal governments, government-owned corporations,
Indian tribes, and educational and religious institutions where
the employee performs work connected with the institution's
educational activities. Further, Title VII applied to employers
of 25 or more persons only. The Equal Employment Opportunities Enforcement Act amends Title VII of the 1964 Act and was
signed by the President on March 25, 1972. The major items
in this Act are: (1) EEOC was given enforcement power through
the federal courts; (2) coverage was extended to firms with 15 or
more workers and unions with 15 or more members (effective
one year after the President signs the law); (3) coverage was
extended to state and local government employees; (4) coverage
was extended to public and private educational institutions.

107. The UN Declaration on the Elimination of Discrimina-
tion Against Women (1967). Quoted by, among others,
Anna-Greta Leijon (74, p. 7). As of October 1969, the
International Court of Justice was composed of 15 men.

108. Unbought and Unbossed (263).

109a and b. This information can be derived from the current edition of The Official Congressional Directory, or contact The League of Women Voters or your local public library.

109c. Margaret Chase Smith.

110. FALSE. Emanuel Celler opposed it.

                *   *   *

Related Readings, Questions 93-110
   Bird, C.   Born Female (rev.)
   Chisholm, S.   Unbought and Unbossed.
   Evans, E.G.   Day Care.
   Lamson, P.   Few Are Chosen.

Mannes, M.   But Will It Sell?

*   *   *

111. all of these.

112. homosexuality.

113. all of these. Thus, <u>Mademoiselle</u>'s November 1971 cover-listed (in crimson) story, "A Lesbian and a Homosexual Talk About Sexuality" is misleading as well as inaccurate.

114. homosexual.

115. adult male homosexual.

116. 3 to 4.

117. Canada (and only Illinois and New York among states)

118a. young people

118b. 10 (<u>Village Voice</u>, May 20, 1971. Ellen Frankfort's column).

119. lesbians. Sappho was a woman poet of ancient Greece who lived on Lesbos and flourished around 600 B.C.; known for love lyrics. See also <u>New York Times</u> Letters to editor in reply to Ms. Klemesrud, April 11, 1971.

120. The concerns of "straight" women and homosexuals are linked in the same basic concern of obtaining human equality. The same society, culture, environment determine everyone's role, define her or him, aculturate them all. As a letter from Columbia Women's Liberation (April 29, 1971 <u>Spectator</u>) put it, "As Feminists, we feel that Gay people's oppression is also our oppression. The male-supremicist culture inflicts stereotyped roles on all members of society, Gay and straight. As women we are fighting against these roles. We strongly support any group which also struggles to end sexist oppression."

121. because they like it. (Everything You Always Wanted to Know about Sex but Were Afraid to Ask [McKay, 1969], p. 343, exact quotation: "Most girls become prostitutes because they like it.")

122. in one state ("The story of 'I'--Or, A Sensuous Man Pursued" by John A. Hamilton. New York Times IV:4, July 11, 1971). Prostitution has been legalized in Nevada, England, Scandinavia and some other countries around the world. In England street-soliciting is a crime, but sexual acts between consenting adults are not; prostitutes affix appropriate calling cards to doors in Soho.

New York Times I:43, August 1, 1971, in an article entitled "Prostitutes in Nevada to Test a Drug to Prevent Venereal Disease," states that Nevada allows prostitution in some rural counties, but that it is outlawed in Las Vegas and Reno. "Nevada has the third-highest rate of venereal disease in the nation, but the houses of prostitution contribute very little to the problem," Dr. Edwards (Chief of the State Bureau of Preventive Medicine) said. He said that most of the disease was transmitted by unsupervised street walkers, itinerant women and amateurs."

In France, "In 1957 there were 1,200 cases of syphillis reported. Compulsory medical checks were abolished in 1960 and now there are 6,000 cases in Paris each year," according to Stag, Sept. 1971:40.

*   *   *

Related Readings, Questions 111-122

Broderick, C.	The Individual, Sex and Society.
Chasseguet-Smirgel, J.	Female Sexuality.
Herschberger, R.	Adam's Rib.
Horney, K.	Feminine Psychology.
Linner, B.	Sex and Society in Sweden.
Marshe, S.	Girl in the Centerfold.
Miller, I.	A Place for Us.
Millett, K.	Sexual Politics.
Wyden, P.	Growing Up Straight.

*   *   *

123. Ann's mother (McCalls:43, March 1971). And if you didn't get it, you haven't come a long way, baby.

124. He was Helmer; She was Nora--A Doll's House, by Henrik Ibsen, 1879 (221).

125. the role is forced on them. 1,021,000 white women and 706,000 black women are the sole support of families in poverty (Bureau of the Census, 1969). Most women endeavor to fill this role as best they can, but they hardly

welcome it. It is forced on them, contrary to the so-called
Moynihan Report, which conveys the male head of family as
the norm, "the" male role; thus, the woman family head
becomes "deviant," and is described in the Report within a
section titled, "The Tangle of Pathology." Comments such
as "There is much evidence that Negro females are better
students than their male counterparts" (page 31) and "In a
matriarchal structure, the women are transmitting the culture" (page 76) take on the character of guilt-by-association.
Rather than dominating the ghetto child's family experience,
the female sustains it. Read "Like a Lot of Negro Kids,
We Never Would Have Made It Without Our Momma" by
Dick Gregory in <u>109</u>.

126.   Part of the myth of woman's inferiority has been dependence on the male for a lot of things, including orgasm--
the sexual caste system falls apart with the researches of
Kinsey, Johnson & Masters, and others, as well as in rap
sessions, when the importance of the clitoris, for example,
is freely discussed. In fact, women can have multiple
orgasms.

127.   The "nuclear family" is a sociologist's term referring
to today's family: husband/wife and children, self-contained--
even isolated--highly mobile. The significance of the nuclear
family is that in the past, women have managed a virtual
"factory" at home and sometimes worked alongside males
outside the home as well. Now employment has moved out
of the home--if a woman needs/wants to be employed, she
must go out of the home to find employment. Old roles are
part of such old social myths as females are born weak,
passive, and dependent and thus need to have their lives
directed.

128.   myth.

129.   rationalize.

130.   Some examples: It's a man's world. A woman's place
is in the home. Suffragettes who demanded the vote were
"mannish" women. Feminists who demand ratification of the
Equal Rights Amendment are called lesbians, dykes, females
who can't get a man. "We must have our manhood first."
Basically, woman "feels," while man "thinks." Women who
want careers and to enter professional schools will only get
married/pregnant anyway. Boys' sports include football,
soccer, hockey, wrestling, swimming, baseball, golf; girls'

sports include field hockey, tennis, softball (as listed in Darien, Connecticut, Public Schools' teacher application). In 1925 the argument against spending money to educate women was that there had never been a woman genius. Women aren't seriously attached to the labor force; they work only for "pin money."

Women are out ill more than male workers; they cost the company more. Women don't work as long or as regularly as their male co-workers; their training is costly-- and largely wasted. Women take jobs away from men; in fact, they ought to quit those jobs they now hold. Women should stick to "women's jobs" and shouldn't compete for "men's jobs." Women don't want responsibility on the job; they don't want promotions or job changes which add to their load. The employment of mothers leads to juvenile delinquency. Men don't like to work for women supervisors. (Most of these myths are dispelled by 123.)

131a. TRUE (U.S. Dept. of Highways, quoted in, for example, 81, p. 557).

131b. FALSE. The National Safety Council reports that no such statistics are available. The breakdown of accidents is according to collisions with pedestrian, other motor vehicle, railroad train, fixed object, etc. Probable causes or contributory factors are shown as being alcoholism, reckless driving, drug addiction, falling asleep at the wheel.

132. all of these. An interesting commentary on New York City's marriage-licensing appears in 81, p. 536f.

133. Cholera (although some may feel the answer should be "all of these!")

134. "A strange discrepancy between the reality of our lives as women and the image to which we were trying to conform ..." (165, p. 9). ("The passive woman who does nothing is very destructive" is by Kate Millett.)

135. TRUE. Annie Gottlieb's "Female Human Beings," New York Times VII Part 2:1f, Feb. 21, 1971: "as feminist writers from Mill to Rossi to the Red-stockings have said again and again, women are the only oppressed group that have lived divided from one another and in intimacy with their masters, 'in a chronic state of bribery and intimidation combined' [Mill]. The goal of their lives being to capture and keep one man apiece, women were even

further divided: as hostile and mistrustful as two men com-
peting for some prize or honor, only more so, because
women fought for an undignified reward. As long as women
were kept apart, free women would remain isolated ... and
a 'movement' could be dissolved."

*   *   *

Related Readings, Questions 123-135

Bernard, J.	The Sex Game.
Brecher, R.	An Analysis of Human Sexual Response.
Friedan, B.	Feminine Mystique.
Gornick, V.	Women in Sexist Society.
Ibsen, H.	A Doll's House.
Janeway, E.	Man's World, Woman's Place.
Merriam, E.	After Nora Slammed the Door.
Peck, E.	The Baby Trap.
Rainwater, L.	The Moynihan Report and the Politics of Controversy

*   *   *

136. Aphra.

137. The sources of myth-making in our society have
changed; no longer are they the noble poet, or the matinee
idol in the pulpit, or the orpheum circuit. Now they spring
from newspapers and magazines, motion pictures, and especially television. TV does not just entertain or inform.
Public service messages, commercials, drama, talk-shows,
selected-news--they help to create the myths we live by.
For example, the idea that women want to be the same as
men; the idea that, were the Equal Rights Amendment ratified,
women would be in big trouble with such things as existing
labor laws--they need "protection"; the idea that women want
to have their cake and eat it too when it comes to such
things as military service and jury duty; the idea that women
professional librarians are mousey hush-hush clerks; the
idea that Feminists are all white, middle-class; the idea
that (only) women abandon babies.

138. all of these. "Mod Donna" opened April 24, 1970 at
the New York Shakespeare Public Theater, Joseph Papp di-
recting. See Marylin Bender's article, "Women's Liberation Taking to the Stage" in New York Times of March 26,
1970, as well as the book-of-the-play by Ms. Lamb (226).

139. frequently misused in the print media to imply contraception--especially by confession, romance, and movie magazines.

140. For example, the presence of a woman on the "news team," often a "double token" (female black or Puerto Rican); "specials" such as "Women Are Revolting" (Nov. 8, 1970, New York City Channel 5, 7-8 P. M., WNEW-TV and other airings): male moderator, footage of an actress bouncing along pulling out/off her bra shown approximately 20 times in the hour, approximately 13 commercials in that same hour; continuing programs for women (with predominantly male panels) on radio and TV, such as "For Women Only," built around topics which for the most part should concern everyone, e.g., sleep, music and the community, water pollution; listing of women in the credits following TV productions--notice that the policy-making producers, writers and directors are still male for the most part, while the "assistants" and "researchers" are Sally, Irene and Mary.

141. age: 50 in 1970 (born 1920); occupation: attorney; religion: Jewish; political party: Democrat; marital status: "Mrs." Yes, she won--19th N. Y. Congressional District (Current Biography, July 1971:3f).

142. Many ads imply rewards of love, romance/sex, social acceptability, job advancement, status (or the opposite). The following are a few examples: The best cigarettes are thin and rich like women... (Virginia Slims); "Jane, I HATE you! Your floors look so grreat!" (Beacon Wax); "After, I felt proud..." (Klear); "Lemony smells clean, and that says something nice about you" (Joy); "...gives you more time to love your baby"* (Baby Scott); "My husband says my windows look real nice"* (Ajax); "My wife--I think I'll keep her" (Geritol); "Oh a lotta love went into it, Charlie ..." (Crisco oil); "Diapers with love built in" (fabric softener). [*These two are doubly insulting--the allocation of "time" to love, and the assignment of a "colloquialism" to a black woman.]
    Also "I'll never get married, Aunt Hildy.... [drags in, clutching head]. Every time the weather changes, I get this sinus headache." "Achhh [pitiful pursing of the lips] und just ven your boyfren vas all ready to prohpoze" (Sine Aid); "'My hair never looked better,' says Sarah, 'and it makes me feel younger.' Would you believe she has daughters in their twenties?!" (Silk & Silver); "This is the life--going camping with your boy" (Rice-A-Roni); "You're

not getting older ... you're getting better" (Loving Care);
"Some women can drive a man to drink. She can do just
the opposite. She doesn't look at all extraordinary, does
she? A typical schoolmarm, you might guess. Or just
somebody's Aunt Mary" (General Telephone & Electronics).
          Even "public service announcements" come in for
their share of dehumanization, e.g.: "Every tree's a family
tree--fathers go to work, children play, mothers stay home,"
says Smoky-the-Bear, urging Dallas residents to prevent
forest fires (NBC-TV, June 21, 1971).

143. Godey's Lady's Book. It is a "woman's magazine."

144. announcer on the TV soap-opera, "The Doctor."

145. Profiles in Courage, containing chapters on seven
men, with a chapter on 11 "additional men of courage."
Surely there were courageous women in a period of over a
century and a half? And of course the author prefaced with
thanks to Gloria and Jane for "typing and retyping." Countless junior high school boys and girls are assigned this in
paperback.

146. Bill Cosby (NBC-TV, Dec. 31, 1970, 12:45 PM, New
York City, among other airings). Shelly Berman, introducing his wife on "It's Your Bet" (Jan. 12, 1971): "And
here's my domestic help." Cosby is also responsible for
"One good thing happened to me this year--my wife finally
gave me a son--I think I'll have him dipped in gold," said
publicly on the national Emmy Awards telecast, June 7,
1970, ABC-TV.

147. middle-aged men. Dwight Whitney's "Six Authors in
Search of a Character," TV Guide:22-6, Oct. 31, 1970: "If
anyone doubts that a handful of middle-aged men dominate
the field, all he has to do is look at the Writers Guild of
America West roster...."

148. a negative term. Devised by the Male Mass Media
and utilized by them and some Duped Dames to deride the
contemporary Movement of women towards sexual equality.
The threatened male's assumption that women want to be like
him, or the same as he is, is absurd and egocentric. The
media would never be so crass or imprudent as to degrade
the contemporary movement of blacks towards racial equality
with a flip term like "Black Lib."

149. is male-oriented.   Feminists object to "Sesame Street"
for all of these reasons, but especially because it is male-
oriented.   They must work to change such programing and
the media's rationalization for it, e.g., writer Anne Sanders
in The American Way (inflight magazine of American Airlines, June 1971) justifies it this way: "For good reasons,
'Sesame Street' was developed as a male-oriented program.
This was done in order to counteract some negative effects
of the female-dominated family experience common to ghetto
children.   They offer masculine identification, then, often
at the expense of Susan, the show's female cast member.
According to the feminists, they could accomplish the one
without sacrificing the other."   Considerable has been written
about "Sesame Street's" negative aspects, but it hasn't appeared in controlled-circulation type magazines such as
The American Way; see, for example, the writings of Arnold
Arnold and Monica Sims.

150. the getting of (sexual) pleasure from being dominated,
mistreated or hurt.

151. all of these.

152. Shirley Chisholm, in her Unbought and Unbossed
(263, p. 33).

153. male chauvinism.

154. Coitus.
I disagree with you.   ("She's paranoid" = "She disagrees
     with me.")
You warm up too slow.
He disagrees with her.   (Same thing, slightly higher on the
     socioeconomic scale, would be "She needs to see a
     psychoanalyst.")
She accepts the status quo without question like a good girl
     should.
He made a bad contract.
She's audible.   (The fact that women like Bella Abzug,
     Shirley Chisholm and Gloria Steinem are audible and
     chic is even more threatening.   When men like David
     Susskind say some of the Women's Liberation women are
     "shrill," they mean about the same thing Harvard-style,
     i.e. they don't conform.)
She lost the baby.   ("It's just one of those things..." would
     have meant "She's pregnant.")
Just that.

Anything on the male side of the double standard, especially
    prostitution.
The female who does the office or other shitwork.

155.   Albert Einstein (page 105 of his Cosmic Religion
[1931]).

156.   Jean-Jacques Rousseau (57, p. 105).   And in his
Social contract, Rousseau advocates the overthrow of such a
state!   His attitude to the relationship between the sexes not
only fostered narcissism, but actually encouraged masochism
as well.

157.   TRUE.   Remarks of Ms. Catherine East, "A Better
World for Women" at the Women's City Club of Cleveland,
January 16, 1969.

158.   misogynist.

159.   Robert Frost.

160.   patriarchy.

161.   Machismo.   A Latin male considers "muy macho" real
praise.

162.   That women may have to go on a sex-strike in order
to achieve world peace generally and equality in particular.
Lysistrata, by Aristophanes, the third and concluding play
of the War and Peace Series, circa 411 B.C., tells of the
women of Athens led by Lysistrata, who determine to take
matters into their own hands in order to stop a 21-year war.
Lysistrata's successful scheme consists of rigorous application to husbands and lovers of self-denial.   (Dudley Fitts'
English version, published by Harcourt, is recommended.)

163.   FALSE (The MBA, March 1971, p. 48: editorial,
"A Myth That Dies Hard," by Susan Davis).   Coordinated
through the Department of Commerce, they include more
than 100 programs offered by various government agencies:
loans, set-aside contracts, technical assistance grants, etc.
"A feminist asked Secretary of Commerce Maurice Stans what
it would take for women to qualify for the minority enterprise programs, which offer financial and technical assistance
to minority businessmen (i.e. blacks, Indians, Chicanos,
Puerto Ricans).   Secretary Stans put his arm around her,
smiled patronizingly, and replied that everyone knows that

women control the country's wealth.   In other words, women
don't qualify." Women, of course, do not control the country's wealth.

164.   Robert Southey.

165.   they constitute a small numerical majority; this com-
plicating factor is unique to Women's Liberation and not
present for other minorities (the term minority can be used
in connection with women--e.g., employment-minority).
True equality of the sexes would mean giving up many things
that men of various races, religions, nationalities can share
or adjust to tolerably well.   A woman serves as a man's
psychological punching bag--a receptacle for just about everything he wants to unload ... pressures and tensions, both
physical and emotional.   She has to suffer his inequities--
e.g., husband comes home and unloads his job problems,
possibly involving discrimination and inequity he's experienced
at work.   In a broader sense, the cop, security guard,
supervisor, etc., commands a woman in a way he would
not a man.   A physically small man "deals with" a woman
in a way he cannot a larger man ... a diminishing progres-
sion.

166.   Plato, in The Republic.

167.   all of these.   It's just a matter of which ones can be
changed, e.g., enforcement of the Civil Rights Act, ratification of the Equal Rights Amendment, unity among women
of all races, or boycott of products and politicians.

168.   All I wanted out of this was a son.   NBC-TV News
8:30 A.M., June 14, 1971 "Today Show." See also New
York Times during this period.   Later they all died.

169.   There's Cobina Wright, Junior and Senior.   (What
does this mean to you?   Are men more concerned about
immortality than women?)

170.   Every mother's son.   Be a man.
       Take your medicine like   The manly art of ...
           a man.   Man in the street.
       Man O'War.   Man-hour.
       Mankind.   Gentleman and a scholar.
       Brotherhood.   Congratulations, it's a boy!
       12 good men and true.

171.   40% can be expected to leave yearly under these policies, thus reducing the number qualified for raises, pensions
and other benefits (34, p. 212).   The stewardess continues
to be the classic example of the sexual object.   Is sex a
bonafide qualification?   Male stewards are found in other
countries and on at least one American line.   Where stew-
ardesses are now permitted to marry, the sign listing flight
crew name may say "Miss" (one time when "Ms." would
work to the airlines' advantage) and they will announce themselves using first and last names (while a male voice comes
on strong with "This is Captain Smith").   On the 747 it's
a male voice that announces itself as "flight service director,
a member of American Airlines management."   And on a
recent American Airlines 747 flight, the comedy portion of
the recordings offered Bob Newhart in "The Man Who Looked
Like Hitler" routine of a conversation aboard a plane: "They
are really hiring beasts, nowadays, aren't they?"

*   *   *

Related Readings, Questions 136-171

Figes, E.	Patriarchal Attitudes.
Kendall, E.	The Upper Hand.
Lamb, M.	The Mod Donna & Scyklon Z.
Mill, J.	Essays on Sex Equality.
Rogers, K.	The Troublesome Helpmate.
Woodward, H.	The Lady Persuaders.

*   *   *

172.   feminism.

173.   caste.   A discussion of the significant difference
between slave and caste status can be found in 98, p. 49f.

174.   Stokeley Carmichael (81, p. 35).

175.   Eldridge Cleaver (81, p. 36).

176.   Martin Luther King, Jr.   (My Life With Martin
Luther King, Jr., by Coretta Scott King, page 60).

177.   Shirley Chisholm (263, p. 165).

178.   2 - 1 - 3.

179.   TRUE (New York Times IV:4, March 7, 1971: "Now,

27% of all black families--three times the white figure--
are headed only by a mother").

180.   A black woman refused to give up her bus seat.

181.   Saint Thomas (151, p. xvi).

182.   money-raising and church-housekeeping (98, p. 136f).
The New Feminism is having an impact here also, however,
e.g. members of the Unitarian Universalist Women's Federation have initiated efforts for abortion-law repeal within
several states.

183.   she was a woman   (World Almanac & Book of Facts,
1971, p. 821).

184.   the daily Orthodox Jewish prayer for a male (176,
p. 73).

185.   the Hindu Code of Manu (176, p. 64).

186.   from the writings of Pope John XXIII (81, p. 35).
Read Michael Novak's The Experience of Marriage: Thir-
teen Couples Report (Macmillan, 1966), the testimony of
some American Catholics.

187.   attributed to Martin Luther   (Burton Stevenson's
Home Book of Quotations, 9th ed., p. 2195).

188.   Saint Paul   (I Timothy 2:11-12 [King James Version]).
If you really want some maleness, read a letter from Paul.
He goes on, "For Adam was first formed, then Eve.   And
Adam was not deceived, but the woman being deceived was
in the transgression."

189.   fornication by the wife.   Matthew 19:9 (King James
Version): "And I say unto you, Whosoever shall put away
his wife, except it be for fornication, and shall marry another, committeth adultery: and whoso marrieth her which
is put away doth commit adultery."   The same statement is
attributed to Jesus in Matthew 5:32, but when Mark (10:11)
and Luke (16:18) report this conversation, they say nothing
about the exception for fornication.

190.   Elizabeth Cady Stanton.

191.   A good thought-question.   One might also note the

male clergy who elect to wear clerical collars, symbolic
jewelry, etc., indicative of their specialty and special status
on some occasions--likewise M.D.'s with white coats worn
over regular clothes, even in the streets, off-duty, in hot
weather.

192.   the Hare Krishna Movement (Back to Godhead: The
Magazine of the Hare Krishna Movement, no. 36, p. 32, no
date [c1970].   Published monthly by Iskcon Press, a division
of the International Society for Krishna Consciousness, Inc.,
38 North Beacon, Allston, Mass. 02134).   The outer, back
cover of this magazine is a full-color illustration of a black
male-like "demon" and white Sri Balarama: "Sri Balarama
is shown killing the Pralambesura demon with one blow of
His fist."

193.   The masculine Godhead: Genesis says that God created men in His own image and as "male and female."
Nevertheless, God has usually been portrayed as a man,
referred to with such "masculine qualities" as sternness.
Christians furthered the process by asserting that God became human in the person of a male.
       Ethical hypocrisy: according to feminist theologians,
Christian leaders developed an ethic based on such passive
virtues as humility and obedience, but then used them as a
means of subduing the other sex.   "While exhorting others,
chiefly women, to practice Christian virtues, they have
themselves pursued power, creativity and self-fulfillment on
levels far removed from obedience, self-abnegation or, for
that matter, chastity," wrote Barbara Sykes in The Episco-
pal New York, the diocesan newspaper.
       Religious symbols: feminists maintain that the funda-
mental symbols of Christianity are permeated with male
chauvinism, e.g., the story of Adam and Eve blames women
for the presence of sin in the world.   Catholics complain
that the figure of Mary has been idealized into a "sexless"
projection of male vanities, and that the usual picture of
her kneeling before her son is an affront to the role God intended for women.   (New York Times IV:6, May 9, 1971,
"Women's Lib: Was It Really Eve's Fault?" by Edward B.
Fiske.)

194.   Fu Hsuan ... Confucius (176, p. 61).

195.   Socrates.

196.   Buddhism and Christianity.

197. celibate priesthood (176, p. 82). Thus the insistence
that priests remain celibate is based on something far beyond "tradition"; equality between priests and nuns is also
out of the question.

198. Aristotle.

199. check the telephone directory or "Information."

200. all of these.

＊   ＊   ＊

Related Readings, Questions 172-200
Angelou, M.   I Know Why the Caged Bird Sings.
Cade, T.   The Black Woman.
Carson, J.   Silent Voices.
Daly, M.   The Church and the Second Sex.
Doley, S.   Women's Liberation and the Church.
McCarthy, M.   Memories of a Catholic Girlhood.
Mace, D.   Marriage East and West.

Part II

DOCUMENTATION FOR HUMAN EQUALITY

This Part II describes standard reference tools generally available in public and community college libraries
and relevant to the needs of all involved in the new feminist
movement--especially writers, informal researchers, planners, speakers, public figures, teachers and students. It
is not intended as a guide for deep scholarly research. An
attempt has been made to characterize each tool in the context of the Women's Liberation Movement; while it is important to know how to use the key to the news which The
New York Times Index, for example, can provide, it is
even more important to understand its limitations. Reference works reflecting recognition of the potential and ne-
glected market of specialized tools for, by and about women
have begun to appear on the market: some, like Foremost
Women in Communications and Notable American Women, in
conventional channels and others, like The Dictionary of
Sexism, less so. New indexes and other reference works
have recently appeared reflecting the interests of librarians,
publishers and bibliographers in all of the social change
movements; while they may not be in the "average" library
reference collection, some will be pointed out.

Parts of this section may be a review for some--the
inevitable result of our uneven library backgrounds. The
potential power of libraries and library skills is diminished
by school library programs whose quality varies from state
to state and community to community. It follows that the
young by-product instructor often does not integrate teaching
and library use. The holder of an advanced academic degree may have been exposed to a few standard references
in her or his subject and possibly some basic bibliographic
tools for getting around in it. Mere awareness, however,
rarely leads to intimacy. The human tendency is to assume
that we know all about that to which we have merely been
exposed.

The principles of organizing books and the information

73

their contents provide are basically the same in almost
every library. A graduate of a high school providing a
quality school library program has had the opportunity to
learn the principles basic to the use of any library, as well
as to acquire related skills of their application to both
sources and locators of information. It does not matter,
for example, whether a library's card catalog has subject-
cards whose first lines are in red or in all caps--the point
is consistency and that the user understands the concept of
the subject-approach. It does not matter whether Simone
de Beauvoir's The Second Sex has the author-card filed
under "D" or under "B"--the point is that all of her titles
are under one or under the other, with a cross-reference
("SEE") leading to the one utilized. It does not matter if
one has never used specialized indexes--the point is that a
basic index such as Readers' Guide has been introduced and
mastered in school as a standard locator of information
whose principles are applicable to other indexes.

*   *   *

Current Events

"There is no equality except in a cemetery."
(Rep. Emanuel Celler, New York Times,
August 11, 1970, p. 23.)

NEW YORK TIMES INDEX

        The daily and Sunday editions, including the Magazine
Section (VI) of The New York Times newspaper are analyzed
by The New York Times Index in an alphabetical approach to
their contents in terms of subject-matter. Of course, the
New York Times Company employs renowned writers and
subject-specialists whose bylines are important assets, but
the emphasis in newspaper reportage is on the proverbial
who-what-where-when-why. The Index is necessarily published twice a month with annual cumulations (interfiling
of back issues) since it is tied to a periodical. It can be
used retrospectively to 1913, and is especially useful for
its references to important speeches, which are often entirely reprinted. The location of coverage in other newspapers can be derived from the Index and brief synopses
within answer some questions without reference to the
newspaper. Access to book-reviews is a useful feature,
especially if the complete or accurate author's name or the

title is unknown; listings are grouped under the descriptor
(the <u>Index</u> term for subject-heading) "Book Reviews." Initial use of the <u>Index</u> is not simple, but it takes only a little
practice; note the instructions included in each supplement
and regular volume.

No amount of skill in using the <u>Index</u> will replace
systematic newspaper reading. Research necessitates using
an index to locate exactly an item only vaguely remembered,
or to "cover" subject matter, but one needs to build critical
reading into the day's routine. Are the (male) media selective (biased?) Do they discriminate against women?
Notice the dearth of women's bylines, pictures and employment "opportunities" in Section III: "Business & Finance"
of the Sunday issue. The slant given to coverage of women
is identifiable--for example, on May 9, 1970 a rally was held
in Brooklyn's Prospect Park in connection with the Equal
Rights Amendment. It was well attended and covered by
television news. As chairman of the House Judiciary Committee, Representative Emanuel Celler's negative influence
has been great, and the group confronted him as a Brooklyn
resident. Indexing covering issues of <u>The New York Times</u>
from May 1 to 15, 1970 mentions only his 82nd birthday
celebration.

In 1969, the New York Times Company established
new records in revenues, earnings and advertising. The
company's Annual Report indicates that "During the year
several important changes were made in the management
of the News Department, bringing able young men into posts
of greater responsibility." Women appear in eight of the
approximately 29 photographs of in-plant operations--cooking,
serving food, typing, looking up something in the library,
telephoning, waiting in and exiting from the Medical Department. On the other hand, females are portrayed as using
all (except <u>The Golf Digest)</u> of the company's several
products.

A statement from Human Rights for Women, Inc.
(1128 National Press Building, Washington, D.C. 20004)
describes a group of New York feminists who

> started a sit-in in the offices of Grove Press on
> April 13 [1970] claiming that Grove Press pub-
> lishes pornographic literature which is degrading
> to women, sadistic, and misogynic. Grove Press
> called the police and nine women were arrested,

charged with "criminal trespass" and "criminal
mischief."

The women were detained by the police until the
following day, transferred from precinct to precinct four or five times so that their attorneys
could not locate them, denied food for fourteen
hours (one of the women was a stress diabetic)
and forced to strip and squat for the alleged purpose of searching for weapons or narcotics, although there was no narcotics or concealed weapons charge. Five of the women had their periods
and were ordered to remove their tampons for
search and were refused replacements.

One of the young women refused to submit to the
"strip and squat" order, which is used by some
police departments to intimidate, humiliate and
break down women charged with even minor of-
fenses. Unable to cope with her, the police
matrons separated her from the other women and
turned her over to "the men" [male police]. One
of the policemen threatened "to beat her face to
a pulp" if she did not submit....

Finally, a police lieutenant ordered that she be
spread-eagled and shackled to the cell bars....

The New York police department may have set a
record for the number of violations of constitutional
rights in a single incident.

When the women were released, they reported
their harrowing experiences to the press and
threatened to sue the police department. The
charges of criminal trespass and criminal mischief against the women were dropped.

Locate the coverage The New York Times gave to this "incident" via The New York Times Index; how much can you
glean from the entry in the Index itself? Turn to the newspaper and decide whether adequate and fair coverage was
provided in the context of the statement above. Some requests for information which can be located via The New
York Times Index follow, with their "solutions." Think
each through before starting.

Regarding the Grove Press incident ...

Because the incident occurred on April 13, 1970, look first in the Index April 1-15, 1970 Supplement, or in the 1970 cumulated annual volume, under "Grove Press" [quotation marks indicate subject-headings under which information may be found]. Answer: Ap 14, 55:3 [Meaning April 14th issue, page 55, column 3]. Turn to the issue of the New York Times for April 14, 1970, page 55, 3rd column.

"Mod Donna" has been called "the ambisexual liberation musical." Its first performance was in the New York Shakespeare Festival Public Theatre on April 24, 1970. What kind of reviews did it get? Did editors assign any women to review it?

April 16-30 Supplement = 0. April 24th was a Saturday-- perhaps reviews appeared in a Sunday issue 8 days later, i.e. May 1-15 Supplement. "Theater--Reviews."
Answer: C Barnes My 4, 48:1; G Glueck My 10, II, 1:1; W Kerr My 10, II:1. G Glueck = Grace Glueck by reference to the newspaper itself; you may already know that Barnes and Kerr are well-known male reviewers.

There was considerable speculation and innuendo at the time of Dorothy Kilgallen's death in 1969; of what did she die?

1969 cumulated volume. "Kilgallen, Dorothy" Nov 16, 1969, 49:1.
Answer: "... reaction of a combination of alcohol and barbiturate ... 'acute ethanol and barbiturate intoxication'."

Is the Proud Eagle Tribe a radical women's liberation group?

October 1-15 1970 supplement (or 1970 volume) "Proud Eagle Tribe (Organization)" Oct 15 70. See also Harvard University "Harvard" O 14, 30:6; O 15, 20:4.
Answer: statement in indexing indicates that explosions in the Harvard library may be linked

to a revolutionary women's group, the Proud Eagle Tribe, which is linked to counter-insurgency.

There were ten women members in the House of Representatives on August 10, 1970, when the Equal Rights Amendment was voted on. How did they vote?

August 1-15, 1970 Supplement. "U.S. Constitution--Proposed Amendments--Women" Ag 9, 11, 12, 13. August 11:24. Answer: of 10 women House members, 9 voted for the Amendment; the 10th, Lenor K. Sullivan (Dem. /Missouri), had announced opposition and was absent.

You are watching a TV show in which a panel from the media interviews political figures--it is pre-election 1970, and Herman Badillo's response to a question includes reference to the tragic incident at Kent State, and, in his words, "the killing of the young men." No one challenges him. How can you check out your doubt about this statement? (He was elected to represent the people of the 21st New York Congressional district.)

May 1-15, 1970 "Kent State University." page 49. Answer: "... Ohio National Guardsmen fatally shoot four students, including two co-eds ..." in bold type, within the indexing.

READERS' GUIDE TO PERIODICAL LITERATURE

Readers' Guide indexes the contents of approximately 160 well known, general magazines reflecting the range of subject-matter and treatment of the contemporary scene-- from Atlantic to Ebony, Good Housekeeping to Ladies' Home Journal, Look to Newsweek, they are the magazines most read by Americans and available in most libraries. (These six titles as well as several others indexed are also available as talking books, in braille, or on magnetic tape.) Bound cumulations cover each year, as well as larger periods of time, retrospectively to 1900. Author and subject-

entries for each article and title-entries for stories are all
in one alphabet. Emphasis is again on the subject approach.
Information to locate each article is provided: the name of
the magazine, its date and volume number, pagination; in
addition, the presence of such useful materials as maps,
portraits and other illustrations, and bibliographies is noted.
Entries are under very specific subjects (for example, "Women's Liberation Movement") and are multiple-listed,
making it easy to find any specific single article, or all
articles published within a time-span on any one subject.
Cross-references (SEE and SEE ALSO) lead to the desired
information or to additional relevant information. The
H. W. Wilson Company specializes in such tools for many
of the disciplines and makes available a free brochure,
"How to Use the Readers' Guide to Periodical Literature
and Other Indexes."

An entire special issue of
Atlantic was devoted to
"the woman question" in
1970, someone says. Can
you locate it bibliograph-
ically?

"Women--U.S.": in indexing
covering 1970. Woman's place;
symposium. Il Atlantic 224:81-
112+ Mar '70 Disc 225:94-7
My '70.

You read of a "blatantly
Victorian" issue on the
Negro woman in Ebony
during 1966. Can you lo-
cate it from this information?

Volume 26 "Negro women":
Negro woman; symposium,
with Intro. by J. H. Johnson
21:25+ Aug '66.

Who has been called the
king of abortionists?
(Provide full name)

Volume 29 = "Abortion": King
of the abortionists; clinic operated by R. D. Spencer il Newsweek 73:92 F 17 '69. "Spencer":
Answer: Robert King Spencer.

The perpetuation of sex-
role stereotypes plays an
important part in keeping
women down. The rela-
tionship of family size and
sex-role stereotypes is an
aspect of this. You are
interested but hesitate to
use scholarly journals.
Would it be possible to

Volume 29 = 0. Supplement
covering indexing from Jan.
16-April 16, 1970: Family
size--SEE "Family, size of."
Answer: Family size and sex-
role stereotypes bibliog Science 167:390-2 Ja 23 '70 F E
Clarkson and others.

locate an up-to-date article
in a popular magazine, yet
one which is authoritative
and might even include a
bibliography?

You hear there's an article
in Esquire magazine some-
where about a woman with
concave breasts ...

Volume 25 "Woman with concave breasts; a story" SEE
Wegner, Robert E. Esquire
63:84 F '65.

What body of the United
Nations seems to have re-
sponsibility for the condition of women? Which
periodicals indexed in
Readers' Guide provide information about it regularly?

Any cumulation: "United Nations
--Commission on the Status of
Women." Answer: UN Mo C,
Dept of St Blt = The UN
Monthly Chronicle and The De-
partment of State Bulletin.
(See list of periodicals indexed
in front of each volume.)

Gloria Steinem did an interview with Hugh Hefner in
1970; can you locate it?

Nov. 10, 1970 Supplement or
major cumulation covering 1970:
Steinem, Gloria SEE "Hefner,
Hugh Marston" (or directly to
"Hefner.") What Playboy
doesn't know about women could
fill a book; interview by G.
Steinem. Il por McCalls 98:
139-4 O '70.

Host Mike Douglas, in
"welcoming" guest Kate
Millett to his show re-
ferred to her mother's
attitude toward her daughter's activities as "she
should wash her hair,"
stating that his source was
"Time or Newsweek." Did
he give an accurate cita-
tion? Impression?

Nov. 10, 1970 Supplement or
major cumulation covering 1970:
"Millett, Kate" Time 96:18-19
Ag 31 '70. Answer: "The
attention rubs off on her family,
too; in St. Paul, her mother
states her firm support of
Kate's work, but wishes she
would 'dress herself up. Kate's
missing the boat if she appears
on the Mike Douglas show without her hair washed'."

ALTERNATIVE PRESS INDEX

Underground movement newspapers and periodicals

which "amplify the cry for social change and social justice"
are indexed by this new publication, a quarterly available at
a special rate to Movement groups and people. The print-
out format is not as difficult to cope with as in many publi-
cations, and a "How to Use" is provided at the beginning.
Especially relevant periodicals indexed include Broadside,
I. F. Stone's Bi-Weekly, Leviathan, Liberation, Liberator,
Mother Earth News, Monthly Review, Motive, Movement,
New York Review of Books, Old Mole, Ramparts, Rat, This
Magazine Is About Schools, and The Village Voice. No
Women's Movement periodicals per se are indexed, although
relevant articles are cited via such subject-headings as
"Women's Liberation, " "Sexual Revolution, " "Employment--
Women, " "Radical Women, " "Abortion, " "Day Care Centers, "
"Divorce, " and "Prostitution. " During API's first year,
there were no entries under "Rape"; "Prostitution" was
strictly Vietnam/male. The system of subject-headings
seems to be still evolving.

Judge Harrold Carswell received much publicity be-
cause of his alleged racist
attitude, but not much for
his sexist. Locate at least
one author who dared to
point out this possibility...

Vol. 2, no. 1 Jan-March 1970,
p. 49 "Women's Oppression":
Carswell--Also a male supremacist R Furst Guardian 22
19 p5 2/7/70. Answer: R.
Furst wrote "Carswell--Also a
Male Supremacist, " which appeared in The Guardian, February 7, 1970 issue, beginning
on page 5.

Subject-Matter Summaries: Encyclopedias

Rosetta Stone was made by the Egyptians.

INTERNATIONAL ENCYCLOPEDIA OF THE
SOCIAL SCIENCES

The standard encyclopedias available in most American libraries, peddled door-to-door in suburbia, and copied
by high school students vary in their approaches to the subject of women as well as in the amount of coverage--pos-
sibly the result of male editorial policy-making and writing.
An interesting case in point is provided by one of the few
really new encyclopedias, The International Encyclopedia of

The Social Sciences [New York: Macmillan and Free Press,
c1967; information from Prospectus, preface, other preliminary pages, and contents table].   Most encyclopedias
have adopted so-called continuous revision, issuing newly-
copyrighted sets consisting of some almost never-changing
basic articles, some new articles on such events as the
moon-landings, and some updated articles with additional or
changed facts, e.g., the development of heart-transplants
in surgery and the death of General DeGaulle.   When material is added, something has to go or the set expands
endlessly.   Cross-references, past-tenses, indexing, etc.
are not always maintained, and a chopped-up effect can
result.

     In considering the need for a completely new ency-
clopedia (new as opposed to the old "Encyclopedia of the
Social Sciences" which was published 1930-35,) the Ford
Foundation provided funds to enable a special group of eight
men to study the matter.   The ten policy-making editors of
the new encyclopedia were men.   Down on the nitty-gritty
level of people listed on the "staff" were several women.
Articles on topics crucial to woman and her place in the
social sciences include Fertility Control, Fashion, Animal
Sexual Behavior, Social Aspects of Sexual Behavior, Psychological Aspects of Sexual Deviation, Labor Force Participation, Social Aspects of Sexual Deviation, and Prostitution
--all written by men, the last two by the co-author of the
negative reply to McCalls' article asking "Is a women's
revolution really possible?"   No, he [John Gagnon] replied,
"truly free women would undermine society."*

ENCYCLOPEDIA AMERICANA (associated with The Ameri-
     cana Annual)

     The last complete revision of the Americana was pub-
lished 1918-20, but it also employs continuous revision.   It
has a detailed, alphabetical index-volume.   The majority of
articles are lengthy but not exhaustive.   There is an em-

_____
*"Is a women's revolution really possible?   Yes says the
young liberated woman who no longer wants to be a man's
'toy, pet, or mascot'," by Leslie Aldridge Westoff.   "No,
say two eminent sociologists, who claim that truly free women would undermine society," by John Gagnon and William
Simon.   McCalls, October 1969:76f.

phasis on contemporary American places, organizations and
institutions, as well as on science and technology. Remember it as an encyclopedia to turn to for information on
American places, histories of different centuries, glossaries
of technical terms and texts of documents. Substantial
articles from the 1966 copyright include Woman Suffrage, by
Esther W. Hymer, who is identified as U.N. Observer,
United Church Women; Feminism, by Felix Grendon, who
is not otherwise identified; and Women, Legal Rights of,
also by a man--Monrad G. Paulsen, professor of law at
Columbia University. Emma Goldman is considered a
"Russian anarchist" in the brief 1955 edition entry.

Evaluate comparatively each of the articles on Women
(Woman) in the major encyclopedias by considering the
qualifications and sex of the author; bibliography; related
questions and assumptions, e.g., role and scope, and em-
phases--such as on suffrage, ancient history, the Equal
Rights Amendment.

Biography

Or Mother was a "Miscellaneous Writer."

> The bigger the job, the less likely it is to be
> filled by a woman. This means that women at
> the top are exceptional among women. It also
> means that the elite of any group can assume that
> it is stag; the few women at the top can be ig-
> nored or treated as exceptions. Yet there are
> always some women up there....

And they are what Ms. Caroline Bird goes on to describe
as in the loophole classifications of Dynastic women, Token
women, Gimmick women, Sex women, and Office wives and
housekeepers [in: Born Female; The High Cost of Keeping
Women Down (McKay, 1968), p. 102-3, and Chapter 5].
While there is a variety of biographical directories on the
market, directory-type information usually consists of such
data as the biographee's name, address, and current position. If the biographee provided the information by filling
in a questionnaire, additional personal information (and
slant) may be included, possibly some details of her or his
work, specialization, or other common interest around which

the directory is built, e.g. "Men of the REIGN," "All the
Men of the BIBLE," "DIRECTORS in the City of New York,"
"Soviet Men of SCIENCE," "McGraw-Hill Modern Men of
SCIENCE."

WHO'S WHO IN AMERICA; A BIOGRAPHICAL DICTIONARY
    OF NOTABLE LIVING MEN AND WOMEN.
WHO'S WHO OF AMERICAN WOMEN; A BIOGRAPHICAL DIC-
    TIONARY OF NOTABLE LIVING AMERICAN WOMEN.

    It is Who's Who in America that most people have in
mind when they refer to someone's "making Who's Who."
(Who's Who is an annual published in London listing mainly
distinguished living Englishmen.) Notable, living Americans
are listed alphabetically, with brief biographical data, including addresses, as provided by the biographees themselves. Separately-published geographical and vocational
indexes, necrologies and cumulative indexes provide greater
access to this information.

    There are, however, comparatively few women who
seem to be notable, living and American in any given two-
year period. Five per cent of the "prestige elite" listed in
the 1967 Who's Who in America were women--down from
6 per cent in 1930 [Bird, op. cit., p. 103]. This may be
due to the scope being determined in part by formula-
coverage of certain job-titles. A biographee can be dropped
if she/he changes job or field. But more importantly, the
categories of jobs are those which generally do not include
women--all members of the President's Cabinet, United
States Congress, governors, ambassadors, heads of major
universities and colleges, bishops and chief ecclesiastics
of the principal religious denominations, and principal officers of national and international businesses. The Marquis
Who's Who Company is in business: it also publishes Who's
Who of American Women structured along the same lines.
Whether Who's Who of American Women supplements, complements or overlaps Who's Who in America is a good
question.

AMERICAN MEN OF SCIENCE
DIRECTORY OF AMERICAN SCHOLARS

    American Men of Science is an example of a bio-
graphical directory which has come to be in almost every

library. It has appeared in 11 editions (the 12th begun in 1971 and was retitled American Men and Women of Science), its multi-volumes covering United States and Canadian women and men in the physical, biological, social, and behavioral sciences. A glance at the specific fields within these four disciplines reads like a roster of male-domination: agriculture, economics, engineering, medicine, nucleonics, physics, political science. The Directory of American Scholars complements American Men of Science in its coverage of scholarship in the humanities: drama, English, foreign languages, history, law, linguistics, philology, philosophy, religion, speech.

BIOGRAPHY INDEX

Where does one turn for leads to relatively authoritative and detailed biographical material on contemporary women and the men who determine their way of life? An index, rather than a directory, is needed in this type of situation. The Biography Index is, according to its subtitle, "a cumulative index to biographical materials in books and magazines." Each issue lists in-print materials (books currently available on the trade-market) under a main, or "name" alphabet of biographees. The alphabetical index by occupations provides an additional avenue of access to this information. There are further breakdowns under Occupation--nationality, for example. Information on both living and deceased persons is indexed. In addition to the citations (leads) provided, information is contained within the entries themselves, e.g., the subject's birth and death dates, occupation, maiden and complete name. Volume 7 lists a magazine article about a Mary Lindsay under the revealing entry: "Lindsay, Mary (Harrison), 1927?-   wife of Mayor John Vliet Lindsay." Patricia (Ryan) Nixon's occupation is "president's wife." Marie (Sklodowska) Curie, however, made it--she is a "chemist."* References to portraits, other illustrations and bibliographies are included in the indexing. One would expect the library which has The Biography Index in its reference collection to also have a good representation of the books and magazines it indexes.

---

*A fascinating examination of the built-in bias of another subject heading scheme is Prejudices and Antipathies: A Tract on the LC Subject Heads Concerning People (Scarecrow Press, 1971); author Sanford Berman includes a chapter, "Man/Woman/Sex."

CURRENT BIOGRAPHY

Current Biography is one of the few contemporary biographical tools which provides considerable background about the life and work of each subject. Its scope is not limited by nationality, sex or occupation--the subjects are leaders in their fields and in today's news. Documented biographical treatment in depth utilizes newspapers, magazines, books and occasionally the subjects themselves as sources which are identified at the end of each article. Included are specific details of the biographee's career; such practical information as pronunciation if the name is unusual, address, birth-date; critical evaluations of her/his work; her/his views, attitudes, opinions; and a recent photograph. Current Biography is published every month except August and cumulates into a yearbook with a helpful cumulated Index every five and ten years. In fact, a biographee can appear more than once, for example, Dr. Benjamin Spock, in 1956 and 1969. The Index to Women of the World from Ancient to Modern Times: Biographies and Portraits, compiled by Norma Olin Ireland, includes women described in Current Biography and in New Yorker magazine's "Profiles" as well as in some books for young people.

DICTIONARY OF AMERICAN BIOGRAPHY

Subjects of lengthy biographies are deceased American women and men who have made significant contributions to American life in a variety of fields. DAB is noted for the good writing of its identified authors, accuracy and its bibliographies. It includes about 700 biographies of women out of a total of nearly 15,000 entries. It was modeled to some extent on another useful set, The Dictionary of National Biography, which encompasses inhabitants of the British Isles and its Colonies and also excludes living persons--Mary Wollstonecraft is listed under her married name, Godwin, with her occupation given as "miscellaneous writer."

Is it true that Senator Edward Kennedy was suspended from Harvard for cheating?

Current Biography 1963 Annual (via 1960-9 Index): "Kennedy, Edward Moore" p. 217. Answer: yes; asked a classmate to take a Spanish examination for him. They were both caught and suspended. Kennedy was reinstated.

Who is Leontyne Price's husband? How do you pronounce her first name?

Current Biography 1961 Annual (via 1961-9 Index): "Price, (Mary) Leontyne" p. 374-5. Answer: Mr. William Warfield. Lē on' tēn.

By what male biblical name was Harriet Tubman known? Why?

Dictionary of American Biography (c1936) p. 27: "Tubman, Harriet." Answer: Moses, because she led 300+ slaves from bondage to freedom in the North and Canada.

Is it true that Congresswoman Shirley Chisholm has her doctorate? What is Mr. Chisholm's occupation? It is true that she is a contest-winning amateur ball-room dancer? Is it true that she has an English education? Locate at least ten references for further information about her.

Current Biography 1969 vol. (via 1961-9 Index): "Chisholm, Shirley" p. 92-5. Answer: she has an honorary Doctor of Humane Letters from Pratt Institute (1969) and has her MA from Columbia University (elementary education). He is an investigator for New York City Department of Social Services. Yes. Attended Barbados elementary school. Bibliography on page 95.

Harriet Blatch was the daughter of what famous women's suffrage worker? What was her full name? Where was she born?

DAB Suppl. 2 (vol. 22) p. 43-4: "Blatch, Harriet Eaton Stanton." Answer: daughter of Elizabeth Cady Stanton. Born Seneca Falls, N.Y.

Newscaster Harry Reasoner authored the book, "Tell me about women." On what did he base this?

Current Biography. 1966 Annual (via 1961-9 Index): "Reasoner, Harry" p. 322-4. Answer: one reviewer said it was "probably partly autobiographical." (P.H. Bickerton in the Springfield Republican, May 12, 1946.)

Locate a book for children which contains a biography of Elizabeth Cady Stanton.

Biography Index. Vol. 7 p. 19: "Stanton, Elizabeth (Cady) 1815-1902, Feminist--Juvenile Literature." Answer: McNeer, May Yonge, Give Me Freedom

(Abingdon, 1964), p. 61-76
Il por (This is just one example.)

Susan Sontag is said to be   Current Biography. 1969 annual
the author of Freed; The   cumulation: "Sontag, Susan"
Mind of the Moralist   p. 413-15. Answer: by agree-
(Viking), but the title is   ment with Philip Ruff, her ex-
not associated with her   husband, only his name appears
name anywhere.   on title page.

Government Publications

The Women's Bureau is Part of
the Labor Department

        Government publications are sometimes referred to
as "documents," but they represent a source--a publisher--
rather than any one type of output. Knowing about them, because of their varied subject-matter, formats, sources and
levels of sophistication, can be time-consuming and yet rewarding. While public libraries in the past may not generally have collected government publications and the associated indexes to their contents, they are becoming more
aware of this source of inexpensive publications relevant to
the layperson's needs. Government publications--from and
about the various levels (e.g., city, county, state, federal)
and parts of American government--are especially relevant
to the status of women. Education, politics, employment
and health are some areas of mutual concern. Sources of
statistical information at the federal government level are
important in documenting the existence of discriminatory
practices. A United States government publication has an
issue-date but not a copyright and can be quoted freely.

SELECTED UNITED STATES GOVERNMENT PUBLICATIONS
PRICE LISTS (series)

        Two free titles come to mind. Selected U.S. Govern-
ment Publications is distributed bi-weekly to anyone request-
ing her/his name be placed on the mailing list. It highlights
"best-sellers" among the United States federal government's

standing titles--a current, small selection of popular books
and pamphlets. Price Lists is a series of more than 70
federal government publications now in print. The inclusion
in each List of pamphlet materials, as well as its up-to-
dateness, makes it an extremely useful publisher's catalog of
special interest to women (e.g., no. 31 Education; 33 Labor;
33A Occupations, Professions and Job Descriptions; 70 Census; and 86 Consumer Information). The Government puts
out a flier listing all the Price Lists, with labels for establishing oneself on either or both of these two mailing-
lists: "How to Keep in Touch with U.S. Government Publications."

HANDBOOK ON WOMEN WORKERS

Probably of most interest to women is The Handbook
on Women Workers, the major publication of the Women's
Bureau, which is part of the Wage and Labor Standards Administration of the U.S. Department of Labor. "This in-
valuable ... paper-covered 'Bible' brings together the salient
Government statistics on women's income, education, employment, occupations, and legal status" [Bird, Born Female
(1968), p. 251]. Individuals should request a single, free
copy from the Bureau; ask also for "Publications of the
Women's Bureau Currently Available" (Leaflet 10, latest
revision).

The 1969 Handbook, to quote from the Foreword by
Ms. Elizabeth Duncan Koontz, Director of the Women's
Bureau (1972), "is designed as a ready source of reference. Part I deals with women in the labor force; Part II,
the laws governing women's employment and status; Part
III, the Interdepartmental Committee, the Citizens' Advisory
Council, and the State commissions on the status of women;
Part IV, organizations of interest to women; Part V is a
selected bibliography on American workers. This 1969 edition includes information that has become available since
1965. Knowledge about the work women do, the circumstances of their working, and the direction of changes in
their work is essential--if society is to make maximum use
of the potential of women as a human resource and if women
themselves are to take advantage of the greater opportunities
now available to them." Many Women's Bureau publications
would serve the reference librarian and her/his patrons
well; examples of other highly relevant and recent titles are:

Continuing education programs and services for women.
Pamphlet 10, 1971.   70¢ US GPO 2902-0042
Fact sheet on the earnings gap. Dec. 1971rev. WB71-86.
US GPO 1971. 0 419 373.
Laws on sex discrimination in employment; Federal
Civil Rights Act, Title VII State Fair Employment
Practices Laws executive orders. US GPO 1970
0-383-902. 30¢.
Summary of State Labor Laws for Women.   Annual
Underutilization of women workers. Revised 1971.
35¢ US GPO 1971   0-413-102.

OFFICIAL CONGRESSIONAL DIRECTORY

The Congressional Directory is useful in identifying
and reaching personnel. For each member of the Congress,
there is biographical material and indication of committee
assignment(s). The biography includes a statement of the
district's boundaries and an up-to-date population estimate;
state maps show these districts. State delegations are
itemized. Another section lists names and often addresses
of Congress(wo)men's administrative assistants and secretaries. The organization and personnel of Congress and its
committees, all of the executive bodies and miscellaneous
commissions and boards, and the Judiciary are provided.
The United States Government Organization Manual is another source of information; annually revised, it is particularly useful for the names of administrators.

STATISTICAL ABSTRACT OF THE UNITED STATES

The Statistical Abstract is an annual digest of data
collected from statistical agencies of the U.S. government
and a few private agencies by the Bureau of the Census of
the Department of Commerce and covering population, vital
statistics, immigration, finance, railroads, commerce, etc.
It is the type of publication included in Selected U.S. Government Publications' listings. Many of the tables in the
1970 edition present their data in a retrospective, comparative manner. Page v lists the various publications which
should be used to supplement The Statistical Abstract (e. g.,
County & City Data Book) and page 961 provides a guide to
state statistical abstracts. A glance at Section 2: Vital
Statistics, Health, and Nutrition (commencing on page 45)
reveals the type of relevant information provided. Tables

of information and data include:

Illegitimate live births, by age and race of mother: 1940-1968

Children ever born to women ever married, by selected characteristics of women: 1960 and 1969 (those characteristics including amount of education, status in the labor force, race, location, and type of residence.)

Expectation of life at birth: 1920-1967, by sex and race.

Marriages and divorces, 1940-1969, by ages, sex, children.

Physicians, by sex and age, by place of graduation: 1967 (including Canadian and other foreign, from unpublished American Medical Association data).

Infant, maternal, fetal, and neonatal death rates, by race: 1940-68.

Heart disease, arthritis (both types) and hypertension in adults by sex and age groups.

MONTHLY LABOR REVIEW

Special issues of this magazine are summaries of special reports in the field of labor in the United States. Each issue contains a bibliography of recent labor literature. Statistics of employment, labor turnover, earnings and hours, work stoppages, prices, cost-of-living (average cost of the necessities of life, e.g., food, shelter, clothes, medical expense) are provided. While there has been considerably more emphasis on its coverage of other labor groups, women have received consideration, e.g., "Women at Work," a special section of the June 1970 issue. (Readers' Guide will produce others.)

DOCUMENT AND REFERENCE TEXT: AN INDEX TO MINORITY GROUP EMPLOYMENT INFORMATION

DART is an Equal Employment Opportunity Commission publication which includes in its coverage several hundred titles dealing with women, who constitute but one of several minority groups encompassed. The 1967 edition was supplemented in 1971. Neither volume is available in the libraries of Columbia University, as one example.

What is the number of your
Congressional district? Who
are your representatives?
Senators? How many Con-
gressional districts are
there in your state? (Likewise, who are your state-
level representatives in the
legislature?)

Official Congressional Directory.
Current edition. Your state,
alphabetically. (Ask your reference librarian for the corres-
ponding state-level title--simply
request your state's "handbook"
or "manual.")

What age-group and which
sex suffer most from
hypertension?

Statistical Abstract, 1970.
Table of contents. Section 2:
Vital statistics... p. 79.
Answer: 1960-62 Adults 18-79
years of age. 1960-62 Males
17.2%, females 12.2% (% of
adults 14.6%). Age 75-79,
27.5%.

Which sex had longer life
expectancy in 1970?

Statistical Abstract, 1970.
Table of contents. Section 2:
Vital statistics... p. 53.
Answer: 1967 female--74.2
years (male 67). Ask your-
self related questions, e.g.,
Is this true of Caucasian and
Negro races? The answer is
there.

What are the sexes of the
Commissioners of the
Equal Employment Oppor-
tunity Commission? What
is the address of the EEOC
and its telephone number?

Official Congressional Directory,
92nd Congress (convened Jan.
21, 1971). Table of contents:
independent agencies section.
Alphabetical arrangement, i.e.
p. 625: "Equal." Answer:
Judging by first names, 4 men
and 1 woman. 1800 G Street,
Washington, D.C. Phone 343-
3539 (Code 183 x 33539).

Each Congress(wo)man has
an administrative assistant
and apparently a secretary;
how do their sexes seem
to be distributed and do
they correlate with the
sex of the employer?

Official Congressional Directory,
92nd Congress. Abridged contents: xx. Section: Lists of
representatives; administrative
assistants and secretaries. p.
329, "Administrative assistants..."
Answer: p. 335, Bella Abzug,

for example, has both a female
administrative assistant and
secretary, judging by first
names. Overall males seem
to turn up more as "Administrative Assistants" and women
as "secretaries." See, for
example, Edward Kennedy,
Emanuel Celler.

Handbooks, Directories and Other Tools

Or, "A Good Cigar is a Smoke."

Although no handbook on the Women's Rights Movement has been compiled--the so-called "Civil Rights Handbook" [J. A. Adams and J. M. Burke, Civil Rights; A Current Guide to the People, Organizations and Events (New
York, Bowker, 1970)] relates mainly to race--a number of
works exist which can provide specialized information relevant to the interests and concerns of workers and students
in the Movement. The latest edition in each case should
be sought out, although older editions occasionally are useful comparatively.

ENCYCLOPEDIA OF ASSOCIATIONS

The main volume of this "encyclopedia" encompasses
national organizations of the United States with many classifications: business, social welfare, religion, horticulture,
athletics, education, health, government, science, labor and
hobbies. An alphabetical "key-word" index may initially be
difficult for the layperson, but makes it possible to identify
organizations devoted to a particular subject of interest as
well as to locate a specific organization after a little practice. "Woman," "Women," "Abortion," "Day care," "Divorce," and "Alimony" are examples of key-words. There
is a loose-leaf up-dating service. The vast number of
women's auxiliaries and other handmaiden and appendage
groups can be clearly seen here.

WORLD ALMANAC & BOOK OF FACTS

This is the most common, well known library and
home reference tool besides the unabridged dictionary and--
in the library--the card catalog. Don't by-pass any of them.
Up-to-date miscellaneous information for the preceding year
emphasizes statistics of government, industries, population,
schools, sports, etc. Its emphases on both the past and
things American contradict the title. One volume of miscellaneous information can be valuable if one bears in mind
that use of the index is essential, and that its reliance on
secondary and even tertiary sources limits both reliability
and up-to-dateness somewhat. An article on women's
achievements in 1970 was included in the 1971 World Almanac.

BOOK OF THE STATES

General articles on various aspects of state governments are supplemented by manuals which are available for
complete information on individual states. For each state,
The Book of The States provides the routine things (picture
of the governor, seal, nickname, motto, flower, bird, etc.)
and the names of chief officials and information on the
state's legislative reference service. State labor legislation
affecting employment of women is summarized, and published
separately as a reprint by the Women's Bureau. State
manuals--published by official state agencies or by commercial publishers--are useful and important tools as well,
and a majority are available for the asking, or at low prices
any library can afford. A checklist of current state manuals, with specific information on how to obtain them, appeared in Special Libraries (February 1971); hopefully,
Frederick G. Cook, its author, will keep it up-to-date.

CONSUMER REPORTS
CONSUMER BULLETIN

These are two popular magazines indexed in Readers'
Guide. The Reports' annual December issue, " Buying
Guide, " is well-known. Their cumulative indexing over the
months is convenient. False-labeling, product advertising
particularly via television and exorbitant claims are some
of the techniques used by ad agencies and Big Business to
lure women consumers. Just a glance at an issue can help
counteract such power. An untitled Food and Drug Adminis-

tration listing of drug products which the FDA had decided, after evaluations by the National Academy of Sciences-National Research Council Drug Efficacy Study Group, lacked substantial evidence of effectiveness (as defined in the Federal Food, Drug and Cosmetic Act) was printed on November 1, 1970. Some products had been removed from the market; others were subjects of actions contesting findings or making changes. Almost all were familiar names, e.g., Colgate-Palmolive's Brisk Activated Toothpaste, Chlorophyll Toothpaste with Gardol, Dental Cream with Gardol. This list was publicized only in Consumer Reports (February 1971, p. 11f). Nor does it restrict itself to concern with major appliances; prosaic products are regularly evaluated and rated, e.g., disposable diapers (February 1971), instant potatoes (July 1971) and door locks (February 1971).

DIRECTORY OF MEDICAL SPECIALISTS

Physicians holding certification by American Speciality Boards are listed according to their speciality, geographically within Boards, and then alphabetically by surname. It reveals, for example, that a backlash book such as Fascinating Womanhood [Helen B. Andelin, Andelin Foundation, Box 3617, Santa Barbara, Calif. 93105; see Look March 9, 1971, p. 19] is dubious indeed when it points to statements of praise by "professionals" who cannot be located. (Neither of the two male MD's quoted in the Fascinating Womanhood brochure aluding to its use in "psychotherapy" and "emotional problems" is a certified psychiatrist; nor is "Dr. H. C. Diehl of Colorado Springs," who praises G. C. Payette's How to Get and Hold a Woman, sold direct only via advertising in New York Times, VII, p. 33, May 2, 1971.)

BARTLETT'S FAMILIAR QUOTATIONS

The main part of Bartlett's is arranged chronologically by the authors themselves, with special sections for anonymous, Biblical, etc. quotations, placing an importance on thorough and extensive indexing. There are said to be four or five entries per quote in the Index, so that it is possible to locate or identify a quotation, passage, phrase or source with a minimum starting-point, as well as to provide a "suitable" quotation for any occasion. Note the sub-title: "collection of passages, phrases, and proverbs traced to their sources in ancient and modern literature." Bartlett's

is for easy locating, if you have little lead, of the right
phrase or the sayings of famous people from 2000 B. C. to
the date your edition was published.   Interesting footnotes
trace history and usage.   Such a tool is enlightening when
one studies the centuries of slander, humor and falsity ac-
cumulated about women.   The publisher, Little, also puts
out A Guide to the Use of "Bartlett's Familiar Quotations."

DICTIONARY OF AMERICAN SLANG

Of the several handbooks defining and describing the
development of American slang, this one, by Harold Wentworth and S. B. Flexner, is perhaps the most relevant for
modern woman's needs.   It includes colloquialisms, jargon
and taboo words with full definitions and often the date of
first use and a citation to printed sources.   It has, in fact,
been involved in censorship and called "controversial" but
is to be found in most libraries.   The little lady who accepted the challenge to open her ears for a week's time to
the terms commonly used by men to demean women found
DAS helpful with most of the following: baggage, ball and
chain, biddie, bird, bitch, broad, cat, cow, cunt, dame,
dog, doll, flibbertigibbet, fish, gal Friday, hen, lay, little
tramp, mother, my old lady, my woman, piece, pussy,
puta, researcher, slut, tail, tart, whore and our women--
heard in an office, precinct-house, old folks' home and
supermarket; passing a construction project; watching the
TV credits, a Young Lord on the News, Dick Cavett, and
David Susskind's program.

FOUNDATION DIRECTORY

Non-profit and non-governmental foundations are
listed by states; the index to fields of interest reveals
nothing under Women.   Nevertheless, this tool, together
with "The Annual Register of Grant Support," which began
in 1969 and includes governmental and business agencies,
may provide leads to funds to support important Women's
Liberation projects.

Who said "A woman is
only a woman but a good
cigar is a smoke?"   From
what is it taken?

Bartlett's Familiar Quotations,
14th ed., index: "Woman..."
ref. to p. 871b.   Answer: "The
betrothed," by Rudyard Kipling,
Stanza 25.

Women physicians seem to concentrate in the practice of which specialties?

Directory of Medical Specialists, vo. 14, 1970. Browse through The Directory, especially the sections devoted to your part of the country/state. You can usually identify women by their first names, attendance at female colleges and medical schools, memberships, etc.

How do the Association for the Study of Abortion and the Association for Humane Abortion differ?

Encyclopedia of Associations, 6th ed., "Abortion" key-word index; p. 657. Answer: Association for the Study of Abortion was formerly (1965) named the Association for Humane Abortion.

Who said "Power corrupts absolutely?"

Bartlett's Familiar Quotations, 14th ed., index: "Power corrupts..." ref. to p. 107fb. Power corrupts, poetry cleanses, from J. F. Kennedy address. Footnote refers to p. 750a: "Power tends to corrupt and absolute power corrupts absolutely." Answer: Letter to Bishop Mandell Creighton, April 5, 1887, from John Emerich Edward Dalberg-Acton, Lord Acton, 1834-1902.

Which state, having previously rejected the 19th Amendment, got around to ratifying it in 1970?

World Almanac & Book of Facts, 1971, index: "Women--Achievements in 1970": p. 820-1. Answer: Georgia (p. 320, 3rd paragraph).

How many Congressional districts are there in the state of Hawaii? On the island of Hawaii? What is a Congresswoman's salary?

World Almanac & Book of Facts, 1971, index: "Congress, U.S. --Members": p. 491-3. Answer: (p. 941, House as of Nov. 14, 1970) Hawaii has 2 representatives, at large, i.e. not numbered districts. 42,500 for "member."

You are watching educational TV airing a young come-
dian--"giving him a chance."
He tells of the "dumb
broads" in his Miami audience, and of a girls' bas-
ketball team--"the Fort
Dix Dykes"--and he imitates
the hissing of Japanese
wives of regular-Army men
.... What is a dyke?
(Steve Landesbert at "The
Improvisation" 'Where
clowns commence' Feb.
13, 1970, Channel 13,
NET/New York City, "Here
and Now.")

Dictionary of American Slang
(Wentworth), "Dyke," p. 168.
Answer: Female homosexual
who plays the male role.

Did Marie Antoinette really
say "Let them eat cake?"
Rousseau quotes her this
way...

Bartlett's Familiar Quotations,
14th ed., index: "Cake, let
them eat, p. 436b. At length
I recollected the thoughtless
saying of a great princess,
who, on being informed that
the country people had no bread,
replied, "Let them eat cake...."
Jean Jacques Rousseau, 1712-
1778, Les Confessions (1781-
1788) VI. Answer: "This re-
mark is usually attributed to
Marie Antoinette, after her
arrival in France in 1770, but
the sixth book of the Confessions was written two or three
years before that date."

Is it true that the population density of Puerto Rico
is greater than that of
New York?

Book of the States 1970-71.
Check out states individually:
p. 614--Puerto Rico = 796 per
square mile; p. 593--New York
= 382.7. Answer: Yes.

In what states is it possible to marry with no waiting after licensing and
with no tests?

Book of the States 1970-71.
Answer: Nevada

Bibliographic Access

Bibliographic control is easier than it
used to be but still not 100%.

A bibliography on a subject of interest to a researcher,
graduate student, partisan or subject-specialist is the basis
for access to the literature and any further work.   Whether
selective (e. g. , all the landmark books in a given field) or
comprehensive (e. g. , "everything" ever published in every
format), the problem of keeping it up-to-date becomes end-
less.

The "average" public or community college library
is often unable to justify purchase of more than a few of the
standard tools supporting bibliographic control, because they
serve the public indirectly and are relatively costly.   The
librarian must select those few titles with which the staff
can function.   Thus, all the titles discussed may be found
in the collections of only larger libraries; the others--
notably The National Union Catalog and The Cumulative Book
Index--could not be included.   About 1970 many publishers
began to utilize "International Standard Book Numbers
(ISBN)"; one should exist for each book title and appear
on the verso (back) of the title page.   Basic bibliographic
information includes author, full title, publisher, and date
of publication.   The ISBN, the most recent copyright date
and Library of Congress catalog card order number (ap-
pearing on verso), the price, pagination, the presence of
bibliography, illustrations and indexing, the names of a
series of which it may be part, and the illustrator, joint
author, etc. , are also helpful in identifying and acquisition-
ing books.

Many style manuals are available to assist in the
format of bibliography-making. * Technique is basically a

---

*The following are in print and recommended (always seek
out the latest edition): Richmond, P. H. , Bibliography and
Footnotes; A Style Manual for Students and Writers, Uni-
versity of California Press; Seeber, E. D. , Style Manual for
Students, Indiana University Press; Turabian, K. L. , Stu-
dent's Guide for Writing College Papers, University of
Chicago Press; and also: Chapter 15, "The Rule of Citing:
Footnotes and Bibliography," in J. Barzun's The Modern
Researcher, Harcourt.

question of recognizing the difference between comprehensiveness and selectivity, and defining scope. A listing of every
book, for example, ever published on the subject of women
would not be feasible, although perhaps theoretically possible.
Better to limit its scope to every book in English currently
in print on the subject of women.   Even more workable might
be every article which appeared in general magazines in 1970
on the subject of Women's Liberation.

THE BIBLIOGRAPHIC INDEX

        Although The Bibliographic Index is not available in
every library, it must be mentioned here because it is one-
of-a-kind: the compilation of any comprehensive and of
most selective bibliographies would begin here.   It lists
currently-published bibliographies on many detailed subjects,
including both "separates" and "parts," in English and foreign languages, under subject and other relevant approaches.
("Separates" appear as publications themselves, usually in
magazines, but also as pamphlets; but most bibliographies
are "parts," appended to or included in such other publications as books and articles.)   Knowledge of new editions of
bibliographies and supplements to others is possible because
The Bibliographic Index is itself a serial, with supplements
and cumulations.   A useful companion-tool usually found in
larger and academic libraries is Theodore Besterman's
World Bibliography of Bibliographies (4th ed., 1965-66),
which lists only "separates," and includes only previously-
published, hence often older, bibliographies.

PUBLISHERS TRADE LIST ANNUAL
BOOKS IN PRINT
SUBJECT GUIDE TO "BOOKS IN PRINT"

        PTLA lists by publisher almost all books currently
in print on the United States trade market.   Related titles
are the well-known BIP, and its subject guide.   BIP consists of two alphabetical lists (author, title) of the books
contained in PTLA, including adults' and children's books,
paperbacks, reference works, and some foreign-language
titles.   The Subject Guide to BIP analyzes the contents of
BIP (excluding poetry, fiction and drama) by listing the
books under a series of alphabetical subject-headings such
as are utilized in a library's card catalog.   Thus a book
may be listed under several subject headings, because it

may well be about more than one single thing; for example,
a book on woman's history might also be about her legal
status and laws effecting her.   An incredible number of
books under subject-headings beginning with "Woman" and
"Women," with their subheadings, are to be found in the
1970 edition of SG-BIP; even allowing for the overlap which
is the result of their frequently being about more than one
aspect of their main subject-matter, and discounting the fact
that many are biographies, the list is impressive.   It is
important to remember that neither BIP nor SG-BIP is a
book selection tool (libraries have them for verification and
acquisitions purposes)--a comprehensive list is the anti-
thesis of selectivity.   Libros en Venta is a combined Books
in Print/Subject Guide of Spanish-language books published
in the Americas and Spain.

ALTERNATIVES IN PRINT: AN INDEX AND LISTING OF SOME MOVEMENT PUBLICATIONS REFLECTING TO-DAY'S SOCIAL CHANGE ACTIVITIES

     Although AIP lists relatively few titles devoted to
Women's Liberation, it does provide access to a variety
of formats, including films and pamphlets not otherwise
available.   Examples of subject-headings under which Movements and their publications can be located are: "Abortion,"
"Birth control," "Childhood education," "Children's literature," "Consumers," "Divorce," "Family," "Homosexuality,"
"Marriage," "Pregnancy and lactation," "Sexual revolution,"
"Venereal disease," "Women in industry," and "Women's
liberation."   To quote from AIP's publicity, "Following the
appearance of ... Alternate Press Index, members of the
Social Responsibilities Round Table of the American Library
Association felt the library profession should be involved
directly in supporting and facilitating access to alternative
ideas of life styles and intelligent social actions.   A demand
for these materials is now being made by many concerned
individuals, students, and Third World patrons of all libraries...."   AIP requires manipulation, because titles are
listed under Movement Groups, rather than directly under
subject-matter.

BOOK REVIEW DIGEST
BOOK REVIEW INDEX

     The consensus of qualified specialists' and reviewers'

critical reaction is often needed in evaluating and using a
book. The locations in periodicals of all of the reviews
which have appeared on a book can be useful information.
These two broad types of services are those of (1) the
index, which locates, and (2) the digest, which summarizes.

The Book Review Digest and the Book Review Index
supplement each other to some degree. While BRI provides
only citations to many reviews of current books, BRD is
both an index and a digest, but on a more limited scale.
Periodicals from which its reviews are taken are limited
to about 70 "regulars." For each book, a brief descriptive
note is followed by citations to several reviews and excerpts
from as many as are necessary to reflect the balance of
critical opinion. Frequently other types of review-informa-
tion (e.g., the name of the reviewer, the length of the review) are sought in addition to the references to the reviews
themselves. Books suitable for young adults are indicated.
The currency of the monthly (except for February and July)
issues as well as the convenience of the annual cumulated
volume are two of BRD's attractions for the user not involved in pure science/technology or deep scholarly research.

MOTION PICTURES AND FILMSTRIPS (Library of Congress)

Issued quarterly, with annual and five-year cumulations, this is actually a reproduction of the catalog cards for
8, 16 and 35mm motion pictures, and filmstrips currently printed by the Library of Congress. Entry is alphabetical by titles, with an extensive subject-index which includes such subject-headings as "Abortion," "Alimony,"
"Day-care," "Divorce," "Hefner," "Self-defense," and "Women." A list of distributors and their addresses is appended.
Each main-entry contains a vast amount of reliable information about the film and a summary. A counterpart is available for phonograph recordings and music.

What was the Catholic re-action to Mary Daly's re-cent book, The Church and the Second Sex, i.e., criti-cal reviewing?	Book Review Digest, 1968 (if year of publication is unknown, approach cumulated indexing for largest period possible, in this case, 1961-9.) "Daly, Mary." Answer: America magazine contained a review, by a wo-man, which was positive. A

periodicals directory such as
Ulrich's International Periodicals
Directory, provides information
as to religious periodicals
(America is Catholic).   Other
reviews can be located by using
Book Review Index.

Did American mass media
generally assign men or
women to critique the 1963
best-seller, The Feminine
Mystique? What, if any,
were negative comments?

Book Review Digest, 1963. Index reveals author is "Friedan,
Betty." Turn to F's.   Answer:
both males and females seem
generally assigned. Examples
of two women were Lucy Freeman and Marya Mannes. (BRI
would not help here, as it began publication in 1965.) Negative comments: "sweeping gen-
eralities," "drilling insistence
of style."

In considering The Bi-
ography Index, reference
was made to May Yonge
McNeer's juvenile book,
Give Me Freedom. Is it
in print? If so, what is
its cost and standard
book number?

Books in Print, 1970. Author
section: "McNeer, May."
Answer: yes. $3.24 with
library binding; 0-8382-0288-8.
Note also that here you can find
an indication of suggested appropriate grade-level range
(6-9).

You are interested in
woman as she is por-
trayed in books for chil-
dren, as well as the re-
actions (acceptance) by
reviewers of these books.
Track down examples of
this.

Book Review Digest, 1968 provides an example: Subject index: "Woman--Biography--
Juvenile Literature." The author, Rich, is given. Turn to
Author section, the main alphabet: "Rich, Josephine." Women Behind Men of Medicine
(Messner). Answer: "...
content and style combine to
make ... truly fascinating for
girls, grade 10 and up."
Maureen Reiners. Best Sellers
27, p. 395 1/1/68 130w. Another reviewer (Louise Spain
in Library Journal 9/15/67)
points out (as a positive aspect

of the book) a Japanese mother whose only wish was to serve her researcher son, by drinking a potentially poisonous experimental draught.

You are asked to prepare a bibliography on lesbianism to support a discussion on the relationship between homosexuality and Women's Liberation. You have checked a number of standard locators of titles and locators of information and found leads to materials, but you recognize the need to use up-to-date primary sources and less conventional things such as pamphlets. Under what will you look in Alternatives in Print?

Answer: "Homosexuality," "Gay power movement," "Women's Liberation."

Where can you obtain such things as bumper stickers, posters, buttons and tapes to publicize birth control? Under what will you look?

Alternatives in Print. Answer: "Birth control," "Abortion," "Sexual revolution," "Birth environment movement," "Council for Christian and social action," "Zero population growth," "Women's Liberation."

An article, "Double Jeopardy; To Be Black and Female," by Frances Beal, appears in Morgan's anthology, Sisterhood Is Powerful. But how can I get a copy of it (my library doesn't have a copying machine for the public to use yet--the book has a long list of reserves--or I can't afford to buy the paperback...)?

Alternatives in Print. "Women's Liberation." Since AIP breaks down entries within subject by sources, it's lucky that D.C. Women's Liberation isn't far along in the alphabet. Answer: 25¢. Note instructions re enclosing postage. "Movement publishers" list elsewhere in issue: D.C. Women's Liberation = Box 13098, T Street Station, Washington, D.C. 20009.

Part III

A BASIC BOOK COLLECTION

Preliminary Note

     Reading--critical, comparative, analytical reading--
is one of the few techniques toward self-liberation at everyone's free and easy disposal in the United States. Everyone
has some prejudices, some built-in misinformation which
have shaped her or his attitudes, habits and ultimately,
life-style. Woman's life, like man's, is one of indoctrination and often brainwashing. She is conditioned from childhood to be passive and submissive, to tread lightly around
the Male--father, brother, husband, supervisor, employer,
policeman, counsellor, principal, manager. Often her religion programs her assumptions and reactions. If she does
visit the public library occasionally, she may also select
and reject automatically, unthinkingly, unquestioningly. To
say of any book, "I don't want to read it--it won't interest
me," is to imply powers of a seer. How can anyone predict
with certainty whether a book will interest, have relevance
for her or him? Reading can be consciousness-raising.
Cases in point are the following writings representative of
many libraries. The woman who considers herself above
liberating and finds nothing offensive, sexist, discriminatory
or male-chauvinist in them needs help:

Aristotle.	Ethics.
Baker, Stephen.	How to live with a neurotic wife.
Bross, Barbara.	How to love like a real wo- man. In Cosmopolitan, June 1969.
Brown, Helen Gurley.	Sex and the new single girl.
Deutsch, Helene.	Psychology of woman.
DeLeeuw, Hendrik.	Woman; the dominant sex.
Devlin, Patrick.	Enforcement of morals.
Dingwall, Eric John.	The American woman...
Farnham, Marya.	Modern woman--the lost sex.
Freud, Sigmund.	Three essays on the theory of sexuality.

Goldman, Eric F.	Party of one; our American woman. In <u>Holiday,</u> May 1961.
Hemingway, Ernest.	Men without women.
International Conference on Abortion.	The terrible choice...
Lobsenz, Herbert.	Vangel Griffin.
Mailer, Norman.	American dream.
Nietzsche, Friedrich.	Will to power.
Noonan, J. T., Jr., et al.	The morality of abortion...
Peck, Joseph.	Life with women and how to survive it.
Robinson, Marie.	Power of sexual surrender.
Rodell, John.	How to avoid alimony; a survival kit for husbands.
Root, Waverley.	Women are intellectually inferior. In <u>American Mercury,</u> October 1949.
Rousseau, Jean-Jacques.	Emile, Book 5.
Ruark, Robert.	Women.
Ruskin, John.	Sesame and lillies.
Searle, Ronald.	Female approach.
Sparrow, Gerald.	Women who murder.
Spillane, Mickey.	The body lovers [one example].
Tiger, Lionel.	Men in groups.

A Basic Book Collection

The scope of the following collection is broad, and it has been planned to delineate the contemporary situation. A balanced selected collection of only a few hundred, available books for knowing about women which will please all judges is impossible. Countless biographies have been written about women--ground out for markets of all ages-- and are therefore de-emphasized here in order to provide space for autobiography and other types of works. History and biography of the Woman's Movement are included insofar as they lay the foundation and set the scene for today. Woman's "place" in various aspects of literature seems to have been dabbled in by many authors; hopefully, the works of those people who have had something constructive, enlightening or inspiring to say have been identified. Here are books not so much by and about women as they are for women ... all women ... and for men and young people as well. Not the <u>Woman's Guide to Wall Street</u>-type of book,

nor handy-dandy books on how to be a "working mother,"
which are designed to make money. The message is not
guidance in making a better "adjustment," but one of des-
perate need for radical change. Bibliographies per se are
not included in this limited collection, although the presence
of bibliographic support is indicated for a number of books.
Foreign imprints and information on the status of women in
other countries were considered for the enlightenment they
bring to the American condition. Fiction, poetry and drama
can bring us closer to the inner feelings of the woman
author, who, over all, has been emphasized.

The Women's Studies participant may regard some of
the books which follow as basic reading and landmark titles.
Public and community college library directors should be requested to acquire any not already in the libraries' collections. They are readily-available readings and references
on a vital, contemporary issue effecting every American.
In order to assure the utmost in simplicity of acquisition,
titles recommended here and published before 1970 are almost all listed in Books in Print (1970) or readily available
through indicated channels. Ordering information, often including availability of paperback format, has been provided
here. The sequence in which they might be read most
profitably will vary with the individual; the annotations point
up aspects of special interest. References to and excerpts
from reviews are scattered throughout to provide a representation of opinion and exposure to the limitations and potential of these resources. A broad range of subject-matter
and types of writing are represented in this classified list;
an alphabetical arrangement (index) of titles and authors
contained in the collection is included in Part VI, Appendix
2. Threatened, repulsed or busy men may need special
selections pointed out, e.g., Elizabeth Janeway's Man's
World, Woman's Place is undeniably straight fact and not
opinion. (Although, of course, an attempt has been made
to include authors whose opinions are documented as well
as timely.) Titles also available in Spanish are occasionally
pointed out. Books with content, style and reading-level
well suited to junior and senior high school-age people as
well as to adult readers are identified. Abridgements have
generally not been included in this collection.

Each entry consists of:
sequence no., AUTHOR (and dates)
TITLE
["HS" = content, style and reading-level suited to

junior and senior high school-age people as well as
adult readers.]

PUBLICATION DATA

Includes original publisher, date, pagination, whether
bibliographic support ("bib") and indexing are provided. The Library of Congress catalog card number frequently accompanies these data, especially
since International Standard Book Numbers are not
yet available for all books.

ACQUISITION DATA

Where several publishers' editions are available, the
original and/or hardcover is listed first. Books are
often published in several versions, e.g., abridged,
edited for various grade-level ranges, text, etc., and
in several formats, e.g., bindings, illustrations,
large-print, etc. See Books in Print for a full selection. ["S" = also available in Spanish; information
derived from Libros en Venta.]

ANNOTATION

A brief indication of the book's thesis, point-of-view,
special features and the like is added last; frequently,
citations to further specialized reading are given.
An attempt has been made to evaluate the book in
order to make a reader's selectivity more efficient.

For convenience, consecutive numbers have been
assigned to the titles in the Basic Book Collection; these
numbers are utilized in the Awareness Inventory Answer
Key (Part I) in citing some of the sources of data information, as well as in the Index to the collection (Part VI,
Appendix 2).   The basic arrangement is by Dewey Decimal
Classification number and then alphabetical by author.

000 GENERALITIES

010 Bibliographies & Catalogs

(1)   Leonard, Eugene Andruss, 1888-   , et al.
The American woman in colonial and revolutionary times,
    1565-1800; a syllabus with bibliography.
Univ. of Pennsylvania Press   c1962   61-6949
$8   0-8122-7348-6

050 General Periodicals

(2)   White, Cynthia L.
Women's magazines, 1693-1968.
Humanities   1971   348p   bib   index
$10
Sociological study of women's magazines in Britain.   Useful
with Helen Woodward's "The lady persuaders."

(3)   Woodward, Helen
The lady persuaders.
Obolensky   c1960   189p   59-13761
$4.95   0-8392-1058-2   Astor-Honor
A survey of women's magazines and the history of their influence on many things.   Note implications of the title.
See also "Women's record..." by Sarah Joseph Hale, editor
of "Godey's lady's book," and Cynthia L. White's "Women's
magazines."   An index and updating would enhance its
utility today.

100 PHILOSOPHY

130 Pseudo- & Parapsychology

(4)   Freud, Sigmund, 1856-1939
"Femininity," in New introductory lectures on psychoanalysis,
        edited by James Strachey.
Norton   c1965   202p   bib
$4.50   0-393-0105-4; $1.95/pap   0-393-09651-3
So much passion has been expressed about the Austrian
psychiatrist and founder of psychoanalysis, Sigmund Freud,
that one owes it to oneself to read, minimally, this example
relevant to the indictments.   The radical Freudian model
of the female is a faithful replica of an ancient patriarchal
tradition, extending from Asia to Europe and part of Africa
and exported to the New World; it is a time-honored attitude
that dishonors women no matter what they do or do not do--
women are fit for nothing except motherhood, they envy
males and use motherhood and wifehood to avenge themselves
on the superior sex.   It is unfortunate that psychoanalysis in
particular and psychiatry in general are being rejected by
some women today mainly because of the legitimate case
against Freud, for women, as an indoctrinated and manipu-
lated group, are especially in need of the self-knowledge
which psychotherapy can help them achieve in their "catch
up" struggle for human equality.

(5)   Maccoby, Eleanor Emmons, 1917-
The development of sex differences.
Stanford Univ. Press 1966 351p 66-22984
$8. 50   0-8047-0308-6
Studies re the possible biological determinants of tempera-
mental sex differences, sex differences in intellectual functioning, nature of learning process that develops sex-typed
behavior, analysis of children's sex roles, concepts and
attitudes, and sex differences and cultural institutions.   Part
Two consists of an annotated bibliography compiled by Ro-
berta M. Oetzel of hundreds of research studies in sex differences over a period of approximately 30 years.   It is
not difficult to demonstrate on the basis of such studies
that girls are more conforming, suggestible, dependent--
more anything than boys.   Such a review of the literature
points up the need for new research into new and different
questions by qualified researchers.

(6)   Marcuse, Herbert
Eros and civilization: a philosophical inquiry into Freud.
Beacon   1955   277p   55-10920
$7. 50   0-8070-1554-7; $1. 95   (pap V209)   Random
Believes a non-repressive society can be created in which
man's (and woman's) instincts can be freely gratified.
(Eros = love directed toward self-realization.)

(7)   Mead, Margaret, 1901-
Male and female; a study of the sexes in a changing world.
     HS
Morrow   1949   477p
$7. 50; 1967 $2. 95   (pap A160)   Apollo; 1968   95¢   (pap
     5176)   Dell. S
No repertoire of reading would be complete without a taste,
if not a dose, of Margaret Mead.   Despite her references
to the Women's Liberation Movement as "they, " she has
made some personal contributions.   "Male and female" is
easy reading.   See especially the final section, "The two
sexes in contemporary society"--the social anthropologist's
point of view.

(8)   Missildine, W. Hugh
Your inner child of the past.
Simon & Schuster 1963   317p   bib   63-11144
$6. 95
"This remarkable book, by easy to understand descriptions
and case histories, helps you see how your 'inner child of
the past' governs your thoughts, feelings and behavior pat-

terns of today. It helps you free yourself of the parental
tensions set up in childhood by even the best intentioned
parents." [Choice TV series.]

(9) Szasz, Thomas Stephen, M.D., 1920-
   [All of Dr. Szasz's books have relevance for women
   and for those who fear and judge them. Dr. Szasz
   is professor of psychiatry at the State University of
   New York Upstate Medical Center, Syracuse, and
   has appeared on the Dick Cavett television show.]
The ethics of psychoanalysis; the theory and method of
   autonomous psychotherapy.
Basic 1965 226p 65-16890
$6.95 0-465-02072-0
No value judgments ... psychotherapy as social action ...
more self-knowledge = communication.

(10) Szasz, Thomas Stephen, M.D., 1920-
The myth of mental illness; foundations of a theory of personal conduct.
Harper 1961 337p 61-9714
$8.50 1961 0-06-014197-2 Harper; $2.25 1967 (pap
   6199) Delta Dell
Read Anne Sexton's "Live or die" in relation to this; see
especially "Religion and Oppression" (p. 198f). See also
his "Law, liberty and psychiatry; an inquiry into the social
uses of mental health practices"
(Macmillan, c1963, $7.50 and $2.25/pap).

(11) Thompson, Clara M., M.D.
Interpersonal psychoanalysis; the selected papers of Clara
   Thompson, edited by Maurice R. Green.
Basic c1964 398p bib index 64-22399
$10 0-465-03394-6
Major contributions re homosexuality. See especially Part
IV: Psychology of women, and Part V: Problems of
womanhood. In 1941 her "Role of women in this culture"
appeared in Volume 4 of Psychiatry, and in 1943, her
" 'Penis envy' in women," in Volume 6.

150 Psychology

(12) Bardwick, Judith M.
Psychology of women; a study of bio-cultural conflicts.
Harper 1971 242p index 70-137799
$7.95 06-040496-5; 06-040496-3 pap

This is a book about self-esteem, the lack of it, and the
resultant effects on behavior. Its chief contribution is
probably the bringing together of data relevant to sex differences.

(13)   Chasseguet-Smirgel, Janine
Female sexuality; new psychoanalytic views.
Univ. of Michigan Press   c1970   220p   79-10794
$8.95   0-472-21900-6
This is not an easy book to read, possibly because it has
been translated from another language (French) and there
is no access to information via an index.   Six essays are
tied together and introduced by a review of the various approaches to female sexuality through new psychoanalytic
views, both Freudian and non-Freudian.   (C. J. Luquet-Parat,
Bela Grunberger, Joyce McDougall, Maria Torok Christian
David.)

(14)   Horney, Karen, M. D. ,   1882-1952
News ways in psychoanalysis.
Norton   c1939   313p   index
$5.95   393-01015-5; $1.75/pap   393-00132-6
Chapter 6, "Feminine psychology," answers 'penis-envy'
theory; Chapter 16, "Psychoanalytic therapy," is also important, as well as Chapter 1, "Fundamentals of psychoanalysis," if women are to avoid falling into the pit of re-
jecting psychoanalysis and psychiatrists simply because
Freud founded the former and was a latter.   Likewise, her
"Are you considering psychoanalysis?"   Karen Horney was
a woman psychiatrist who "departed so radically from his
[Freud's] views that she fell out of grace with him, left
Berlin, came to the United States in the early thirties and
subsequently founded the American Institute of Psychoanalysis....   All analysts work with Freud's basic discoveries,
i.e., the significance of dreams, free association, psychic
determination....   She found that the women here did not fit
the patterns Freud had described, and could account for this
discrepancy only on the grounds of acculturation....   She
could very well be regarded as one of the first women
liberators ... who ... had a pervasive, profound belief in
the liberation of all persons." [Helen A. DeRosis, M. D. ,
New York Times VI:6, March 7, 1971.] Horney's "Feminine psychology" is also in print (Norton, 1967, $5.95) and
available in Spanish.

170 Ethics (Moral philosophy)

(15) Group for the Advancement of Psychiatry. Committee
on Psychiatry and Law.
The right to abortion; a psychiatric view.
Scribners c1970 74p index 72-108128
$4.95
The G.A.P. has a membership of approximately 300 psychiatrists organized in the form of working committees which
have authored several titles. (See also its "Sex and the
college student.") This title is especially useful for care-
fully-reasoned condemnation of so-called liberalized laws.
Moral, practical, and brief. Alice Rossi a consultant.

(16) Paul, Leslie
Eros rediscovered; restoring sex to humanity.
Association Press 1970 191p index 75-132392
$5.95 8096-1785-4
Social analysis of contemporary attitudes; why our norms
change.

(17) Thomas, William Isaac, 1863-1947
The unadjusted girl; with cases and standpoint for behavior
analysis.
Little c1923 261p
$1.75 0-06-131319-X (pap TB 1319) Torch Harper Row;
Reprint Series in criminology, law enforcement, and
social problems no. 26, 1969, $12. 0-8785-026-X
Patterson Smith.
Pioneering sociologist on determination and individual psychology. Everyone desires: new experience, security, response, recognition. Lack of "adjustment" equates with
failure to conform in our society.

(18) Woolf, Virginia, 1882-1941
Three guineas.
London: Hogarth Press c1938 285p
Harcourt 1963 $1.95 (pap 0-15-690177-3)
Were Ms. Woolf living today, some threatened male might
well label her "shrill." "Three guineas" also relates philo-
sophically to woman's need for independent and creative
work. Ask how can war be prevented? She answers how
a woman can. See also Herbert Marder's "Feminism and
art; a study of Virginia Woolf" (Univ. of Chicago Press,
1968, $6.50).

114 Womanhood Media

200 RELIGION

220 Bible

(19) Deen, Edith
All the women of the Bible.
Harper 1955 410p bib index 55-8521
$5.95 0-06-061810-8
Contents: (1) in-depth studies of women in the "foreground";
(2) alphabetical list; (3) chronological list of nameless women; (4) extensive bibliography (316 women); (5) index. In
general a reference type, scholarly work, i.e., not evan-
gelical, although traditional role for woman is assumed.
Seen through male-God, Adam, conventional Christ-glasses,
but a tool for putting into historical Judeo-Christian biblical
context women's influence as "daughters, wives, mothers,
widows." Use for identification and the bibliography.

(20) Hoppin, Ruth
Priscilla, author of the Epistle to the Hebrews and Other
    essays.
Exposition Press 1969 158p index
$6 0-682-46983-1
Shows that a woman authored part of the Bible and explores
the lack of recognition of women in theology.

240 Christian Moral and Devotional Theology

(21) Wood, Frederic C., Jr.
Sex and the new morality.
Association Press 1968 157p 68-17779
$4.95; $2.25/pap
A supplementary title is John Charles Wynn's "Sexual
ethics and Christian responsibility; some divergent views"
(Association, 1970, $6.95).

250 Christian Pastoral, Parochial, etc.

(22) Gibson, Elsie
When the minister is a woman.
Holt 1970 174p 75-80361
$4.95 03-081-846-X
Based on a questionnaire to 270 ordained women in various
denominations; indicates some of their problems, e.g., mar-
riage, prejudice.

260 Christian Social and Ecclesiastical Theology

(23) Beaver, Robert Pierce, 1906-
All loves excelling; American Protestant women in world

mission.
Eerdmans   c1968   227p   bib
$2.95   (pap 1012)

(24)   Cunneen, Sally
Sex: female; religion: Catholic.
Holt   c1968   171p   bib   68-10075
$4.95   0-03-065490-4

(25)   Daly, Mary
Church and the second sex.
Harper   c1968   187p   index   68-11737
$4.95   0-06-061675-X
The various forms of prejudice and discrimination against
women within the Roman Catholic Church are reflections of
a long history of anti-feminism.   Dr. Daly, an assistant
professor of theology at Boston College, explores the case
against the Church as seen by Simone de Beauvoir in "The
second sex," then outlines the man-centered past of the
Church.   The failure of women to oppose such exploitation
is considered (discussion p. 125f); in addition to "fear char-
acteristic of those who are in a subordinate position, and
ignorance of the facts," she points to "a strong probability
that preoccupation with self-interest obscures the problem
for many who vaguely feel that the given system has worked
out well enough for themselves, and are too comfortable to
bother to abstract from their own condition and see the more
general aspects of the situation."   Writing from the point of
view of a Roman Catholic, she asks that women be ordained
as priests.   A skillful speaker as well as writer; watch for
her on television.   She is also a modern feminist, and has
been part of N. O. W. task force studying the discrimination
against women in all religions.

(26)   Doley, Sarah Bentley, ed.
Women's liberation and the church; the new demand for
    freedom in the life of the Christian church.
Association press   1970   158p   bib   70-129441
$5.95   8096-1814-1; $3/pap   8096-1813-3
An anthology: race, Christianity.

300 THE SOCIAL SCIENCES

(27)   Alt, Herschel and Edith Alt
The new Soviet man; his upbringing and character develop-
    ment.

Bookman Associates   c1964   304p   index   64-24068
Twayne $6.
Not so much about the new Soviet man as about men and
women and children, especially the children--how their upbringing and character development produce Soviet people of
today.   While the Soviet experience has relevance for the
United States and other countries in sharpening their own
assessment of the conservation of children's lives, this survey of child-rearing demonstrates that the Soviets have not
yet faced the basic concerns of human nature: the impact
of the system on control of the family, the child, and of
everyday life.

(28)   Beard, Mary Ritter, 1876-
Woman as force in history.
Macmillan   1936   369p   bib   index
$1.50/pap   (03054)   Collier books   S83 Macmillan
Ingenious title (not "a force").   By the noted historian and
sociologist.   One of the many books dealing with women's
contributions throughout the history of the Western World--
this, however, is outstanding.   Its age does not limit it
in any way.   Well documented; includes excellent bibliography.
For all these reasons, it should be required reading and
owned as a personal reference book where possible.   (Small
print of paperback format only a slight drawback.)

(29)   Benjamin, Lois
So you want to be a working mother!
McGraw   1969   141p   74-3628
Funk & Wagnall   95¢   (pap 63)
This is a classic example of the book written by a brainy
gal who's done it without even realizing what "it" really is.
Over and over again she repeats the fact that she is doing
three or four things by herself.   The day of feeling guilty
as an employed mother seems to have passed.   Now one
attempts to convince oneself (and readers) that it's fun,
rewarding.   Nevertheless of its type not bad and provides
an example of need for "critical reading."

(30)   Benson, Mary Sumner, 1903-
Women in eighteenth-century America; a study of opinion
     and social usage.
Columbia Univ. Press   c1935   343p   bib   index   65-27114
Kennikat Press $11.   0-8046-0026-0
A reissue of an American history classic, issued also as a
Columbia University thesis.   History and condition of women
in the United States reflected in modern literature for the
most part.

(31)   Benson, R. O. D.
In defense of homosexuality; a rational evaluation of social
    prejudice.
Julian   1965   239p   bib   65-21551
Now available as "What every homosexual knows" (Ace,
1970, $1. 25 /pap).

(32)   Bernard, Jessie Shirley, 1903-
The sex game.
Prentice-Hall c1968   372p   bib   index   68-13219
$6. 95   13-807503-4
An exploration of the many opinions and concepts held about
sex roles, and of the many and various relationships be-
tween the "two great collectivities that we call the sexes. "

(33)   Bernard, Jessie Shirley, 1903-
Women and the public interest.
Aldine-Atherton   1972   343p
$8. 95   #25024
Examines and challenges the roles assigned to women in our
culture.   The "general welfare" and "pursuit of happiness"
don't jive with the status quo.

(34)   Bird, Caroline and Sara Welles Briller
Born female; the high cost of keeping women down (rev. ed.).
McKay   1970   302p   index   71-134801
$6. 95
About economics today.   Readable but nevertheless packed
with relevant and documented data.   See especially "The
androgynous life" and "Up from slavery. "   A basic course
book.   Chapters often reprinted as parts of Women's Liberation anthologies, but should be chewed and digested from
cover-to-cover.   Libraries having first edition should retain
both.

(35)   Bohannan, Paul, ed.
Divorce and after.
Doubleday   c1970   301p   bib   index   71-111149
$6. 95
Contributors are men and women.   Women are Jessie
Bernard, Margaret Mead, Herma Hill Kay.   Fields are
sociology, anthropology, psychology, medicine, law.   Includes
in its consideration the way other societies--Eskimo,
Swedish, Kanuri--deal with "the problem"; also, the role
of the family court, prospects for divorce "reform. "   Good
for its attitude towards divorce as a fact--a process of
relationships.

(36)   Brown, Donald R. , ed.
Role and status of women in the Soviet Union.
Teachers College Press   c1968   139p   68-27326
$8.95   8077-1128-4
The authors of this collection of essays were participants
in a symposium held at Bryn Mawr College.   They are
specialists in Russian literature and language, psychologists,
sociologists, and historians who are familiar with the Soviet
Union.   The general role of woman in relation to man, and
a comparison of the roles of Soviet and American women inevitably come up.   But it is the consideration of sex role
in a changing (developing) culture which should interest us
most.   Faculty planning committee of three men, with the
usual clever comment (concluding remarks by Robert A.
Feldmesser) by the male who'd discovered something: don't
call 'em females.   No index.

(37)   Brown, Helen Gurley
Sex and the new single girl.
Geis   1970   273p   76-126750
$5.95
A few titles in this Collection have neither utility nor direct
relevance--they are pointed out for their "negative value"
and identification.   Know thy enemy.   Gurley-Brown books
are ground out for a market; if this latest appeals to you,
better try consciousness-raising by comparing it with, for
example, "The working girl in a man's world; a guide to
office politics" (OP) by Jan Manette, who recognizes it's
a man's world and the woman employed in it is "the girl."
Letty Cottin Pogrebin's "How to make it in a man's world"
(Doubleday, c1970, $5.95) might be somewhere in between
--suited for the defensive housewife who needs to have the
arguments knocked down for her.

(38)   Buck, Pearl Sydenstricker, 1892-
To my daughters, with love.
Day   1967   250p   67-24634
$4.95
The mother of seven daughters, Ms. Buck should be qualified to write on youth, love and marriage, children, woman's
role, values.   She has written, "remember that women of
all races in our democracy, the United States, were forced
to stand aside in their struggle for enfranchisement while
Negro men were given the vote" [p. 155].   "The mother,"
by Ms. Buck (J. Day, 1934, $5.95; 50¢ pap), is a so-
called woman's story: the long wait for return of a husband
who never shows--the deserted, cheated woman who slaves

away and ultimately gets ... a grandson. The "universality
of mother love" which pervades this philosophy does not
appeal to many liberated women.

(39)   Bullough, Vern L.
The history of prostitution.
University books   c1964   304p   bib   index   64-16619
$7.50
A standard, by a male. See also Charles Winick's The
lively commerce" (Quadrangle, 1971, $8.95).

(40)   Burger, Ninki Hart
The executive's wife.
Macmillan   c1968   265p   index   68-23629
$5.95; 1970 $1.50 (pap 00814)   Collier Macmillan
The author (female) specializes in writing for/about women.
Cover commentary, "a lively guide to a wife's important
role in her husband's career," and chapter titles like "A
labor of love" should be clues. She tells how to handle
your husband's gambling, financial irresponsibility and
philandering, and how to pass the Wife Test for his new job.
Everyone should read at least one such book and realize
that there is sufficient demand for a major publisher to
keep it in print. Then read something like Margaret Hel-
frich's "The generalized role of the executive wife" (Marriage
and Family Living 1961:23-4, 384-7).

(41)   Cade, Toni, ed.
The black woman; an anthology.
New American library   c1970   256p   70-121388
95¢ (pap Q4317)   Signet
By and about the black woman as a woman; notes on contributors briefly highlight each. Stories, poems and
essays by Abbey Lincoln, Nikki Giovanni, Kay Lindsey and
others. A variety of topics as well: politics, racism in
education, the black man, the myth of the "castrating"
black woman, and woman's share in black power. See
especially Cade "on the issue of roles." There are many
anthologies about women and many books about black women
but this is different and a vivid contrast to such books as
"Black woman" (photographs by Chester Higgins, Jr., text
by Harold McDougal) and "To be a black woman; portraits
in fact and fiction," edited by Mel Watkins and Jay David.

(42)   Carson, Josephine
Silent voices; the Southern Negro woman today.

Delacorte Press   c1969   273p   69-17530
$6.95   (7899-6)   Delacorte-Dell
Based on lengthy research throughout the South, during which
the author lived among, travelled with, and interviewed many
black women.   Detailed picture of the lives of workers on
Delta plantations, teachers, housewives, women in Negro colleges, domestic servants, nurses, old women attempting to
become literate, highly literate women of various ages.
Unusual and interesting for the reactions to and treatment
of the Caucasian female author by blacks in general and
women in particular.   Question: "Do you know many bookish
Negro people, or Negroes who read a lot, I mean?" Answer: "Well, a few, of course, but you know, the posses-
sion of a book is something different from reading it out of
the library.   If you can buy your own books then you are in
a different ... category as a reader.   Wasn't long ago anyway when most Southern Negroes had no access to a library.
No, I would say that was one of the most cruel punishments
--not being able to use a library, not knowing about a library even ..." (p. 105-6).

(43)   Chesser, Eustace, M.D.
Love and the married woman.
Putnam   c1968   286p   bib   index
1970   95¢   (pap Q4166)   Sig NAL
So-called marriage manuals are a glut on the market; they
are sometimes even misogynous and pornographic.   This
is, however, an example of the real thing--by a male,
London, psychologically-oriented physician.   Good drawings.
A "catch up" for the person whose knowledge of the basic
facts is impoverished or who needs "confirmation."

(44)   Clarke, Edith, 1896-
My mother, who fathered me; a study of the family in three
      selected communities in Jamaica ... (2nd ed.).
Humanities Press   c1966   288p   bib   66-7277
$6.

(45)   Colebrook, Joan
The cross of lassitude; portraits of five delinquents.
Knopf   c1967   340p   67-11120
$6.95
Title is from Federico Garcia Lorca's "The American girls
carried babies and coins in their bellies/ And the boys
fainted stretched on the cross of lassitude."   Not fiction:
a narrative of the fate of five young women caught between
prison and urban slum lives.   A period of four years is

followed by the author without judgment as she looks into
their minds and lives--each an individual, although inter-
related. Real writing.

(46)   Cooke, Joanne, et al.
The new women; a _Motive_ anthology on women's liberation.
Bobbs Merrill 1970   222p   bib   70-125895
$4.95; 95¢/pap M516   Fawcett Premier
(This is not Wasserman's "Bold new women.")   Much of
the material appeared in the March-April 1969 issue of
Motive magazine published by the Board of Education of the
United Methodist Church (Nashville, Tenn.), whose reader-
ship was scandalized. A few additions, e.g., Frances
Beall's article on black women and Robin Morgan's poems,
were made. "The realities of Lesbianism" by Phyllis and
Del Martin should be noted. Good further reading bibli-
ography. In some ways similar to Morgan's "Sisterhood
is powerful" but not a duplication. Co-authors are Charlotte
Bunch-Weeks and Robin Morgan.

(47)   Coser, Rose Laub, 1916- , ed.
The family; its structure and functions.
Saint Martin's Press c1964   678p   bib   64-10687
$4.95/pap
Outline of a course given at Wellesley College. Readings
are mostly by men: structural limitations on the family,
limitations on marital selection, role distribution, socialization, societal network. Would fit in best in a first-level
course for conservative types; a far cry from consciousness-
raising, but sociology is basic too.

(48)   Cotton, Dorothy Whyte
The case for the working mother.
Stein & Day c1965   185p   65-14395
$4.95   8128-1033-3
The "working mother" of the title is the employed mother.
Chapter 7 devoted to "leading your double life" recognizes
that it is still a double life. Married to a psychiatrist.

(49)   Cudlipp, Edythe
Understanding women's liberation.   HS
Paperback library c1971   220p   64-529
75¢/pap
The cover claims this paperback is "a complete guide to
the most controversial movement sweeping America today.
Including a list of Women's Liberation organizations and
publications."   The list is very limited, but the book isn't

just another anthology--Cudlipp is a writer.   Examples of
her chapters: Mrs. Housewife, 'You've got a long way to
go, baby'; The double standard at work; Legally, women
do have a leg to stand on; Slow to anger; NOW NOW'er and
NOW'est; How to liberate a woman--or yourself; and Where
WL fails women.   Even these catchy chapter headings don't
quite do justice to the good job she has done in summarizing
the status quo of the WL movement without interjecting herself.

(50)   Dahlstrom, Edmund
The changing roles of men and women, with "The status of
      women in Sweden."
Beacon Press   1971   304p   bib   index   77-159846
$8.95   0-8070-4170-X; $2.95/pap   0-8070-4171-8
First published in Sweden in 1962, based on the Swedish-
Norwegian report, "Life and work of women," and revised
in an English edition in 1967, this was one of the first to
apply the "dual role" approach to the question of sex roles.
The concluding chapter analyzes debate on sex roles in conservative, liberal and radical approaches.   In Sweden, the
debate on the problems of the family has progressed beyond
conflict between woman's two roles--in the home and on the
job--to encompass the two roles of man as well.   Swedish
government efforts to increase man's right to a larger position within the home, as well as woman's right to a career
and family, are surveyed by six Scandinavian experts.
While "foreign," it presents a universal model for personal
humanized existence.   Appended is the "1968 Report to the
United Nations on the status of women in Sweden," reviewing government reforms in the past few years in family law,
education and labor market policy.   The complete report
was published by the Swedish Institute in Stockholm and
written by Maj-Britt Sandlun.

(51)   Diner, Helen
Mothers and Amazons; the first feminine history of culture.
Julian   1965   308p   65-21550
$7.50   0-870-97-017-8
Based on theories of 19th-century anthropologist J.J. Bach-
ofen that primitive sociological organizations are matriarch-
ate, and that the patriarchal family is a comparatively recent development.

(52)   Dodge, Norton T.
Women in the Soviet economy; their role in economic, sci-
      entific, and technological development.

Johns Hopkins Univ. Press   c1966   331p   66-14375
$10   0-8018-0172-9
Women students in higher education institutions, educational
attainment.

(53) Duvall, Evelyn Ruth Millis, et al.
Being married.   HS
Association Press   1960   440p   bib   index   60-8522, 60-
    9107
$5.75
Handbook for young adults who can't afford/reach a coun-
selor.   Co-authors are Reuben Lorenzo and Sylvanus M.
Duvall.

(54) Ellmann, Mary
Thinking about women.
Harcourt   c1968   240p   index
$4.95   0-15-189790-5; 1970 $2.65/pap 0-15-689900-0
The sexual analogy is a mental habit which victimizes
women.   Since the most vociferous source of sexual opinions
is the novel, feminine stereotypes are often based primarily
on modern fiction--what this author identifies as: form-
lessness, passivity, instability, confinement, piety, ma-
teriality, spirituality, irrationality, compliancy, and the
two incorrigible figures of the shrew and witch.   These re-
occur in fiction and criticism from Jane Austen to Ivy
Compton-Burnett, Mary McCarthy and Norman Mailer.
Crammed full of sharp and entertaining gems of thought and
observation as well as technical presentation, e.g., "...
sexual opinions are sexual themselves.   They mate with
each other and multiply--incessantly.   Also, the little ones
look like the big ones."

(55) Epstein, Cynthia Fuchs
Woman's place; options and limits in professional careers.
Univ. of California Press   c1970   220p   bib   index   75-
    98139
$6.95   520-01581-9
Thoroughly documented and supplied with comparative and
historical relationships.   Although most of her data are drawn
from the professions of law, medicine, science, engineering
and university teaching, she also touches on problems of
all employed working women, especially their status.   She
uses a sociologist's tools to identify social factors that
assign women to and keep them in their "place."   Well
suited for Women's Studies.

(56)   Farber, Seymour M. , M. D. and Roger H. L. Wilson,
    M. D. , eds.
Challenge to women.
Basic books   c1966   176p   index   66-17180
$5. 95   0-465-00908-5
Farber was a member of the President's Commission on the
Status of Women, 1962-3.   Focuses on the attitudes and
responsibilities of women as "family arbiters"--problems
that the modern woman must encounter as the homemaker
of an urban family, a breadwinner, a colleague of men, and
a wife [jacket].   There's a variety of authors; especially
good are Eve Merriam (Woman's expectations; mirage or
reality); Mirra Komarovsky (Women's roles; problems and
polemics); Ethel M. Albert (The unmothered woman); and
Kate Hevner Mueller (Education; the realistic approach).

(57)   Figes, Eva
Patriarchal attitudes (no. 1 in "Women in revolt; a series
    on the emancipation of women").
Stein & Day   c1970   191p   bib   index   71-126974
95¢/pap   8128-1332-4   Premier Fawcett
This seems to be number one-and-only in an interesting-
sounding series.   Ms. Figes is concerned with the Women's
Liberation Movement in England and is a novelist and aca-
demician.   She considers the influence of such factors as
Christianity, the rise of capitalism, and the advent of
Freudian analysis, but also examines the basic motivation
which lies behind these and similar manifestations of what
could be described as male chauvinism--and female col-
lusion--through the ages.   To what extent have sexual
taboos and Christian teaching led to the half-conscious idea
that women are in some sense evil?   How far are women
themselves to blame, and to what extent do they want
change?   "Sexual taboos (or a code of morality) cannot be
effective unless they are accepted by society as a whole....
One of the reasons that a patriarchal society has been able
to work for so long is that women are themselves ready to
play the roles assigned to them, never having been made
aware of any alternative.   19th-century moral feminists
protested against the double standard of morality but did
not claim sexual freedom for themselves--they wanted the
male to be as virtuous as they themselves were required
to be. "

(58)   Firestone, Shulamith
The dialectic of sex; the case for feminist revolution.
Morrow   c1970   274p   70-123149
$6. 95

Here is a good opportunity to compare critical reactions of professional reviewers: from the Virginia Kirkus reviewing service: "A sharp and often brilliant mind is at work here. Takes feminist analysis a giant step beyond protesting patriarchial attitudes or condemning Marx and Freud." From the mass media, Publishers Weekly: "An eloquent and tough-minded spokesman for one of the fastest-growing social movements of the time, Women's Lib. Her book will outrage many readers of both sexes, but she can't easily be dismissed." An index would enhance the value/utility.

(59)   Fried, Edrita
The ego in love and sexuality.
Grune & Stratton   c1960   296p   bib   index   60-8586
$8
She also wrote "On love and sexuality" (Grove, 1962, 95¢).
Be sure you know what "ego" really means.

(60)   Gavron, Hannah
The captive wife; conflicts of housebound mothers.
Humanities Press   c1966   176p   bib   index   66-75475
$5.50
A study of young London mothers with children under five years of age.

(61)   Goode, William Josiah, 1917-
Women in divorce.
Free Press of Glencoe   c1956   381p   55-10992
1965 $3.50   (pap 91234)   Free Press paperback
Original title: "After divorce."

(62)   Gray, Madeline
The normal woman.
Scribner   c1967   405p   bib   index   67-10852
$7.95;   1969 $2.45   (pap 168)
Unfortunate title. The author recognizes, however, that there are difficult-but-negative decisions to be made--she accepts situations (perhaps she's making a "good adjustment" or not being "rigid"). "Doctors who have helped me" and "Books that have helped me" are almost all male authors. Some stereotypes. A good beginning-level book for discussion purposes and identification of stereotypes.

(63)   Great Britain.   Committee on Homosexual Offences
        and Prostitution.
The Wolfenden Report, authorized American edition.   Introduction by Karl Menninger, M.D.

Stein & Day   c1963   243p   63-13229
$5.95
Published in 1957 as "Report." Membership of Committee:
Sir John Wolfenden, chairman; clergy (i.e., Church of England); medicine, sociology, psychology, law represented;
men and women. Menninger's introduction essential. Note
material on assult, blackmail, procuring. Part 4: Summary
of recommendations; Reservations.

(64)   Greer, Germaine
The female eunuch.   HS
McGraw   c1970   349p
$6.95
A fun book, but with scholarship and organization. Touches
on everything ranging from her judgment of Masters' and
Johnson's Reproduction Biology Research Foundation labora-
tories' concern with dull sex for dull people (paging Hugh
Hefner...) to her unfortunate discard of all psychoanalytic
theory because of Freud's misunderstanding of women. Male-
reviewer Lehmann-Haupt liked Dr. Greer's argument that
history and civilization, not conspiracy of male egos, have
created the "nightmare from which women are trying to
awake" [New York Times, April 25, 1971]. Feminist-re-
viewer Kempton judged the book "something like art,"
pointed up the "particularly biting chapter on altruism" and
concluded with a reminder that liberty is something one
takes without asking [New York Times VII:4, April 25, 1971].
Author was selected by the London Standard as Great
Britain's Woman of the Year, and lectures in English literature at Warwick University and appears on television.
Born in Australia, briefly married, now lives in England.
This, her first book, already very successful in Britain.
Be sure to understand what "eunuch" means.

(65)   Gruberg, Martin
Women in American politics; an assessment and sourcebook.
Wisconsin State Univ.   1968   336p   bib   index   68-27151
Academia $7.50   0-911880-02-X
Roles women have played as elected and appointed public
officials--an analysis of voting habits and political behavior
of women--especially good for lists of women recently
elected or appointed to important political positions.

(66)   Hays, Hoffman Reynolds
The dangerous sex; the myth of feminine evil.
Putnam   1964   316p   bib   64-18006
$5.95

Men have feared and loathed women since the beginning of
time. Hays examines the institutional and attitudinal forms
that man's fear of woman and her body have taken throughout history.

(67)   Hernton, Calvin C.
Sex and racism in America.
Doubleday c1965 180p bib   64-20576
Grove 95¢ (pap B113)
Especially chapters 2 and 5.

(68)   Hobbs, Lisa
Love and liberation; up front with the feminists.
McGraw 1970 161p 79-139554
$5.95 07-029093-8
Title somewhat misleading; it's not about the Movement per
se. Considers total situation--the pill, overpopulation, child
care, consumerism, marriage.

(69)   Janeway, Elizabeth Hall, 1913-
Man's world, woman's place; a study in social mythology
Morrow 1971 bib index 73-142405
$8.95
Ms. Janeway has generally written novels ("The accident,"
"The third choice," "Daisy Kenyon") until researching this
study of social-psychological forces which influence the
position of women and which have produced the contemporary
demand by women for their rights. Any serious study of
women today will include an examination of mythology; she,
however, is interested in the total mythology by which we
live today. Margaret Mead's review (New York Times VII:
7, June 20, 1971) is relevant reading in itself: "This is
a lucid and fascinating book, a book that draws so skillfully
on the best of our fragmented social science, that, as a
social scientist, it gives me renewed faith that we may in
time, produce an integrated understanding of the world....
[S]he has drawn on the best of modern social science--some
of it rather hard for the layman to find.... She stresses
the way men are permitted--in marriage, in the privacy of
the home--to act out their childish emotions and in so doing
find women over-concerned with emotion." Excellent discussion of the three roles women are asked to play--wife,
mother and housekeeper--and how they overlap and conflict,
all in one place while men are permitted to be one thing at
a time. Basic.

(70)   Komarovsky, Mirra
Blue-collar marriage.

Random 1964 395p bib index 64-20031
$1.95 (pap V361) Vin Random
Almost ten years old. Chapter 2 especially still relevant:
"Learning conjugal roles." Also Chapter 7 re barriers to
marital communication. (But "poverty" is no longer equated
with the blue collar.) Women's roles as they exist in
working-class and family life. See all of her books for
Women's Studies: "Unemployed man and his family; the
effect of unemployment upon the status of the man in fifty-
nine families" (Dryden, 1940, $7.50); "Women in the
modern world; their education and their dilemmas" (Little,
1953, OP).

(71) Kraditor, Aileen S. , ed.
Up from the pedestal; selected writings in the history of
      American families. HS
Quadrangle c1968 372p bib 68-26443
$8.95 8129-0062-6; $2.95/pap
An ingenious and apt title which has been reused on several
occasions. Has been called a superb collection of documents
(Scott). Inequality of the sexes still exists because the
family structure has remained basically unchanged.

(72) Kronhausen, Phyllis & Eberhard Kronhausen
The sexually responsive woman.
Grove c1964 255p bib 64-13777
$5.95 GP313; 95¢ (pap U 7035) Ballantine
The wording of the title is strictly a come-on but nevertheless a useful book which documents the existence of
sexually active women today. Simone de Beauvoir chose to
write in the Preface, "the authors grant her an autonomy--
both physiological and psychological ... absorbing and fascinating reading." See especially Chapter 15: The future
of female sexuality.

(73) Lee, Nancy Howell
The search for an abortionist.
Univ. of Chicago Press c1969 207p bib index 74-75135
$7.50 226-47001-6
This is a report of research--not scintillating reading, but
definitely readable--and significant because (1) countless
references are made to it, and (2) it is a documented study
of 114 women who underwent abortion. Their reasons, reactions, and the ways in which they made contact with the
abortionist are included. Factors working on a woman in
search are psychological, medical, social, financial, legal.
The recovery also included. For a picture in the format of
a novel, see Wertenbaker's "The afternoon women."

(74) Leijon, Anna-Greta
Swedish women--Swedish men, translated by Paul Britten
    Austin. HS
Swedish Institute for Cultural Relations with Foreign
    Countries 1968 160p
Swedish Information Service. Single paperback copies gratis.
"Most people think of Sweden as a most advanced country in
the matter of sex equality, but part of the intent of this book
is to show how far Sweden still is from real equality even
though far advanced over other countries. There are still
three ideologies concerning the roles of the sexes--the traditional; the moderate which holds that woman has two roles,
mother and to have a profession; and the radical which assumes that the sexes should no longer have separate roles
in society. The author points out changes which could contribute to a society free from sex roles" [Jeanne Spiegel in
"Sex role concepts."] Includes UN Declaration on the Elimination of Discrimination Against Women, 1967. See also
Linner's "Sex and society in Sweden."

(75) Lenin, Vladimir Ilich U., 1870-1924
The emancipation of women; from the writings, with an
    appendix "Lenin on the woman question," by Clara
    Zetkin.
International 1970 136p
$1.45/pap 7178-0290-6

(76) Lifton, Robert May, 1926- , ed.
The woman in America. HS
Beacon press c1964 293p index 12-30299
$2.95 (Beacon press paperback 249) 4197-1
This is the book form of the Spring 1964 (vol. 93, no. 2)
Proceedings of the American Academy of Arts & Sciences
as they were published in its journal, Daedalus, Stephen R.
Graubard, editor. A readable symposium. Includes Erik H.
Erikson's questionable "Inner and outer space; reflections
on womanhood"; and contributions by several women in-
cluding Alice Rossi's "Equality between the sexes; an im-
modest proposal."

(77) Linner, Birgitta
Sex and society in Sweden.
Random c1967 204p bib index 66-11711
Pantheon $7.95
The book was written to describe the Swedish national sex
education program to American readers. Shows how one
country recognizes the facts of life. Extensive appendices

contain Swedish Board of Education "Handbook," sample les-
sons for age range groups, and Ms. Linner's address to a
U.S. Senate Subcommittee. For an interpretation on the
professional level, see her "Sexual morality and sexual
reality--the Scandinavian approach" (Amer. J. of Ortho-
psychiatry, July 1966). The "Handbook on Sex Instruction
in Swedish Schools" is available from the National Board
of Education, Fack 104 22, Stockholm 22.

(78) Marx, Karl, et al.
The woman question; selections from the writings of Karl
     Marx, Frederick Engels, V. Lenin, Joseph Stalin, re-
     vised edition.
International 1951 96p 51-5114
$1. /pap
Women, family, morals. "Marx, Lenin, Engels and Stalin
develop essays expounding the theory that the emancipation
of women is crucial to the development of true socialism"
[Library Journal:2589, Sept. 1, 1971].

(79) Moody, Anne, 1940-
Coming of age in Mississippi. HS
Dial Press c1968 348p 68-55153
1970 (pap 1484-5) Delta Dell
Not directly about women except how they are used by both
Negro and Caucasian men, a point which the author seems
to miss--wife abuse, incest, adultery, gambling away income, child abandonment and beating, discarded wife, sex-
segregated church, double-standard assumptions galore. An
autobiography which Virginia Kirkus aptly declared "should
make its identification on any terms with readers of any
age."

(80) Moore, Bernice Milburn, 1904-   and Wayne N.
     Holtzman
Tomorrow's parents; a study of youth and their families.
Univ. of Texas c1965 371p bib 64-19414
$8.50 0-292-73409-3
Working mothers and housewives compared.

(81) Morgan, Robin, ed.
Sisterhood is powerful; an anthology of writings from the
     Women's Liberation movement. HS
Random c1970 602p bib 70-117694
$8.95; $2.45/pap Vintage U539
This is the anthology to date, balanced, with something for
everyone--a resource as well (see appendices, which can be

updated by Women's Studies participants).   An absolute basic,
even to the apt title.   Sections: The oppressed majority;
The way it is; The invisible woman; Psychological and sexual repression; Go tell it to the valley: changing consciousness; Up from sexism; Emerging ideologies; The hand that
cradles the rock; protest and revolt (including historical documents).   Good age-range among contributors--teens to
forties--and a variety of life styles and occupations as well;
articles, poems, photos, manifestos.   The editor is an active
feminist.   The timid soul or the Duped Dame who passes this
up on the library's New Book Shelves is cheating no one but
herself.   For insights, information (e.g., how to conscious-
ness-raise), courage, sisterhood.   Read Morgan's opening
remarks re getting it published: "Sex and love have been so
contaminated for women by economic dependence that the
package deal of love and marriage looks like a con and a
shill.   We will not be able to sort out what we do want
from men and what we want to give them until we know that
our own physical and psychological survival--at home and
work--does not depend on men.   Like all oppressed peoples,
we need, first of all, self-determination" [p. 28].   See
also her "Women in revolt" (Random, 1969, $1.95/pap).

(82) O'Neill, William L.
Everyone was brave; rise and fall of feminism in America.
Quadrangle 1969 369p bib 71-78313
$7.95
Historian O'Neill in a kind of epilogue expresses the opinion
based on his work that there are three basic conditions
which must exist before women are equal: (1) a welfare
state which compensates mothers for their service to society;
(2) an environment which will inspire women to utilize their
opportunities; and (3) self-exploration and knowledge.   "Sexual parity ... would mean revolutionizing our domestic life.
Perhaps we do not want it, do not need it, and should not
have it.   Nonetheless, such a revolution is what equality
presupposes."   See also his "Divorce in the progressive
era" (Yale Univ. Press, 1967, $6.50) and "Woman move-
ment" (Barnes and Noble, 1969, $5.75).

(83) Packard, Vance
The sexual wilderness; the contemporary upheaval in male-
     female relationships.
McKay 1968 553p
$6.95; 1970 $1.25 (pap 0-671-78010-7)   PB
Packard contends that whereas in the past sex roles were
sharply defined, today, rules, standards and requirements

for each sex are blurred. Now males and females conceive
of their role(s) in life as affected by this change. How this
change came about and what is needed in the future for personal fulfillment and a strong society are the main concerns
of his study.

(84)   Peck, Ellen
The baby trap.
Bernard Geis   1971   245p   78-148926
$5. 95
The motherhood myth, according to the author, is responsible for the growing population crisis and divorce rate. She
and her husband chose not to have children, and then found
it necessary to write "The baby trap" to defend the right to
that choice. She describes the baby trap as set by the
media, baited by manufacturers, and reinforced by relatives.
See also Edgar R. Chasteen's "The case for compulsory
birth control" (Prentice-Hall, 1961, $5. 95).

(85)   Pilpel, Harriet Fleischel and Theodora Zavin
Your marriage and the law.
Rinehart   c1952   358p   52-5565
Rev. ed. , 1965   95¢ (pap 08113)   Collier Macmillan
Marital duties, responsibilities and rights as seen in American law. American Civil Liberties Union distributes "When
should abortion be legal?" (25¢) by Ms. Pilpel with Kenneth
P. Norwick. "Legal rights of married women" by Daniel J.
deBenedictis is also recommended, emphasis on property
rights (Cornerstone, 1969, $1. 25). Ms. Pilpel's "A copy-
right guide" (Bowker, 1969, $3) is also useful.

(86)   Rainwater, Lee and Karol Kane Weinstein
And the poor get children; sex, contraception and family
     planning in the working class.
Quadrangle   1960   202p   bib   index   60-10881
$5.   0-8129-0041-3; $2. 45/pap   0-8129-6051-3   QP208
A study sponsored by the Planned Parenthood Federation of
America of attitudes toward sexual and contraceptive prac-
tices in the so-called working class; a relationship was
found to marital power structures.

(87)   Reed, Evelyn
Problems of women's liberation; a Marxist approach (5th
     rev. ed.).
Pathfinder   1970   96p   78-143808
$3. 95; $1. 45/pap
Are the oppression of women and the institution of the family

"natural" to society? Anthropologist Reed examines the
roots of women's oppression--articles on women and the
family, the myth of female inferiority, sex and class. But
note that Germaine Greer calls these "arguments couched
in typical Marxist doctrinaire terminology buttressed by
phony anthropology and poor scholarship...." True, the
author makes no bones of Marxist analysis of women's role
past and present in society, the history of reasons for their
oppression under capitalism and of course the way to "emancipation." Her pamphlet, "The myth of inferiority: women's
role in pre-historic societal development" is available from
New England Free Press (15¢).

(88)   Ross, Ishbel
Sons of Adam, daughters of Eve; the role of women in
    American history.
Harper   c1969   340p   bib   index   67-13691
$7.95   0-06-013668-5
The reaction of a woman who reads this status-of-women
survey with no coaching other than the publisher's jacket
should be interesting. In a way, it's like taking a subjective
"awareness inventory." The author's conception of the
American woman's base of real power has it resting in her
capacity to "advise and sway men on the personel level...";
the woman who is informed and interested in many areas,
but basically happy at home spreading her aura of family
stability is the woman of today! She considers women
effective promoters of causes, occasionally gifted in the
arts, moderately well established in the professions, but
generally failures in politics....

(89)   Rover, Constance
The Punch book of women's rights.   HS
A S Barnes   c1967   128p   70-83509
$5.   498-07503-6
Here is a collection of articles, anecdotes and cartoons
about the injustices done to women in the 19th century. Ms.
Rover is an author, senior lecturer in government at North-
Western Polytechnic (London) and member of the Fawcett
Society and other women's organizations. The humorous
satire appeared in Punch, the famous British humor magazine. All the usual aspects of then and today--but including
the problem of the single woman, not much touched upon
in the U.S.A. Suffrage only part of the 19th-century British problem; the exploitation of women teachers and bitter
poverty in the lives of governesses and seamstresses in
contrast to the banality of the lives of well-to-do young

ladies come through.   Ms. Rover has also authored "Women's suffrage and party politics in Britain, 1866-1914,"
available in the U.S. (Barnes, 1967, $7.50).

(90)   Schwartz, Gwen Gibson and Barbara Wyden
The Jewish wife.
Peter H. Wyden   c1969   308p   79-96789
$6.95;   1970   (pap 392)   Paperback library
Two non-Jewish women married to Jewish men got together
and produced this "first fully documented report on the
successes and problems of history's most misunderstood
woman," and then one of the husbands published it.   Interviews with 50 American Jewish wives are the basis for their
contention that modern Jewish wives have little in common
with the stereotyped women, "the bulky matriarchal carica-
ture ... comical, predatory ..." portrayed in other books.
Chapter titles are revealing, however: Isn't it nice to be
perfect?; She worries, worries, worries; Everything must
be organized; She loves luxury (i.e., success = $.); Cul-
ture, culture, culture (Great Books and movies); Guilt,
guilt, guilt.   The authors completely skirt mental/emotional
health and where the men are.   Lyn Tornabene's "What's a
Jewish girl?" (Simon & Schuster, 1966, $2.95) and Dan
Greenburg's "How to be a Jewish mother" (Price Stern, 1965,
$2.95) are also revealing in their own ways.

(91)   Scott, Anne Firor, 1921-
The American woman; who was she?
Prentice Hall   c1971   182p   70-133056
$5.95; $2.45/pap
"Poets and novelists rarely overlook women.   Historians
almost always do" [p. 1].   A documentary history of
Feminism--catchy, somewhat inaccurate title, but ... an
anthology/chronology of 20th century.   First section, "The
background"; second section, " Women's work," includes
an overview of 1800-1900.   Selections of all types of writing,
e.g., contemporary best-sellers, biography and autobiography,
journal articles, other anthologies, older books, classics
and United States documents.   Some reprints; mostly by
women.   But even the most well read will discover some
new fact here.   Read her Introduction.   Author was appointed by President Johnson to the Citizens' Advisory
Council on the Status of Women.

(92)   Scott, Anne Firor, 1921-
The Southern lady; from pedestal to politics, 1830-1930.
Univ. of Chicago Press   1970   247p   bib   index   73-12370

$5.95   0-226-74346-2
The author, a Southern lady, is a writer on the status of
women. Her purpose is to describe the culturally-defined
image of the Southern lady and to trace the effect this definition had on women's behavior from 1830-1930. The realities
of women's lives were often at odds with the image--the
struggle of women to free themselves from the confines of
cultural expectation might have been described in any part of
the U.S., but the 19th-century South provided women whose
role was unusually confining and sanctions which were especially effective. Thus, their efforts to free themselves
were more complex than elsewhere. Women who left a
record were generally part of the educated or wealthy
families; diaries, letters and manuscripts of pre-Civil War
were used as resources. After the War, public records
provided documentation. The final chapter, "The new woman observed," and the bibliographic essay are especially
useful in a book so crammed full of documented research it
might well have turned out dull reading were it not for the
writer's involvement and presentation.

(93) Sex Information & Education Council of the United
      States (SIECUS)
Study Guides. Title varies: "Discussion Guide."
50¢ each; each with Bibliography.
No. 7, for example, "Film resources for sex education,"
      1971.

(94) Snow, Helen Foster [Pen name is NYM Wales]
Women in modern China.
Paris: Mouton 1967   264p   67-18165
Humanities $6.
There is a surprisingly large number of books on women's
status in other countries, including Asia. Some by local
males, e.g., K.N. Venkatarayappa's "Feminine roles"
(Bombay: Popular Prakashan, 1966) are incredibly misogynous; others by outsiders are often put together to sell.
Ms. Snow is eminently qualified as geographer, scholar,
resident, traveler, writer and woman. Her study encompasses the emancipation of Chinese women (a quick survey),
women and the farm, women and Christianity, women and
the Kuomintang, women and education, and "bound feet and
straw sandals." The glossary is useful and supportive of
other readings.

(95) Stambler, Sookie, comp.
Women's liberation; blueprint for the future.

Ace   c1970   283p
95¢/pap   90840
Ms. Stambler is a young woman who seems to have thrown
together an anthology of reprints of mostly periodicals articles.   On closer examination, it turns out to have real
punch: Stambler's Introduction, Women on women, Women
on men, Women on law and education, Women on sex and
sex roles, Women on liberation, Women and the arts, Women's struggle: an historical overview.   See especially
Redstockings Collective's "How women are kept apart, "
Marlene Nadle's "Prostitutes, " Alix Shulman's "A marriage
agreement, " and Rosalyn Baxandall's "Cooperative nurseries, "
for consciousness-raising.   The book is available only as a
paperback with minute print.

(96)   Stenton, Doris Mary
The English woman in history.
Macmillan   1957   363p   index
$6.50   Fernhill
The author is a fellow of the British Academy.   Her purpose here is to describe the place of women and their influence from early to modern times, by which she means
beginning with "the famous description of the women of the
Germanic tribes written by the Roman historian Tacitus"
and ending in 1869 with the publication of Mill's "The subjection of women" because there are already many subsequent studies.   Her conclusion: what was needed was a
husband, best dead, but if not, the skill to manipulate him.
Not enough attention given to the woman of the masses, however.

(97)   Taves, Isabella
Women alone.
Funk   1968   316p   68-15777
$5.95   (710630); $1.95   (pap 901070, F 75)
As often happens, the jacket blurb reveals someone's pre-
conceptions about woman's place: "Every year thousands
of married women suddenly find themselves widows or divorcees.   Thrust from the mainstream of society into a
mysterious sub-culture of 'fifth wheels, ' they face a life
filled with new moral and social problems...."   There is
much in this "Widows' and divorcees' handbook" for all
women alone--help for all except, of course, the married
ones.

(98)   Thompson, Mary Lou, ed.
Voices of the new feminism.

Beacon c1970 246p bib 76-119679
$5.95 0-8070-4172-6; $2.45/pap BP411
Thompson is associate director of the Unitarian Universalist
Women's Federation (Boston), which sponsored "Voices...."
It is not an organizational statement, however. Rather, it
is an examination of "the major aspects of sexual inequality"
and a presentation of "a comprehensive statement of the
adjustments which must be made for the sake of social health
and simple justice" [publisher's comment]. Each contributor
is an expert in her field as well as an accomplished writer
who might have commanded royalties and publicity for her
article elsewhere: history, Joyce Cowley; ideology, Betty
Friedan, Roxanne Dunbar, Alice S. Rossi; problems and
goals, Elizabeth Duncan Koontz, Pauli Murray, Martha
Griffiths, Doris Pullen, Mary Daly; emerging life styles,
Caroline Bird; and program for the future, Thompson,
Shirley Chisholm, Lucinda Cisler. Only some of the
articles are reprints. See especially Roxanne Dunbar's
"Female liberation as the basis for social revolution." A
basic for Women's Studies. Pauli Murray in her "The liberation of black women" makes the point that of approximately
800 full-length articles published in the Journal of Negro
History since its inception (1916), only six have dealt directly with the Negro woman, only two have considered Negro
women as a group. Betty Friedan in her "Our revolution is
unique" discusses the National Organization for Women.
Doris Pullen in "The educational establishment: wasted women" believes that women's colleges should lead the way as
models of educational opportunity.

(99) Walters, Patricia, et al.
Women in top jobs: four studies in achievement.
Fernhill 1971 328p index
$12.
Considers women as company directors, examines the posi-
tion of women managers in two large firms and analyzes how
they do in senior posts in the BBC and the Administrative
Civil Service. Walters is in the Department of Sociology,
Government and Administration, University of Salford, Eng-
land. (Library Journal June 15, 1971.)

(100) Ward, Barbara E.
Women in the new Asia; the changing social roles of men
    and women in South and South East Asia.
Paris: UNESCO c1963 529p bib
$10
"Men, women and change; an essay in understanding social

roles in South and South East Asia" is followed by 19 essays
re countries, mostly by women of the countries--family,
marriage, career, combining marriage and career, changes.
The third part of the book is devoted mainly to female
emancipation and demography. An appendix, "Family planning in South and South East Asia," is followed by Suggestions
for Further Reading, which include a substantial number of
works published in English and/or in the United States about
these countries. See also Snow (94).

(101) Ware, Celestine
Woman power; the movement for women's liberation.
Tower   c1970   73-18102
95¢ (pap T095-18)
"One of the founders of the Stanton-Anthony Brigade, a
forerunner of New York Radical Feminists, Ms. Ware attempts to introduce the entire feminist movement and its
beginnings.   Although she doesn't succeed, she does provide
an interesting refresher course and a superficial overview
of the movement" [Library Journal:2593, Sept. 1, 1971].
Other 1971 publications about the Women's Liberation Movement worth looking into are: Marian Christy's "Behind the
bra-less revolution" (Cowles, $5.95), Karen De Crow's
"The young woman's guide to liberation" (Bobbs Merrill,
$2.95), Helen Eustis' "What you should know about the
Women's Liberation Movement" (Scholastic Mag.), Judith
Hole and Ellen Levine's "Rebirth of feminism..." (Quadrangle books, $10), Lucy Komisar's "The new feminism"
(Watts, $5.95) and Leslie Tanner's "Voices from women's
liberation" (Signet, $1.50)

(102)   Wasserman, Barbara Alson, ed.
The bold new women (rev. ed.).   HS
World   1970   304p
95¢ (pap M 495)   Prem Fawcett World
Don't confuse title with Cooke's "The new women," although
both are contemporary anthologies of the women's move-
ment.   The present title contains many, but not all, re-
prints of works by such bold and courageous new women as
Susan Brownmiller, Rosalyn Drexler, Joyce Elbert, Maria
Irene Fornes, Vivian Gornick, Hannah Green, Stephanie
Harrington, Rona Jaffe, Pauline Kael, Sally Kempton, Jane
Kramer, Doris Lessing, Marge Piercy, Barbara Long, MIM,
Edna O'Brien, Harriet Sohners and Susan Sontag. [Most are
also represented in this Basic Book Collection.]

(103)   Wollstonecraft, Mary, 1759-1797
A vindication of the rights of women.

Original 1792.   Source Library of the Women's Movement
     1970   471p $18   (Also: $1.75/pap   0-393-00373-6
     1967   C.W. Hagelman, Jr., ed.
"A pioneer work in the history of the rights of women.   It
is the point from which historians date the woman question
as a political force" [Source Library...].   "I shall ... consider women in the grand light of human creatures, who,
in common with men, are placed on this earth to unfold
their faculties."   "A vindication ..." was written by Ms.
Wollstonecraft as reply to Rousseau's views on women's
education (i.e., non-education).   Her daughter was Mary
Wollstonecraft Godwin Shelley.

(104)   Woolf, Virginia, 1882-1941
A room of one's own.
London: Hogarth Press   c1929   199p
Harcourt $4.75   0-15-178731-X;   1921   95¢/pap
     0-15-679973-1.   S
Ms. Woolf concluded that women, as ignominious and subservient as their pasts had been (1929), have creative lives
before them, provided they still have (1) regular incomes
and (2) rooms of their own--the two keys to freedom, symbols of power to think for oneself and to contemplate.   Of
her, Annie Gottlieb in her excellent bibliographic essay on
W.L. paperbacks wrote, "one of the first to draw connections between the institutionalized barbarity of this century
and its men's frightened contempt for all women and all
tenderness.   She was the first to wonder why friendship
between women was never shown in novels..." [New York
Times VII Part 2:1f, Feb. 21, 1971 "Female human beings"].

320 Political Science

(105)   Adams, Mildred
The right to be people.
Lippincott   1967   248p   index   66-23241
$4.95
Mainly for the second half of the book, a frank discussion
of developments since 1920--what the right to vote has done
and has failed to accomplish for women politically and
socially.   Raises controversial issues.   Appendix contains
Declaration of Women's Rights, Seneca Falls, New York,
1848.

(106)   Faber, Doris
Petticoat politics; how American women won the right to
     vote.   HS

Lothrop   c1967   192p   bib   index   67-22599
$3. 95
Like most books for young adults in this field, it is basically
biography from the past; as usual, there is no indication that
women went to prison and were physically persecuted for
struggling to get the "right to vote" referred to in sub-title.
Writing, print-size, etc. are all otherwise of a mature
junior high school level.   Chapter 15: "A parting debate"
(final chapter) starts, "How have women used their new
power?" and is followed by an imaginary debate between a
politician and a professional, con/pro.   Good, but portrays
women as working, rather than having to work.   Another
source for the Declaration of Women's Rights (Sentiments)
adopted at Seneca Falls, New York, 1848.   Bibliography is
mostly biographies; page 188 contains references to "sources, "
which can be utilized with young people for a take-off to a
discussion of methodology.   Olivia E. Coolidge's "Women's
rights; the suffrage movement in America, 1848-1920" (Dutton, 1966, $4.95) is a good companion title.

(107)   Flexner, Eleanor, 1908-
Century of struggle; the woman's rights movement in the
     U.S.
Harvard Univ. Press   1959   384p   bib
$8.50   0-674-10650-4   Belknap Press;   1968 $3.45/pap
     0-689-70072-5, 117 Atheneum
Generally considered the best authority on the early suffragettes in the history of civil rights for American women.
Brings the history up to the founding of the Women's Bureau
(1920).   Only scholarly work covering entire movement--
breadth prevents dealing with ideological questions in great
depth, however; see also Aileen S. Kraditor's "The ideas
of the Woman Suffrage Movement, 1890-1920, " and Inez
Irwin's "Up hill with banners flying" (O. P.).

(108)   Kraditor, Aileen S.
The ideas of the woman suffrage movement, 1890-1920.
Columbia Univ. Press   c1965   bib   index   65-14410
$9.
Although the suffrage movement had no official ideology,
its history must be viewed and understood as a chapter in
the intellectual history of the American people.   The ideas
of the leaders of the movement were their aspirations and
weapons.   Sheds light on American reform movements in
general.   Most secondary sources on the suffrage movement
are biographies; Flexner's "Century of struggle" is the only
scholarly work, but it covers the breadth of the entire move-

ment and cannot get into the ideology in the detail that
Kraditor does here.   The two major types of suffragist
argument, and the relationship of women suffrage and religion are surprising.   The appended data re the 20 suffragettes on whose ideas the study is built produce interesting
generalizations, e.g., of the 26, 16 were college graduates,
17 married, three divorced, nine never married and 16 at
some time earned their own living in a middle-class occupation.

(109)   Rainwater, Lee and William L. Yancey
The Moynihan Report and the politics of controversy.
MIT Press   c1967   493p   index   67-15238
$12.50; $3.95   (pap 0-262-68009-2, 681)
The 1965 U.S. Department of Labor Office of Policy Planning
and Research report, "The Negro family; the case for national action" (US. GPO 794-628 45¢/pap, often referred to
as "The Moynihan Report") concluded that the Negro family
is a "tangle of pathology" involving "matriarchy" and such
other negatively ascribed factors as delinquency and crime.
(See chapter 4, page 40f; Newsweek summarized the Report, August 9, 1965:32.)   Thinking and reading women soon
began to counter with the thought that most Negro women
become "matriarchs" because the role is forced upon them.
The assumption of instability in matriarchal households is a
masculine defense.   The concept that most women become
matriarchal because they are deviant evolved from the male-
family-head-as-the-norm role.   "A fundamental fact of Negro
American life is the often reversed roles of husband and
wife" [first sentence in Matriarchy Section of the chapter,
"The tangle of pathology," p. 30].   As if to prove this, the
Report continued, "There is much evidence that Negro females are better students than their male counterparts"
[p. 31] and "In a matriarchal structure, the women are
transmitting the culture."   Rainwater and Yancey present
the full text of the original government publication with material which utilizes it as the focal point of "politics of
controversy."   Reading can be dangerous....

(110)   Strachey, Rachel Costelloe, 1887-1940
The cause; a short history of the women's movement in
     Great Britain.
Kennikat Press   1969   (original 1928)   429p   bib
$15.   0-8046-0450-9
Published by G. Bell (London) in 1928 under the authorship,
"Ray Strachey."

330 Economics

(111)   Balabanoff, Angelica, 1878-1965
My life as a rebel (3rd. ed.).
Greenwood Press   c1938   324p   68-23270
1968 $14   0-8371-0091-9
Balabanoff has also written "Impressions of Lenin" (Univ.
of Michigan Press, 1964, $5).

(112)   Canada.   Dept. of Labour, Women's Bureau.
Women at work in Canada; a fact book on the female labour
    force, 1964.
The Bureau   1964   108p   bib
75¢/pap   L38-664
Somewhat comparable to the U.S. Dept. of Labor Women's
Bureau "Handbook," although now old.   Contains: Seventy
years later, Trends in women's employment, Characteristics
of women workers, Women's occupations and training, Women's earnings, Legislation affecting women workers, International labour affairs and women workers.   "Facts and
figures; women in the labour force, 1969" is a bi-lingual
(French/English) pamphlet of data and charts which updates
"Women at work in Canada..." (L 38-3069).   The proportion
of employed Canadian women is less than in the U.S., but
it is steadily increasing; most are 20-24 years old (55.8%)
and married.   "Working mothers and their child-care arrangements" (L38-2970) is an excellent 1970 publication containing "highlights of data," e.g., working mothers comprise
almost 25% of the Canadian female labor force.   "Women's
Bureau 1970" is a misnomer--a bi-lingual pamphlet in response to requests relating to courses and education programs being developed.

(113)   Clark, Alice
Working life of women in the seventeenth century.
London: Routledge (New York: Dutton)   1919   328p   index
    67-31558
$10   (9-678-05039-2)   Kelley   1968
Originally published in England in 1919, this is an economics
classic reprinted.   Each chapter is preceded by an outline-
summary.   The 17th century itself forms a sort of water-
shed between two widely differing eras in the history of
English women: the Elizabethan and the 18th century.   Thus
characteristics of both can be studied in the women who
move through it either in the pages of dramatists or as revealed by personal papers or in public records.   "The conception of the sociological importance of past economic con-

ditions for women I owe to Olive Schreiner, whose epoch-
making book, 'Woman and labour' (repr.), first drew the
attention of many workers in the emancipation of women to
the difference between reality and the commonly received
generalizations as to women's productive capacity." The
author's conclusion (Chapter 7): great productive capacity
of women under conditions of family and domestic industry;
no difference between efficiency of labour when applied for
domestic purposes or for trade; rate of wages no guide to
real value of goods produced. 1919 style but readable.

(114)   Ginzberg, Eli, 1911-   and Alice M. Yohalem
Educated American women; self portraits.
Columbia Univ. Press   1966   198p   66-28964
$6.50
The planners: career or family-oriented, working mothers;
the recasters, adapters, unsettled. These are the "self-
portraits" of the 26 women whose life styles were reported
in Ginzberg's "Life styles of educated women." "Our society
is still not sufficiently geared to permit women to realize
fully their potentialities" [p. 196].

(115)   Harbeson, Gladys Evans
Choice and challenge for the American woman.
Schenkman   c1967   185p   bib   67-29322
$7.95; $2.95   (pap 0-80703-401-6, SK 20)
A study with emphasis on the choice supposedly available
to women, the need to choose, and the right to. Selected
bibliography includes international perspectives.

(116)   Massachusetts Institute of Technology. Symposium
        on American Women in Science and Engineering
Women and the scientific professions. Proceedings, ed. by
        Jacqueline A. Mattfeld and Carol G. VanAken.
MIT Press   c1965   250p   index   65-26968
1967 $6.95   0-262-63012-5; $2.95/pap   79
Considers the personal, sociological and economic factors
involved in a woman's professional career. Divided into
four major sections: (1) commitment required of a women
entering a scientific profession; (2) who wants a woman in
the scientific professions? (3) case for/against the employment of women; (4) "closing the gap." Participants were
men and women: Alice S. Rossi's "Barriers to the career
choice of engineering, medicine or science among women":
women are "punished socially and psychologically instead of
being rewarded as men are for their efforts and achievements..." in seeking higher degrees in fields like science

and engineering. Bettelheim: "the problems facing professional women stem from the fact that these women are expected to enter a masculinely oriented working world as
men...."

(117)   Myrdal, Alva Reimer, 1902-   and Viola Klein
Women's two roles, home and work (2nd. ed. rev.).
Humanities Press   c1968   213p   68-77517
$5. 50; $2. 50 /pap
The current dilemma about women's roles stems not from
what they can do but what they should do.   Women's two
roles in this case are home and work and they are considered from the point of view of women's educational
needs.   Factors impeding the employment of married women
are analyzed and suggestions made.

(118)   National Council of Women Study Project
What's in it?
National Council of Women of Canada
The Council $1. 25
Study guide for individuals and organizations; indicates social
and economic conditions brought forward in briefs to the
Royal Commission on the Status of Women; commission
recommendations to the Prime Minister; and the potential
effects of these recommendations in the Canadian community,
professions, industries and other spheres.   Prepared by
the Canadian Association for Adult Education under contract.
(French-language study guide will be published by La Federation des Femmes du Quebec.)

(119)   National Manpower Council
Womanpower; a statement...
Columbia Univ. Press   c1957   371p   index   56-12740
$7. 50
Although almost 15 years old, this remains an authoritative
work; the Council's recommendations dealt with the ways of
improving development and effective utilization of the nation's
womanpower resources.   Chapters by its staff cover employment opportunities, practices and problems (still) affecting women; high school and post-high school education
and guidance in relation to work; patterns of work and types
of women workers.   Chapter 10 relates to women in the
armed services (not too much in the literature re this subject).   Includes discussion of the influence of traditional
attitudes on distinctions between "men's" and "women's"
jobs, on the acceptance of women as supervisors and their
opportunities to become executives.   This work constitutes

evidence that in 1956 Americans were thinking about women's liberation, whether they called it that or not.

(120)   Simons, Gustave
What every woman doesn't know.
Macmillan   1964   440p   64-20300
$6.95
An eminent tax-lawyer writes for women on every aspect of
the American woman's financial rights and obligations.   "For
the last hundred years in these United States millions of
women have held down jobs and drawn their own checks,
while a benevolent government has bestowed upon them the
right to own their own property and give it away or sell it
as they please.   Women in America are said to do most of
the buying, are the beneficiaries of most of the life insurance, and own a major share of real estate.   Increasing
numbers of supervisory and middle-executive posts are oc-
cupied by women.   A beautiful picture of feminine financial
emancipation is presented.   The only trouble is that it is a
fake and an illusion. "   Simons answers the questions: Why
are women financial slaves?   What is the illusion of financial
emancipation?   How do tax laws discriminate against women?
What are the risks of joint accounts and jointly-owned
property?   Why should a woman think twice before signing
a joint tax return?

(121)   Smuts, Robert W.
Women and work in America.
Columbia Univ. Press   1959   180p   bib   index   59-8116
$5.50
Describes unpaid work of women on farm and in home since
1890 and paid employment in factory, office, professions,
etc.   Radical changes since turn of the century, implications
for woman, her family and society.   Emphasizes causes,
rather than consequences, however; use with Komarovsky
(70).

(122)   Stollenwerk, Antoinette
Back to work, ladies; a career guide for the mature woman,
    by Toni Stollenwerk.
1967   55p   67-31459.
$2/pap   (P18)   Pilot books
This one doesn't have the usual unfortunate emphases on
such things as volunteer work and entering the professions
which require years of preparation.   New and of possible
interest: Sandra Reisner Friedman and Lois C. Schwartz's
"No experience necessary; a guide to employment for the

female liberal arts graduate" (Dell, 1971, $1.25), and
Juanita Kreps' "Sex in the market place; American women
at work (Johns Hopkins, 1971, $1.95).

(123)   U.S. Department of Labor.   Women's Bureau.
1969 Handbook on women workers.   Women's Bureau Bul-
    letin 294.
U.S. G.P.O.   1969   384p   bib   index $1.50/pap   (1
    copy gratis from the Bureau)
This is a basic tool.   Other Women's Bureau publications
of personal interest are constantly being prepared; examples
are: Automation and women workers (Feb. 1970); Careers
for women series: "Why not be ..." (an engineer: Leaflet
41, 1971, 10¢); Changing patterns of women's lives (Leaflet
54, 1971, 10¢); Conozca sus derechos (Leaflet 39-A, 1967,
15¢--Spanish transl. of Know your rights); Day care services; industry's involvement (Bulletin 296, 1971, 25¢);
Facts about women's absenteeism and labor turnover (1969);
Job finding techniques for mature women (Pamphlet no. 11,
Feb. 1970, 30¢); Labor laws affecting private household
workers (1971); The myth and the reality (4p, April 1971,
WB71-113, 10¢); Negro women in the population and in the
labor force (Dec. 1967, 30¢); Para beneficiar las mujeres
en sus trabajos (1969, Spanish transl. of To benefit women
at work); Profile of the woman worker; 50 years of progress (April 1970, WB70-127); and Women workers today
(1971).   Government publications for which a price is listed
may be purchased from the Supt. of Documents, U.S. Government Printing Office, with a discount of 25% on orders
of 100 or more copies of the same publication.   Check or
money order made payable to the Supt. of Documents should
accompany orders.   Publications for which no price is
listed and single copies of others may be obtained from the
Women's Bureau.   Use the document number whenever
possible.

340 Law

(124)   Bureau of National Affairs Editorial Staff
Civil Rights Act of 1964; text analysis, legislative history;
    what it means to employers, businessmen, unions,
    employees, minority groups.
BNA   1964   424p   64-25380
$9.50   0-87179-005-X; $8.50/pap   0-87179-006-8
The Bureau also has in print "State fair employment laws
and their administration ... a BNA operations manual"

(1964, $6.50) and "Equal pay for equal work" (1963, $6.95/ pap).

(125)   Callahan, Parnell J. T.
The law of separation and divorce (2nd. ed.).
Oceana c1967 122p index 67-24914
$3   0-379-11001-6
In the Legal Almanac Series.   Includes definition of terms.
Request a copy which includes changes since press date.
His "Know your rights under New York's new divorce law"
(Oceana, 1966, $1.50) also relevant.

(126)   Cantor, Donald J.
Escape from marriage; how to solve the problems of divorce.
Morrow   1971   index
$4.95
An experienced divorce lawyer, writing with courage, analyzes the marriage contract, the right of divorce, the divorce trial, the strategy of lawyers, and the reforms that
are needed.   Reveals the inequities of a legal system im-
posing itself on the individual morality and norms of marital
behavior.

(127)   DeWolf, Rose
The bonds of acrimony.
Lippincott c1970 160p 72-127083
$4.95
Another book about divorce today, tricky title and all; this
is good of its kind, however.   The Marriage Council of
Philadelphia, a division of the Department of Psychiatry of
the University of Pennsylvania Medical School, has been
studying marriage in Philadelphia since 1932.   Among its
published conclusions are: about 50% of all marriages are
based on convenience rather than love; by the time they reach
forty, 50% of husbands have had at least one "affair"; by the
time they reach forty, 26% of wives have had at least one
"affair"; 63% of women married a decade or more claim
they are less happy than when they were first married.
Lack of an index makes it difficult to use for more than
straight reading, but some people need to be brought up
sharply, which this should do.

(128)   Handbook for state and city commissions on the
        status of women.
Univ. of Wisconsin (Madison) Extension, in cooperation with
     the Women's Bureau, Wage & Labor Standards Adminis-
     tration, U.S. Dept. of Labor c1968 26p

Women's Bureau, Washington, D.C. 20210 free/pap
Seven useful chapters--how to: organize or reorganize a
commission, plan and conduct a conference, conduct and
utilize surveys, produce and distribute a report, pass legislation, implement recommendations, inspire a favorable
press. Introduction says material was developed from a
series of workshops held in 1967 by women. A very useful
little gem, really more than a pamphlet and not something
one can expect to locate via an underground press kind of
index.

(129) Hart, Herbert Lionel Adolphus, 1907-
Law, liberty, and morality.
Stanford Univ. Press c1963 88p bib index 62-18743
$3.75; $1.45/pap 0-8047-0154-7. $1.45 (pap V 319)
     Vin Random
Homosexuality.

(130) Hindell, Keith and Madeleine Simms
Abortion law reformed.
Humanities 1971 269p bib index
$10
History of British fight. Abortion Act of 1967.

(131) Kanowitz, Leo
Women and the law; the unfinished revolution.
Univ. of New Mexico Press 1969/1st ed. 312p index
     70-78551
$8.95 0-8263-0134-7; $3.95 (pap 0173-8)
Most comprehensive exploration of the kinds of laws discriminating on the basis of sex, this isn't another little
handbook of what every woman should know about her divorce. And don't think for a moment there isn't sex-based
discrimination in American law. The New York University
School of Law has inaugurated a course devoted to legal
problems of women; one of the required readings is this
title by N.O.W. member Kanowitz. Appendices contain:
Title VII of Civil Rights Act of 1964, Executive Order
11246--Equal Employment, and relevant cases. Contents:
Law and the single girl, Law and the married woman, Title
VII of 1964 Civil Rights Act and Equal Pay Act of 1963,
Relationship between these, Constitutional aspects of sex-
based discrimination in American law.

(132) Schulder, Diane B. and Floryence Kennedy
Abortion rap.
McGraw 1971 239p

$6. 95; $3. 95 /pap
Account of the testimony given at the abortion hearings to
repeal New York State law. Authors are attorneys who
were involved in the first class-action abortion suit and in
1971 started another similar class lawsuit against the
Catholic Church, challenging its tax-exempt status in light
of its active lobbying. "The book ... is a good beginning;
it reveals through actual testimony the arrogant attitude of
male legislators toward a woman's right to control her own
body, and through the testimony of women, the suffering
they've experienced as a result of such attitudes" [Village
Voice, May 20, 1971].

360 Welfare and Association

(133)   Bremner, Robert H. , ed.
Children and youth in America; a documentary history.
Vol. 1, 1600-1865; Vol. 2, 1866-1932 bib   74-115473
Harvard Univ. Press 1970- $10, $20
There will be three volumes in this series tracing the
history of the nation's attitudes towards its children--legal
status of children, public education, child labor, juvenile
delinquency, birth control, abortion, etc.

(134)   Child Welfare League of America
CWA Standards for day care service (rev. ed.).
The League 1970 123p 79-10080
$2. 50
The Child Welfare League has several other relevant titles:
Dorothy B. Boguslawski's "Guide for establishing and
operating day care centers for young children" (1970, $2. 50);
Florence A. Ruderman's "Child care and working mothers..."
(1970, $7. 50); and Helen D. Stone's "Foster care in ques-
tion..." (1970, $4. 20).

(135)   DeRham, Edith, 1933-
How could she do that? A study of the female criminal.
Clarkson N. Potter c1969 337p bib 68-26886
1969 $6 Potter; 1970 95¢ (pap 0-671-77167-1) Pocket
    Books
Stories based on actual criminal histories with the names
and other forms of identification changed. When a woman
commits a crime, especially murder, most people react with
disbelief and shock. Women, however, do commit substantial amounts of crime, increasing in number. The
author examines seven "rather typical cases" including Carole

Tregoff, who collaborated with Dr. Finch in the murder of
his wife.   Insight, rather than sensationalism, is the author's
purpose.   Conclusion and Suggested Further Reading useful.

(136)   Evans, E. Belle, et al.
Day care; how to plan, develop, and operate a day care
      center.
Beacon   1971   288p   bib   index   76-156448
$6.95   0-8070-3178-X
Resource and guidebook; includes section on how to interview
and select teachers, staffing, outlines of needed equipment
and supplies, legal requirements.   Considers small cooperative units, and can also help parents to evaluate existing
day care programs.   Written with Beth Shub and Marlene
Weinstein.

(137)   Giallombardo, Rose
Society of women: a study of a women's prison.
Wiley   c 1966   244p   bib   index   66-14132
$7.95   0-471-29730-5

(138)   Pierce, Ruth I.
Single and pregnant.
Beacon Press   c1970   222p   bib   index   72-119678
0-8070-2778-2 $5.95;   0-8070-2779-0 BP 407 $1.95/pap
Appendices include Abortions referrals, Planned Parenthood
affiliates (August 1969), Maternity and infant care projects,
and Suggested Readings (which include Spock's "Baby and
child care").   It is (nevertheless) a tool that professionals
can and should alert clients and libraries to.   Compassionate
and relevant in this period, when it is still stigmatic to be
single and pregnant.   Author's attitude of <u>choice</u> of what to
do is good.

(139)   Ward, David A. and Gene G. Kassebaum
Women's prison; sex and social structure.
Aldine   c1965   269p   bib   index   65-12460
$7.95

370 Education

(140)   Bernard, Jessie Shirley, 1903-
Academic women.
Pennsylvania State Univ. Press   1964   331p   bib   64-15066
$8.75   0-271-73050-1
Bernard is author of many books about women and their

status in American society.   Compassionate, understanding,
brilliant analyses of strengths and weaknesses of women
college teachers--"by and large, academic women tend to
be associated with the low-status or low-prestige institutions."   For more recent accounts of woman-as-an-employee
of education, see Alice Rossi's "Status of women in graduate sociology departments 1968-9" in American Sociologist
Feb. 1970; essays by J. Collins and members of the Columbia University Women's Liberation Committee in "The
radical teacher," edited by Florence Howe and Paul Lauter;
and the New University Conference pamphlet, "Free women."

(141)   Breasted, Mary, 1943-
Oh sex education!
Praeger   1970   343p   index   78-101655
$7.95
Breasted is a Village Voice writer who was a supporter of
sex educators when she began her research.   She concluded
that the sex education offered in most public schools is a
form of moral indoctrination, and that most of the educators
are just as interested in controlling behavior of the young as
were most of the fundamentalists.   Reference to the Ana-
heim, California public schools curriculum is made.

(142)   Chicago.   University
Women in the University of Chicago; report of the Com-
      mittee on University Women, May 1, 1970.   Prepared
      for the Committee of the Council of the University
      Senate.   (Contact University Women's Assoc.)
122p
This report is included in this Collection for its own value
as an example of the type of document which should be
sought out and circulated by libraries.   "Women" in this
case were faculty and students; Jo Freeman, as a graduate
student in political science, was a Committee member.   Includes questionnaire.   Appendices, tables and references
also have relevance beyond the University of Chicago campus.
"A dangerous experiment; 100 years of women at the University of Michigan" by Dorothy Gies McGuigan may also
interest the reader [Center for Education of Women, 1970,
$2.50].

(143)   David, Opal D., ed.
The education of women; signs for the future.
American Council on Education   c1959   153p   bib
$2.   0-8268-1262-7
Now a decade old, this collection still has relevance in the

field of education of women. See especially Ann L. Rose
Hawkes' "Factors affecting college attendance; Robert
Sutherland's "Some basic facts"; and Marguerite Zapoleon's
"College women and employment. "

(144)   Lever, Janet and Pepper Schwartz
Women at Yale; liberating a college campus.
Bobbs   1971   272p   75-142486
$6. 95
Lever and Schwartz are women graduate students in sociology
at Yale.   From September 1969 to June 1970, they interviewed 300 men and women, faculty, students and adminis-
tration--a kind of before-and-after of Yale's first year in
which undergraduate women were admitted to regular living
quarters and academic programs.   Notable for revealing
changing concepts of masculinity and femininity, male and
female relationships.

(145)   Sexton, Patricia Cayo
The feminized male; classrooms, white collars, and the
    decline of manliness.
Random   c1969   240p   69-16415
$6. 95
The author, a professor of sociology and education, analyzes the effect on boys of an educational system in which
most of the teachers are women (i. e. , K-12).   She feels
that women teachers discourage the boyish traits and reward what she calls the feminine ones of obedience, neat-
ness, politeness and good grades, and this has an emascu-
lating effect on the boys.   Her answer is to give women a
chance to enter other professions with no limit to upward
mobility, and to encourage men to enter the teaching profession, with the ultimate hope of achieving true integration
between the sexes.   (Jeanne Spiegel's "Sex role concepts. ")

(146)   Smith, Margaret Ruth, ed.
Guidance-personnel work; future tense.
Teachers College Press   1966   176p   66-20497
$4. 75   8077-2176-X
". . . [F]or educators in elementary, secondary, college, and
continuing education who have a concern for both the personal and intellectual growth of persons" [Foreword].   An
anthology of 15 sections; no. 10: Counseling for women's
roles in the 1980's, by Jane Berry.

(147)   Spiro, Melford E. and Audrey G. Spiro
Children of the Kibbutz; a study in child training and per-
    sonality (new ed.).

Schocken   c1965   500p   66-4193
$9. 50   0-8052-3032-7; $3. 45/pap   0-8052-0093-2

390 Customs and Folklore

(148)   Amundsen, Kirsten
The silenced majority; women and American democracy.
Prentice Hall   1971   192p   index   70-153441
$5. 95; $2. 45/pap
"Provides documentation for the powerlessness of woman and
suggests that 'woman power' should be organized at the polls
to help upgrade the character of American life and politics"
[Library Journal:2590, Sept. 1, 1971].

(149)   Andreas, Carol
Sex and caste in America.
Prentice Hall   1971   160p   bib   index   74-160532
$5. 95; $1. 95/pap   Spectrum
Briefly put: woman's position in our society is the product
of conditions (neither physiological nor psychological),
traceable from biblical days to contemporary advertising.

(150)   Baker, Elizabeth Faulkner
Technology and woman's work.
Columbia Univ. Press   1964   460p   index   64-22559
$12.
Women have had to contend not only with the difficulties of
adjusting to new work, but also with the problems of establishing their right to have it.   Factors have been revolutionizing technology, war, emergencies, broadening "facilities"
(note facilities, not educational philosophy), changing attitudes toward the 'place' of women.   Almost ten years old
and in some ways shows its age (e. g., re librarians), but
still relevant.

(151)   Beauvoir, Simone de, 1908-
The second sex, tr. and ed. by Howard Madison Parshley.
Knopf   c1952   732p   index   52-6407
$10; $1. 25/pap   (Q3192)   Bantam. S
"The healthiest, headiest, wealthiest, and wisest book that
has ever been written on women and therefore, also on
men ... ; one of the great expressions of the human spirit
of our culture" [Ashley Montagu].   Controversial exploration
of female cultural, social, sexual life from childhood through
menopause.   The "Introduction" is worth reading and re-
reading, especially re "The Other," the second sex; study
first her use of the word "immanence" (e. g., p. 63). Basic.

(152)   Brenton, Myron
The American male; a penetrating look at the masculinity
    crisis.
Coward-McCann   c1966   252p   bib   index   66-20146
$5.95;   1970   95¢/pap   Prem   Fawcett World
Subtitle as well as some of the jacket comments are "come-
ons" to sell this nevertheless rare book; courageous male
writer, well-documented.   All relevant but see especially
chapters 3, "Notes on the 'feminization' of society"; 4,
"Back to the good old days: the patriarchal myth"; and 4,
"New ways to manliness."   Marya Mannes: "... makes
superb sense and should stimulate fresh thinking by many
sorely in need of Mr. Brenton's insight into the radical
changes affecting both sexes today."   This book is about the
increasingly difficult choices the American male is having to
meet, the invisible straight-jacket that keeps him bound to
antiquated notions of what he must do or be in order to
prove himself a man.   Any woman who is tired of hearing
about the sad plight of the contemporary male and justifica-
tions of the Women's Liberation Movement based on its
benefits for both sexes will probably be wary of this...

(153)   Cassara, Beverly Benner, ed.
American women; the changing image.
Beacon Press   c1962   141p   bib   62-13636
$4.95;   0-8070-4198-X
Anthropologist Margaret Mead asks some basic questions
in her introduction: are women to be seen as individuals
or primarily as wives and mothers?   Are we to continue
providing education for girls comparable to that of boys
and then reward with approval the girl who makes no use
of her education?   A number of women, e.g., Pearl Buck,
Agnes E. Meyer, Ethel J. Alpenfels, Dorothy Hopper attempt to answer these questions in separate chapters relating to their areas of interest.   Published by Beacon Press
for the Alliance of Unitarian Women.

(154)   Cross, Barbara M., ed.
Educated woman in America; selected writings of Catherine
    Beecher, Margaret Fuller and M. Carey Thomas.
Teachers College Press   c1965   187p
$5.95   0-8077-1221-3; $2.50/pap   0-8077-1218-3
"Documents from the writings of three very different women
who not only gave impetus and direction to women's education in America, but helped forge the image women had of
themselves" [TC Press catalog].   See also Helen S. Astin's
"The woman doctorate in America; origins, career and

family" (Russell Sage Foundation/Basic Books, 1970).

(155)   Davis, Elizabeth Gould
The first sex.
Putnam   1971   640p   index   79-150582
$7.95
The author is a professional librarian.   The Library Journal's
use of ridicule in its review (p. 2529, August 1971) is dis-
tressing.

(156)   DeRham, Edith, 1933-
The love fraud; why the structure of the American family
     is changing and what women must do to make it work.
Clarkson N Potter   c1965   319p   bib   64-25197
$5.
The fraud imposed upon women in general through populariza-
tion of the idea that "love" is a valid substitute for action is
felt most keenly by the educated American mother.   Further,
there is the waste of talent and education among American
women.

(157)   Deutsch, Helene
Psychology of women; a psychoanalytic interpretation.
Grune & Stratton   1944-5   44-5287
V1 = Girlhood   (1944) $8;   V2 = Womanhood   (1945)
     $9. S
Provides opportunity for judgment and comparison.   Deutsch
equates "femininity" with passivity and "masculinity" with
activity, since these are "fundamental identities ... in all
known cultures and races..." [p. 224f].   Deutsch, as a
Freudian, denies woman choice; compare with Karen Horney.

(158)   Douglas, Mary
Purity and danger; an analysis of concepts of pollution and
     taboo.
Praeger   c1966   188p   bib   index   66-23887
$5;   1970 $1.45/pap   Pelican Penguin
Douglas argues that there are fewer sexual taboos in a
society where the male can enforce his domination directly
and where society allows a man to punish his wife/woman
with direct physical force.   Not entirely related to women;
however, important.

(159)   Epstein, Cynthia Fuchs and William Goode
The other half; roads to women's equality.
Prentice Hall   1971
$5.95   0-13-642983-1; $2.45/pap   0-13-642975-0

Within a year of "Woman's place ...," Ms. Epstein has
edited, with William Goode, a book dealing with the changing
pattern in women's traditional roles, with cross-cultural
comparisons to women in other societies. Includes discussion of the Women's Liberation Movement in the United
States and other countries.

(160)   Farber, Seymoud M. , M. D. and Roger H. L. Wilson,
    M. D. , eds.
Man and civilization; the potential of women; a symposium.
McGraw c1963 328p bib 63-21477
$2. 95 /pap (19942)
An interdisciplinary symposium, including some women. In
fact, all of the six sections' chairmen were women. Each
section is summarized initially: Roles, Consequences of
equality, and The male revolt are especially good. ("They
don't know what they want," the old refrain, appears.)

(161)   Farewell, Nina, pseud.
The unfair sex; an expose of the human male for young
    women of most ages. HS
Simon & Schuster 1953 212p 53-7817
$3. 50
Pseudonym = Grace Kelin and Mae Klein Cooper. Bernard
Kalb in Saturday Review: "... an amusing, witty, and I'm
happy to report, worthless attack on men..." (May 16,
1953:27).

(162)   Ferguson, Charles Wright, 1901-
The male attitude.
Little Brown 1966 365p 66-21988
$6. 95
The origins of the American male's attitudes towards life.
The United States has often been referred to as a matriarchy, but Ferguson shows that it has always been governed
by men, guided by male precepts and controlled by male
emotions. "He feels that men have made women over into
their own image, and they have formed a society so male
in faith and practice that even if women were given an equal
representation at all levels of government the difference in
public affairs would not be great. Now the criteria are
those of men, and women could achieve posts of importance
only by male tactics and by measuring up to male definitions
of competence. His intent is to trace the historic sources of
current emotion." (Jeanne Spiegel's "Sex role concepts. ")

(163)   Ferriss, Abbott Lamoyne, 1915-

Indicators of trends in the status of American women.
Basic 1971
$12.50; $6.95/pap   0-87154-252-8
Data are drawn mainly from two major surveys: Current
Population Survey and National Health Survey, each of which
is reviewed in appendices. Statistical "evidence" of trends
in the status of women relative to the status of men is the
author's intention. He organizes around what he considers
the "major life activities or concerns of women": education,
marriage, fertility, work, employment, income, organizational activities, recreation, health and illness, and death!
(What might be a better or fuller list?)

(164) Firkel, Eva
Woman in the modern world.
Fides 1956 211p 56-4128
1970 95¢/pap 0-8190-0375-1. S
Translated from German. See also her "Mature woman"
(Dome, 1968, 95¢).

(165) Friedan, Betty, 1921-
The feminine mystique.
Norton c1963 384p index
$6.95; Dell 1970 $1.25/pap 2498-1. S
Heartening to realize that this best-seller remains in-print
in hard cover and paperback a decade later. One of the
founders of the National Organization for Women, Ms. Friedan documented the reassertion of patriarchy in 20th-century
America. So well-known (although the title is not fully
understood by even the most ardent Women's Liberation-
ists--see page 9) that the title is parodied and abused, e.g.,
Cal Samra's "The feminine mistake" (Nash, 1971).

(166) Fuller, Margaret
Woman in the nineteenth century, and kindred papers re-
      lating to the sphere, condition and duties of woman.
Source Library of the Women's Movement 1970 (orig.
      1855) 430 p
$16.50
Margaret Fuller earned her living as a school teacher; began discussion groups ("conversations") for women; co-
edited The Dial with Ralph Waldo Emerson; and was the
first woman to join the staff of the New York Tribune. "A
highly influential work which maintained that women must
fulfill themselves not in relation to men but as independent
individuals, this book is the final form of earlier talks and
writings" [Source Library]. She wrote, "Woman, self-

centered, would never be absorbed by any relation; it
would be only an experience to her as to man. It is a vul-
gar error that love, a love, to Woman is her whole existence;
she also is born for Truth and Love in their universal
energy."

(167)   Gilman, Charlotte Perkins Stetson, 1860-
Women and economics.
Source Library of the Women's Movement   1970   (orig.
   1898)   368p
$15
The author also wrote books on children, home and work--
this is a classic, written in 1898.   Portions are often reprinted.   "In the most important work of the most original
and influential feminist theoretician in the United States,
Gilman argues that marriage is essentially an economic
relationship in which women are shortchanged, and that the
institution of marriage creates a sexual overspecialization in
women.   She concludes with an attack upon the home, and
a description of the ideal human dwelling" [Source Library].

(168)   Ginzberg, Eli, 1911-   , et al.
Life styles of educated women.
Columbia Univ. Press   c1966   244p   bib   index   66-18060
$7
A group of women who were graduate students between 1945
and 1951 were studied by the Conservation of Human Resources Project at Columbia University.   The unique value
of this particular book is that it presents their experiences
and opinions as they reported them.   How such talented
women function in American society is of great interest.
Major findings included: educated women, contrary to popular belief, do not lead constricted, discontented lives, but
have a multiplicity of opinions that permit them to be in
highly advantageous positions to realize whatever goals they
wish to set for themselves.   "Educated American women:
self portraits" follows.

(169)   Gornick, Vivian and Barbara K. Moran, eds.
Woman in sexist society; studies in power and powerlessness.
Basic books   1971   515p   70-157125
$12.50   465-09199-7
Although well-known scholars and writers are included
among the 30 contributors to this anthology, it was thrown
open before publication via the New York N.O.W. News-
letter and other media.   Gornick is a staff writer for the
Village Voice, and Morgan, a magazine editor-writer.   In

range and quality, it stands out; really lays critical foundations for Women's Studies.   Sidney Abbott and Barbara Love
consider the question, "Is Women's Liberation a lesbian plot?"
Phyllis Chesler describes how women are forced into accepting passive, dependent roles or risk being called "sick."
Anthropology, sociology, history, psychiatry, art, literature,
psychology, philosophy, and education are all represented.
This is the "case" for Women's Liberation.   Basic.

(170)   Kinsey, Alfred Charles, 1894-1956
Sexual behavior in the human female.
Saunders   1953   842p   bib   53-11127
$10   0-7216-5450-9; $1.65   (pap 78510)   Pocket Books. S
"The New York Times gave the first report [on the male]
a generous review but refused to advertise it.   The conclu-
sions of the second report [on the female] were much more
shocking to most Americans than those of the first" [Paul
Blanshard, "Right to read; the battle against censorship,"
Beacon, 1955, p. 159; unfortunately out of print].   Both
were landmark titles that changed everything.   Relate to
Masters & Johnson.

(171)   Kinsey, Alfred Charles, 1894-1956
Sexual behavior in the human male.
Saunders   1948   804p   bib   48-5195
$9.50   0-7216-5445-2. S
For every man, there's a woman....

(172)   Lewis, Edwin C.
Developing woman's potential.
Iowa State Univ. Press   1969   389p
$7.50   0-8138-1704-8; $3.50/pap Text ed.   9-8138-1715-3
"The failure of women to recognize an obligation, both to
themselves and to society, to make productive use of their
education and training has produced a cynical attitude on the
part of men responsible for that training.   Only the women
themselves can demonstrate that their attitudes have changed
and that they are willing to accept the responsibility implied
in the education provided them."   Chapter 8 is review and
summary of research on the so-called working mother, with
the comment that the reader should keep in mind the limitation that "there is no way of knowing whether differences
between working and non-working wives and their families
exist because the women in one group are working and the
others aren't, or are due to other important differences
between women who choose to work and those who don't."
Read and react.   Continue on to Kanowitz's "Women and the
law."

(173)   Lopata, Helena Znaniecki
Occupation; housewife.
Oxford Univ. Press   1971   387p   index   77-83046
$9. 50

(174)   Ludovici, Laurence James
The final inequality; a critical assessment of woman's
    sexual role in society.
Norton   c1965   271p   bib   65-20945, 65-84704
$4. 95
Worldwide.   Includes history of religious misogyny.

(175)   McDermott, Sandra
Female sexuality; its nature and conflicts.
Simon & Schuster   1971   224p   77-154551
$6. 95   0-671-20952-3

(176)   Mace, David Robert and Vera Mace
Marriage East and West.
Doubleday   c1960   359p   index   60-5944
1959 $1. 45   (pap C161)   Dolphin
This book about marriage is more broadly about religion/
philosophy of Europe and Asia excluding Moslem culture:
thus, Japanese, Chinese and Indian cultures, Confucian,
Buddhist and Hindu.   Well documented.   See especially
chapter 3, "What is a woman worth?"--as a person, not
much it would seem.   A source book in its way.

(177)   Mill, John Stuart, 1806-1873 and Harriet Taylor Mill
Essays on sex equality, edited by Alice S. Rossi.
Phoenix (orig. 1869)
$1. 95/pap
This excellent new edition includes Mill's famous feminist
essay, "The subjection of women, " of 1869, co-work by his
wife, and a revealing and interpretive essay by Dr. Rossi
about their relationship.   Basic.

(178)   Millett, Kate
Sexual politics.
Doubleday   1970   394p   bib   index   70-103769
$7. 95; $2. 95/pap   Avon   Equinox
Sculptor, critic, college teacher, wife, Ph.D.   Ask yourself what does the title mean exactly?   She argues that the
relationship between the sexes is and always has been a
"political one"--a continuing power struggle in which women
are sometimes idolized, other times patronized, always exploited.   Patriarchal bias as reflected in literature.   Theo-

retical. Women's Studies. See page 62 for her conjecture
of what a full sexual revolution might be like. This is not
light reading, but neither is the subject matter. Lazy
readers and women who give token acknowledgment to the
W. L. Movement (same pay for same job, sure) may hesitate to tackle something meaty and rationalize that it's difficult or boring.

(179) O'Neill, Barbara Powell
Careers for women after marriage and children.
Macmillan 1965 401p bib index 65-11571
$5.95
Old but good (i.e., change in specific fields is so rapid
today that parts of a 1965 publication must be updated to
be relevant). Chapter 4: "Library work" should be dis-
regarded. Appealing format about specific people who have
achieved in these careers. The jacket says it: "For the
woman who wants individual fulfillment as well as marriage."

(180) Osofsky, Howard J., M.D., 1935-
The pregnant teenager; a medical, educational and socio-
    logical analysis.
Thomas   1968   124p   68-9391
$6.75
Author is a feminist.

(181) Putnam, Emily James
The lady; studies of certain significant phases of her
    history.
Putnam   1921   323p
Univ. of Chicago Press $5.95   0-226-68562-4; $1.95/pap
    0-226-68564-0   P362   Phoenix
It is difficult to realize that "The lady" was written in 1910.
See especially the introductory comment, "the typical lady
everywhere tends to the feudal habit of mind. The gentle-
man has never been an analogous phenomenon.... The lady
herself feels no uneasiness in her equivocal situation, and
the toilers who support her do so with enthusiasm. Plays
like "The doll's house" and "The thief" show how clearly
the lady-forger or burgler should be differentiated from
other criminals. The true lady is in theory either a virgin
or a lawful wife." Author had been first dean of Barnard
College. Her view; all ladies are women, but few women
are ladies. The lady is "the female of the favored social
class." Proprietary marriage, which makes women a pos-
session; a patriarchal society, which makes women, like
children, subjects to be ruled; and a class structure which

assigns everyone to specific ranks of unequal worth, "are necessary for the lady to exist." Read Marilyn Bender's "The beautiful people; the fashion explosion of the sixties" (Coward, 1967, $7.95) next; its social context is broader than just fashion. Implicit material on women, in Bender's work, updates "The lady" in a way.

(182) Reeves, Nancy
Womankind; beyond the stereotypes.
Aldine-Atherton 1971
$10; pap ed. available for classroom use only, $4.95
The author, a woman attorney, shows that stereotypes fail the tests and impede women's full participation in life. Absence of women in public life shown by a photographic essay.

(183) Richardson, Herbert W.
Nun, witch, playmate; the Americanization of sex.
Harper 1971 160p 76-85064
$4.95
Central idea: sexuality is as much a function of society as of biology, and that changes in attitudes toward sex accompany other social changes.

(184) Roszak, Betty and Theodore Roszak, 1933-   , eds.
Masculine feminine: readings in sexual mythology and the
    liberation of women.
Harper 1970 316p 74-133277
Colophon $2.45/pap
Argues for the abolition of sex roles and adoption of androgynous equality. An anthology: Juliet Mitchell, Alice Rossi, Judith Brown et al. Alternatives to the family.

(185) Seidenberg, Robert
Marriage in life and literature.
Philosophical Library 1970 307p 70-97939
$5.95 0-8022-2331-1
An untypical view of life relationships.

(186) Seward, Georgene Hoffman, 1902-   , ed.
Sex roles in changing society.
Random 1970
$9.95 30255-9

(187) Stanton, Elizabeth Cady, et al.
History of woman suffrage.
Fowler & Wells 1887-1902 v. 1-4; National American

Woman Suffrage Assoc. 1922 v. 5-6.
Source Library of the Women's Movement. reprint 12v
    $250.
See pages 107-115 of Farrar's novel, "A wondrous moment
then," for description of the influence of volumes 1 to 4 of
this book circa 1919. "The monumental collection of primary
source material of the woman's suffrage movement. This
is an immense compendium of contemporary accounts of the
movement, reminiscences, news clippings, speeches, and
letters" [Source Library]. A classic. Co-authors were
Susan B. Anthony, Matilda Joslyn Gage, Ida H. Harper.

(188) U.S. Presidential task force on women's rights and
    responsibilities.
Report. HS
U.S. GPO April 1970 33p 77-607729
30¢/pap 0-383-452 Pr 37.8:W84/R29
Known by its title, "A matter of simple justice," this report is quoted in serious commentary. A seemingly in-
significant pamphlet, it is a basic document despite the fact
that the President's Task Force on Women's Rights and
Responsibilities has received little publicity. On Dec. 15,
1969 the Report was conveyed to President Nixon by its
Chairman, Virginia R. Allan, and its recommendations remain on paper. Main recommendation: establishment of
an Office of Women's Rights and Responsibilities whose
director would also serve as a special assistant reporting
directly to the President!

(189) U.S. President's Commission on the Status of
    Women.
American women; report of the U.S. President's Commis-
    sion on the Status of Women and Other publications of
    the Commission, edited by Margaret Mead and Frances
    Balgley Kaplan, with an introduction and an epilogue by
    Margaret Mead. HS
Scribners c1965 274p index 65-21367
$6; $4.75 0-8077-2176-X
The President's Commission on the Status of Women (now
the Interdepartmental Committee on the Status of Women)
1965 report, "American women," contains major social
documents of the 20th century and should be widely available. A basic. Possibly Mead's Epilogue is of most interest: includes Homemaking and volunteer service as paid
work; Possibility of guaranteed income; Who should work
outside the home? Present role of homemaking; American
style of living; Should all women marry? Women's right

to choose their lives.   Appendices include Recommendations
of the Commission and consultations sponsored by it.   Two
appendices are especially interesting: Portrayal of women
by the mass media, and Problems of Negro women.   Body
of Report: Civil and political rights; education; federal employment; home and community; private employment; protective labor legislation; social insurance and taxes.   Ample
illustrative charts throughout.

(190)   Young, Wayland
Eros denied; sex in Western society.
Grove   1964   415p   index   64-13775
95¢   (pap Z1005)
Judeo-Christian tradition excludes sex from the range of
the normal.   It may be necessary for some readers to per-
severe until the initial shock of some of the words passes.

500 PURE SCIENCES

560 Paleontology

(191)   Dublin, Louis Israel, 1882-
Fact book on man from birth to death (2nd ed.).
Macmillan   1965   465p   65-16561
$9.50
Much of the supporting data in Ashley-Montagu's "The
natural superiority of women" are derived from this work,
which some women may, but should not, hold against it!

570 Anthropology & Biological Sciences

(192)   Golde, Peggy, ed.
Women in the field; anthropological experiences.
Aldine-Atherton   1971   264p
$8.75
Each of the contributors has been alone--work in the field,
traveling, etc., dedicating their lives and energies to understanding of worlds not their own.   Twelve women anthro-
pologists tell what they do and how they feel.

(193)   Mead, Margaret, 1910-
Sex and temperament in three primitive societies.
Morrow   1935   335p   35-7576
1963 $2.50   (pap A67)   Apollo;   1967   95¢   (pap 777-3)
    Dell. S
Cultural relativism vs biological and psychological universals,
i.e., culture determines the meaning of sex role.

600 TECHNOLOGY (APPLIED SCIENCES)

610 Medical Sciences

(194)   American Friends Service Committee
Who shall live?   Man's control over birth and death; a
   report prepared for the American Friends Service
   Committee.
Hill & Wang   1970   144p   77-106963
$3.95   8090-9706-0; $1.75/pap   8090-1354-1

(195)   Brecher, Ruth and Edward Brecher, eds.
An analysis of human sexual response.
New American   c1966   318p   bib   66-25513
$1.25   (pap Y4054)   SigNAL
Readable discussion of "Masters & Johnson" (see William H.
Masters' and Virginia Johnson's "Human sexual response")
whose work shattered the myth that women are sexually
passive, but was not readable!   Includes other essays--see
the one on the history of the idea of female orgasm.   Non-
technical language but authoritative.   Goes into implications
for bettering human beings.

(196)   Broderick, Carlfred B. and Jessie Shirley Bernard,
   eds.
The individual, sex and society; a SIECUS handbook for
   teachers and counselors.
Johns Hopkins Press   c1969   406p   bib   69-11934
$10   0-8018-1036-1; $4.50 text ed.   6-0-8018-1037-X
A SIECUS (Sex Information & Education Council of the
United States) handbook for teachers and counselors.   Text
and trade editions available.   (Information on the controversial SIECUS is included in "Sources" section.)

(197)   Calderone, Mary Steichen, M.D., ed.
Manual of family planning and contraceptive practice; fore-
   word by Nicholson J. Eastman (illus. 2nd ed.).
Williams   1970   475p
$14.50

(198)   California Committee on Therapeutic Abortion
Abortion and the unwanted child, ed. by Carl Reiterman.
Springer   1971   181p   index   74-146659
$7.50; $4.95/pap
From the Library Journal, Sept. 15, 1971: "In contrast to
the glib and shallow approach of many current books on
abortion, these articles sponsored by the California Com-

mittee on Therapeutic Abortion are sober and scholarly
treatments of the problem by professionals in the field.
The report of a twenty-one year Swedish study of children
born after their mothers were refused abortions is given in
full and forms the basis of many of the arguments...."

(199) Ejlersen, Mette
"I accuse" (Sexual liberation--English tr. by Marianne K.
    Madsen).
London: Universal-Tandem 1969
Award 95¢ (pap A471N)
Translation of Scandinavian best-seller. Woman author describes
female sexuality and dissects male myths in relationship to
it. Main point is that women are their own and only
authorities on their own sexual pleasure.

(200) Group for the Advancement of Psychiatry
Sex and the college student; a developmental perspective on
    sexual issues on the campus; some guidelines for ad-
    ministering policy and understanding of sexual issues,
    formulated by the Committee on Sex and the College
    Student.
Atheneum 1966 178p 65-28368
75¢/pap Prem Fawcett World
J. B. Wheelwright, Chairman. All of GAP's publications
are useful.

(201) Guttmacher, Alan Frank, M.D., 1898-
Planning your family; the complete guide to contraception
    and fertility (newly rev. and greatly exp. ed. of "The
    complete book of birth control").
Macmillan c1961, 1964 329p index 63-14537
$5.95; "Complete book..." 50¢ (PaU2136) Ballantine

(202) Havemann, Ernest
Birth control. HS
Time c1967 118p 67-30369
$1.95/pap
Excellent, easy-to-read series of chapters on history of
birth control, birth control today, the Pill, how to choose,
methods of the future, etc. Note inclusion of abortion as a
method of birth control. Basically, discusses nine methods.
Well-illustrated. A kind of ready-reference for the person
whose background doesn't yet include these facts of life and
has a bit of catching up to do. In short, what every public
school student should have acquired by graduation, neatly
packaged by a company which identifies markets.

(203)   Herschberger, Ruth, 1917-
Adam's rib.   HS
Pellegrini & Cudahy   1948   221p   48-5831
Harper   95¢/pap   P194
An analysis of the position of women in modern society:
because women have been taught from infancy to regard
themselves as receptive, society has educated them to be
frustrated.   Originally published in 1948, recently brought
out again in paper.   Funny essays attack the nomenclature
of popular sex, i.e., the male point of view.   It is possible to laugh at essays which describe the tragedy of sup-
pression of woman's sexuality, which inevitably suppresses
man's tenderness, when they're written this well.   Helpful
for a "beginner" who sees and reads nothing sexist in her
environment!

(204)   Johnson, Eric W.
Love and sex in plain language (rev.).   HS
Lippincott   1968   68p   67-14367
$3.50;   75¢/pap   Pathfinder
Good example of a sex education book used in schools.   He
has also written "Sex: telling it straight" (Lippincott, 1970,
$3.95).   Also for young people: Andre Blanzaco's "VD
facts you should know" (Lothrop, 1970, $3.95).

(205)   Lader, Lawrence, M.D., 1919-
Abortion.
Bobbs   1966   212p   66-18592
$5.95; $1.95/pap   0-8070-2195-4   Beacon
Member of the National Organization for Women, Chairman
of the Executive Committee of the National Association for
Repeal of Abortion Laws, a leading physician activist-ad-
vocate of abortion reform in the fullest sense.   A resource
book for discussion groups and reform-campaigners.   Because it is several years old, it should be supplemented with
up-to-minute material and local information re status quo
and resources.   See also his frequent articles, e.g., "A
national guide to legal abortion" (July 1970 Ladies Home
Journal) and "Undoing the abortion laws" (New York Times:
31, Jan. 4, 1971).   He is also the author with Milton
Meltzer of "Margaret Sanger, pioneer of birth control,"
for young people (Crowell, 1969, $4.50).   For a review
of the laws governing abortion in various countries, see
Ruth Roemer's "Abortion law; the approaches of different
nations" in Amer. J. of Public Health: 1906-22, 1967
(vol. 7).

(206)   Laing, Ronald David, M.D.
The divided self; an existential study in insanity and madness.
Pantheon   1969   237p   bib   69-20194
$5.95
Laing is chairman of the Philadelphia Association, a charity
concerned with developing approaches to problems "created
by defining certain forms of human behavior and experience
as signs of 'mental illness'." How many unidentified women
--suffragettes from the past, feminists of today--have been
branded insane ... queer ... eccentric...?

(207)   Lopate, Carole
Women in medicine.
Johns Hopkins Press   1968   204p   index   68-19526
$5.95   0-8018-0391-8
Data and facts from this book are cited throughout the literature of contemporary Women's Liberation in connection
with education for and employment in the professions.   A
review of the history of American women in medicine is
followed by discussions of why women (do not) enter medicine and the effect of high school counselling, the life of
the pre-med student, and the woman in a "man's school"--
as drop-out, intern, resident, practitioner.   Chapters relate
to marriage and medical career.   Recommendations and the
data of appendices are especially valuable.   A resource in
itself; hopefully, it will be kept up-to-date.

(208)   McCary, James Leslie, 1919-
Human sexuality; physiological and psychological factors of
      sexual behavior.
Van Nostrand   1967   374p   67-28290
$9.75; $8.95 text;   Handbook, $2.50
New York Times IV:12, August 15, 1971: "One textbook
alone is now used at more than two hundred schools."

(209)   Masters, William H., M.D., and Virginia E. Johnson
Human sexual response.
Little, Brown   c1966   366p   bib   66-18370
$10.   S
See also Brecher, Kinsey, and Mary Harrington Hall's "A
conversation with Masters and Johnson" in Psychology Today:
50-8, July 1969, for further clarification.   The evidence
produced by M & J is that women are independent and sexually-active (not passive) creatures.   Their work runs the
gamut in reaction from praise to Germaine Greer's dull-sex-
for-dull-people attitude.   Their "Human sexual inadequacy"

(Little, 1970, $12.50) was touted by Hugh Hefner, and led
to books describing sexual rehabilitation (e.g., Barbara and
Peter Wyden's "Inside the sex clinic; a candid inquiry,"
World, 1971, $10.85).

(210)   Neubardt, Selig, M.D.
A concept of contraception.
Trident Press   c1967   118p   67-11322
$3.95;   95¢/pap   Pocket Books   77025 as "Contraception."
Gynecologist and obstetrician explores every known method
of family planning as of 1966, makes no actual recommenda-
tions, and includes abortion as an "afterthought."

(211)   New York State Abortion Directory
Maternal Information Services, Inc.   1971
Free to poor women, $3-10 by check suggested for others
        and libraries.   By mail.
A free or low-cost abortion directory is an alternative to
the embarrassment and/or high cost of using referral
agencies.   This new publication includes information about
medical care necessary for diagnosis and a description in
lay-language of the vacuum suction method often used in
early pregnancy.   Included are several certified gynecolo-
gists by name, address and phone number, listed by length
of pregnancy to be terminated, procedure used, age-limita-
tions and cost.   Some coverage of states in the New York
region is also provided; low-cost physicians and hospitals
are given preferential listing.   Updating is promised to be
"regular and frequent."   Requests remain confidential.

(212)   Phelan, Lana Clark and Patricia McGinnis
The abortion handbook for responsible women.
Contact books   1969
$3
By and for women.

(213)   Reich, Wilhelm, 1897-1957
The function of the orgasm.
Noonday   1961
$7.50   Farrar, Strauss; $2.95/pap   (N219)   Noonday
        FS&G.   S
Reich was what Robin Morgan has referred to as "a seminal
thinker."   Orson Bean's "Me and the orgone" (St. Martins,
1971, $4.95) summarizes in popular parlance Reich's ex-
perience and philosophy and Bean's personal experience with
Orgone therapy.   Clearly there's not much consideration for
females in it.

(214)   Rosen, Harold, 1908-   , ed.
Abortion in America.
Beacon $2.95/pap   0-8070-2197-0   BP 272
Original title was "Therapeutic Abortion: medical, psychiatric,
anthropological and religious considerations" (Julian, 1954,
348p,   54-772).

(215)   Rubin, Isadore and Lester A. Kirkendall, eds.
Sex in the adolescent years; new directions in guiding and
      teaching youth.
Association Press   c1968   223p   63-11492
$4.95
A collection of articles which appeared originally in Sexology
magazine.   Rubin's "Sexual life after sixty" (Basic books,
c1965, $6.95) is recommended.

650 Business & Related Enterprises

(216)   Baker, Samm Sinclair
The permissible lie; the inside truth about advertising.
Beacon   1969   236p
$2.95   (pa BP396)   6173-5;   7206-6240-0
"An angry professional's documented and eye-opening guide
to the nether world of half-truth which is modern adver-
tising" [Beacon].

(217)   Merriam, Eve, 1916-
Figleaf; the business of being in fashion.   HS
Lippincott   1960   256p   60-13580
$4.95
Clever and perceptive, in her fifties Eve Merriam has 21
books in print at adult and younger levels.   (See "Books in
Print.")   Unfortunately, her "After Nora slammed the door;
American women in the 1960's: the unfinished revolution"
(World, 1964) is out of print.   Likewise her "Double bed
from the feminine side," a book of poems (Marzani and Munsell, 1958).   "Figleaf..." remains in print; obsolescence
is the keyword, says the author, of America's third largest
industry and number one cult (1960).   Her latest, "Nixon
power" (Atheneum, $5.95 and $2.95/pap), is another collection of poems.

(218)   Tierney, Patricia E.
Ladies of the avenue.
Bartholomew House   1971   304p   73-155026
Delacorte   0-87794-028-2 $6.95

Deals with some of the problems of being an account woman
and tells how females in the ad business are treated.

700 THE ARTS

(219)   DeSilva, Anil, et al., eds.
Love and marriage (vol. 5 of Man through his art [World
   Confederation of Organizations of the Teaching Profes-
   sions]).
Graphic   1968   64p   bib   68-11207
$8.95
Preface: "although the art forms ... selected do not in
themselves explain the differing cultural relationships, customs, and value judgments, they do help to show how love
and marriage have been perceived in different cultures and
at different epochs." Love and marriage seem to be most
in evidence as rituals.   One American 20th-century example
selected by Ms. DeSilva and her colleagues is Grant Wood's
"American Gothic."   To be published in this series: The
Family.

790 Recreational Arts

(220)   Tegner, Bruce and Alice McGrath
Self-defense for girls; a secondary school and college
   manual.   HS
Los Angeles:Thor   c1967   125p   index   67-30948
Bantam   75¢/pap   S4856
From the introduction: "Femininity and self-defense: every
culture has its own definition of what constitutes feminine
behavior.   What the culture expects strongly determines
and influences that behaviour....   It was not so very long
ago that femininity was synonymous with helplessness....
This concept was, of course, a highly undemocratic one as
it could apply only to the privileged few.   Elegant, dependent
women were ladies, while their working sisters were merely
females, and the exceptional active woman was dismissed
as an eccentric."   A few entries from the index clearly
reveal the scope of Tegner and McGrath's basic basics:
Adversary, more than one; Basic defense, explanation of;
Bed, defense from; Blocking; Chain, defense against; Chokes,
defenses against; Closet arsenal; Deflecting; Driving alone;
Elevators; Entry, forced; Exercise; Gun attack; Hair pulling,
defense; Kicks, types of; Knife, defenses against; Lights,
for protection; Locks, for protection; Purse weapons; Re-

porting an encounter; Running away; Screaming; Target areas;
Thumb press into throat; Walking alone; Yelling.   Note that
a kick to the groin as the most important thing a girl can
learn for self-defense is a fallacy.   Their "Self-defense for
women; a simple method" (Thor, rev. ed., c1969, $1.95)
is also excellent.

800 LITERATURE & RHETORIC

(221)   Ibsen, Henrik, 1828-1906
A doll's house (In "Ghosts and three other plays" [Doll's
     house, Rosmersholm, Enemy of the people] orig. tr.
     by Michael Meyer).   HS
1966   Doubleday   429p   66-11746
$1.75   (pap A215e)   Anchor.   S
"A doll's house" is a play by the 19th-century Norwegian
dramatist and poet who has been referred to as the "God-
father of Women's Lib" by T.E. Kalem in his review (Time:
48, Jan. 25, 1971) of the production with Claire Bloom.
To critique Kalem's criticism is an exercise in Women's
Studies.   He questions whether Nora's slamming the door
is saving or "indulging herself.... In that final scene in
which Nora accuses Torvald of never having talked to her
seriously about serious things, man and wife are, in fact,
doing just that.   Torvald is changing, seeing his wife as a
person in her own right, and forgiving her.   If she were
really maturing as Ibsen claims, she would forgive him and
try to make a wiser go of things....   [T]he cost Nora is
inflicting on others by her abandonment is clear.   She is
being selfishly irresponsible.   The logic of her act is that
one no longer honors a commitment as soon as it displeases
one to do so.   There are several glaring fallacies in Ibsen's
reasoning.   One is that a woman who has been married for
eight years and borne three children knows absolutely nothing
about life....   Children must be safeguarded and reared,
and a continuity of values preserved.   This is what society
is about...."   Read, react.   "Ghosts," another Ibsen play,
deals with venereal disease.

(222)   Legman, Gershon, 1917-
Love and death; a study in censorship.
Breaking point   1949   95p   49-10742
$1.75/pap   Hacker
When society forbids authors to freely express sexuality,
sadism abounds in the alternative literature produced.

(223)   Rogers, Katherine M.
The troublesome helpmate; a history of misogyny in literature.
Univ. of Washington Press   c1966   288p   index   66-19565
$6.95; $2.95   (pap 0-295-97897-X, WP38)
Not just another book about women via literature, this is a
stimulating survey of misogyny in literature.   Fear and hatred
of women have enlivened literature from Hebrew seers, Greek
dramatists, Old and New Testaments, down to the psychosexual conflicts of the 20th century.   St. Paul was an arche-
typal misogynist.

810 American Literature in English

(224)   Brown, Charles Brockden
Alcuin; a dialogue (type-facsim. reprint of the 1st ed.
    printed in 1798).
New Haven: Rollins   1935   103p
$2.75
Early pleas for woman's emancipation from 18th-century
restrictions.

(225)   Jackson, Shirley, 1920-1965
The magic of Shirley Jackson, edited by Stanley Edgar
    Hyman.
Farrar Straus   1966   753p   66-20163
$10;   1969 $3.95   (pap S7)   Sunburst FS&G
Edited by Shirley Jackson's husband.   Includes short stories
and three of her books.   Her "Hangsman" is also in print
(Farrar, 1951, 75¢ Ace).

(226)   Lamb, Myrna
The mod Donna and Scyklon Z; plays of women's liberation.
    HS
Pathfinder   1971   200p   71-139788
$5.95; $2.95/pap
Mod Donna is a political play; it is also the feminist
musical chosen as one of five Paris Biennial winners out
of a field of 39 productions entered in the competition.

(227)   Lindbergh, Anne Morrow
Gift from the sea.   HS
Pantheon   c1955   128p   55-5065
$1.65   (pap V329)   Random
Contemplation is a wonderful thing.   Woman's sense of
balanced life, patience, faith, solitude come through beauti-
fully, but some women will have to decide what are the in-

gredients of their own "balance," in what they will place
their faith, how they can manage to achieve solitude....

(228)   Oates, Joyce Carol, 1938-
Love and its derangements: poems.
Louisiana State Univ. Press   c1970   60p   75-122357
$4. 50   0-8071-0847-2

(229)   Piercy, Marge
Breaking camp: poems.
Wesleyan Univ. Press   1968   74p   68-16007
Wesleyan Poetry Program Series $4; $2/pap
It takes courage to break camp, whether it's love or politics.
The author is active in the W. L. Movement.   Other ex-
amples of her work are included in Morgan and Wasserman.

(230)   Plath, Sylvia, 1932-1963 (Victoria Lucas, pseud.)
Ariel [Poems].
Harper   1966   85p   0-06-013348-9; $1. 95   pap 0-06-
    013359-7
Since her death, Sylvia Plath has become a major figure in
contemporary literature.   (She referred to herself as an
English poet).   Her estranged husband later brought out her
book of poems, "Ariel," which is the name of her horse,
not Shakespeare's androgyny.   "The art of Sylvia Plath,"
edited by Charles Newman, is a symposium of selected
criticism, an appendix of uncollected and unpublished work
and some biographical material (Indiana Univ. Press, 1970,
$6. 50).

(231)   Sexton, Anne, 1928-
Live or die.
Houghton   c1966   90p   66-22961
$4; $2. 95   (pap 0-395-08180-7)
Poems 1962-1966.   "Sylvia's death" for Sylvia Plath.
"Live"--live or die, but don't poison everything.   Poems
arranged chronologically--autobiographical--strong female
experience.

820 English and Anglo-Saxon Literature

(232)   Brophy, Brigid, 1929-
Don't never forget; collected views and reviews.
Holt, Rinehart   c1966   319p   67-13212
1967 $5. 95   0-03-064145-4   HR&W   (Ever.)
Time magazine called Brigid Brophy "The British Intelli-

gentsia's newest high priestess." This collection of her
views and reviews includes the famous talk she gave at the
time of the Profumo affair, which was later withheld by the
BBC; "The immorality of marriage"; and ideas on monogamy
(she's against it), and women (which appeared in November
1963 Saturday Evening Post). Some of the women are Betty
Davis, Françoise Sagan, Virginia Woolf, Simone de Beauvoir,
and her mother, whom she compares to Lady Macbeth. See
also her review of Norman Mailer's "Prisoner of sex" (New
York Times VII:1, May 23, 1971); in the course of sar-
castically correcting her usage of words there, Mailer refers
to her as "brave and broiling Brigid."

(233) Jellicoe, Ann
The knack, & The sport of my mad mother; two plays.
Delta c1958 88, 87p 64-23978
$1.75/pap Dell
The knack is a comedy, produced in the U.S. by the Establishment Theatre Company in 1964, when it was directed
by Mike Nichols, with George Segal among the cast. Of
course "the knack" is the getting of girls. "The sport..."
(new version) is more complex--fear, rejection, somewhat
symbolic.

(234) Lawrence, Margaret
The school of femininity; a book for and about women as
     they are interpreted through feminine writers of yester-
     day and today.
Kennikat 1966 (orig. c1936) 382p 66-25924
$11. 0-8046-0264-6
Reissued 30 years later, no index. Considers the 19th and
first third of the 20th century "schools of femininity."
Mostly women novelists, although Mary Wollstonecraft and
several women who worked in more than one genre, e.g.,
Olive Schreiner and Dorothy Parker, are included, all of
course writing in English. Author describes a "feminist
pattern" in their fiction writing by utilizing key books of
each author. Interesting today because it reminds us of
the dying and recently dead novelists whose works may tend
automatically to be relegated to a passé category, e.g.,
Margaret Barnes' "Years of grace," merely because the
women lived around 1900 and/or their dialogue isn't au
courant.

(235) Mews, Hazel
Frail vessels; woman's role in women's novels from Fanny
     Burney to George Eliot.

London: Athlone Press   1969   209p   bib   index
Oxford Univ.   Press $6.25
The years between publication of Wollstonecraft's "Vindication of the rights of women" (1792) and Mill's "On the subjection of women" (1869) produced some of England's great
women writers and some new ideas in new fiction.   This is,
however, more than a critique of literature.   It is their conceptions of the female role, and the female standing alone.
Fanny Burney, Maria Edgeworth, Jane Austen, the Brontës,
Elizabeth Gaskell and George Eliot.

(236)   Riley, Madeleine
Brought to bed.
A S Barnes   c1968   bib   68-24466
$4.95   0-498-06925-7
There is a commentary, with illustrative quotations, on every
aspect of childbirth as seen by English novelists since the
18th century.   She considers among other aspects through
her authors the relative welcome accorded boys and girls;
illegitimate birth; infanticide and abortion; doctors and mid-
wives; women in labor; the superstitions and dreams, benef-
icent or malicious, traditionally attendant in childbirth; the
benhavior of husbands.   Excerpts range from amusing to
pathetic.   No index; bibliography is mostly references to
fiction by women.

860 Spanish & Portuguese Literature

(237)   Godoy Alcayaga, Lucila, 1889-1957
Selected poems, by Gabriela Mistral [psued.], tr. by L.
      Hughes.
Indiana Univ.   Press   c1957   119p   57-13189
Indiana Univ.   Poetry Series $1.75/pap   (0-253-29915-2
      PPb15)
Received Nobel Prize in Literature in 1945.

900 GENERAL GEOGRAPHY, HISTORY, BIOGRAPHY

910 General Geography

(238)   Mannes, Marya
More in anger.
Lippincott   1958   189p   58-12279
$4.95
Iconoclast Marya Mannes--the cool, unflappable, verging-on-

chic who can cope with the likes of David Susskind (not that difficult, true, but she is willing and able, with dignity)-- turns to paper and eloquently records her protests and pleas. In 1958 she protested "more in anger" over censorship, politics, ethics, art, television. Although each selection had at least one essay on women as people, the entire book relates strongly if not directly to the current W. L. Movement because it sees and reports. Six years later, her question, "But will it sell?" (Lippincott, 1964, $4.50) was a plea for change from "flabby values and rigid attitudes"-- the "money thinkers" (mainly women, really). Her latest is a book on the psychological development of a woman, "Out of my time," published by Doubleday.

920 General Biography (Collections)

(239)   Bainton, Roland
Women of the Reformation; in Germany and Italy.
Augusburg   1971   288p
$7.95
12" LP record accompanies ($4.95).

(240)   Burnett, Constance Bruel, 1893-
Five for freedom...
Greenwood Press   c1953   317p   68-8734
1968 $12.75   0-8371-0034-8
Description of Lucy Stone's difficult life includes a "fairly typical meeting" at which the fiery leader spoke. Also Lucretia Mott, Elizabeth Cady Stanton, Susan B. Anthony and Carrie Chapman Catt.

no entries 241-249.

(250)   Crawford, Deborah
Four women in a violent time.   HS
Crown   c1970   191p   bib   index   74-127519
$4.50
The "difference" in this collection of biographies for younger people is the violence. Anne Hutchinson, Mary Dyer, Lady Deborah Moody and Penelope Stout were women involved in violence in the 16th, 17th and 18th centuries. Readings provided. "Lise Meitner..." by the same author is also atypical in that it is the account of a female scientist, Lise Meitner, who discovered how to split the atom (Crown, 1969, $3.95).

(251)   Douglas, Emily Taft
Remember the ladies; the story of great women who helped
    shape America.   HS
Putnam   c1966   254p   bib   index   66-10467
$5.95
The author is the only woman ever to precede her husband
(Senator Paul H. Douglas of Illinois) in Congress.   This is
a "Profiles in Courage"-type book à la John F. Kennedy's
femaleless one.   The "ladies" to be remembered and the
reasons in a nutshell: Abigail Adams threatened a feminine
revolt if the ladies were not remembered; Margaret Fuller
made brains stylish among Boston ladies; Belva Lockwood's
efforts helped to force the Supreme Court to admit women
lawyers, starting with herself; Dorothy Dix was a towering
figure in early public welfare; Prudence Crandall was a
first to try integration; it was said of Lucretia Mott that
"mobs could not be mobs" when she presided; Jane Addams
waged war on poverty, and others.   Ms. Douglas is also
the author of "Margaret Sanger: pioneer of the future"
(Holt, 1970, $7.50), which points up Ms. Sanger's fight
to bring birth control to the poor.

(252)   Foremost women in communications, 1969-70 (1st
    ed., 1970), ed. by Barbara J. Love.
Foremost Americans Pub. Corp. in association with Bowker.
    1970   approx 700p   79-125936
$25   0-8352-0414-6
This new directory contains approximately 7,500 biographies
of women in radio, television, newspapers, magazines, advertising, publishing, public relations and related industries,
and boasts an editorial advisory board composed of an actual
majority of women.   Geographical index with a special
section for New York City and a subject-cross index to
areas of professional concentration.   This is a reference-
book type publication--one of a few devoted to women.

(253)   Hale, Sarah Joseph
Women's record; or, Sketches of all distinguished women,
    from the creation to A.D. 1853.   Arranged in four eras
    with selections from female writers of every age.
Source Library...   1970 (orig. 1855)   2v   945p
$43   2v
A "Woman's Bible" written by the editor of Godey's Lady's
Book magazine.   It contains biographies, portraits, and
brief selected writings of some 2,000 women in history.
The range (Creation to 1854) and the 1855 woman's point-
of-view are good.

(254)   Lamson, Peggy L.
Few are chosen; American women in political life today.   HS
Houghton   1968   index   68-30801
$6.95
The chosen few are ten women in American political life
today.   About half are women about whom not too much has
appeared in print.   A further-reading type bibliography would
have enhanced its utility.   Good nevertheless.

(255)   Lutz, Alma
Crusade for freedom; women in the anti-slavery movement.
Beacon   c1968   68-12841
$7.50   0-8070-5486-0
The bold role of women in the agitation which ended slavery
was a major part of that which led to modern feminism.
Lutz is also the author of several biographies of women in
the history of the Movement.

(256)   Notable American women, 1607-1950; a biographical
        dictionary, Edward T. James, ed.
Harvard Univ.   Press   1971   3v   75-152274
Belknap Press   674-62731 $75.
This new project's aim seems to have been a biographical
reference work comparable to the "Dictionary of American
Biography":   the contributions of women to American life
1607-1950, i.e., women who died prior to December 1950.
(DAB contains about 700 women out of 15,000 entries!)
1,359 diverse figures in American life, although not necessarily born in the U.S., e.g., Jean Harlow, Mary Baker
Eddy, Isadora Duncan, Willa Cather, Jane Addams; science,
medicine, literature, labor, politics, art, theater, aviation,
religion, etc.   Only one group was admitted on the basis
of their husbands' renown: presidents' wives (perhaps some
day in the land of opportunity "wives" here can read
"spouses").   Writers of individual biographies are subject-
specialists; there is nevertheless a large proportion of male
editors and writers.

(257)   Smith, Margaret Chase and H. Paul Jeffers
Gallant women.   HS
McGraw   c1968   128p   bib   index   68-31666
$4.75   0-07-059101-6
Ms. Amith is the only woman to have been elected to and
served in both the U.S. House of Representatives and Senate;
she was, like many Congresswomen, first elected in a spe-
cial election after the death of her Representative husband.
Jeffers also co-authored "Gallant men," with Senator Everett

Dirksen, but " Gallant women" does not suffer from this
formula arrangement. The gallant American women were
Anne Hutchinson, Dolly Madison, Harriet Tubman, Harriet
Beecher Stowe, Clara Barton, Elizabeth Blackwell, Susan B.
Anthony, Anne Sullivan, Amelia Earhart, Frances Perkins
and Eleanor Roosevelt; Althea Gibson is a living gallant
woman.

(258) Smith, Page
Daughters of the promised land; women in American history.
Little 1970
$8.95 (801429)
"[The author's] observations are illuminating.... He sees
meaningful connections where a writer less familiar with
the field would observe only disparate and unrelated detail"
[Elizabeth Janeway].

(259) Stoddard, Hope
Famous American women. HS
Crowell c1970 461p bib index 73-87158
$7.50 0-690-28751-8
Biographical sketches mostly contemporary, with many fields
represented. Bibliography at end of each. Good emphasis
on diversification and life.

(260) Willard, Frances Elizabeth, 1839-1898, and Mary A.
       Livermore, eds.
A woman of the century; biographical sketches accompanied
       by portraits of leading American women...
Gale 1967 (orig. 1893)
$29

Individual Biography/Autobiography
(Arranged alphabetically by biographee,
whose surname is underlined)

(261) Angelou, Maya
I know why the caged bird sings. HS
Random c1969 281p 73-85598
$5.95
Marguerite Johnson's autobiography of survival; family life
in the South, Midwest and California; San Francisco; as a
dancer. "The fact that the adult American Negro female
emerges a formidable character is often met with amaze-
ment, distaste and even belligerence. It is seldom accepted
as an inevitable outcome of the struggle won by survivors

and deserves respect if not enthusiastic acceptance" [p. 265].

(262)   Wilson, Dorothy Clarke
Lone woman; the story of Elizabeth Blackwell, the first wo-
      man doctor.
Little   1970   459p   70-97907
$8.95
Affected both medical education and the woman's rights
struggle.

(263)   Chisholm, Shirley
Unbought and unbossed.   HS
Houghton   c1970   177p   79-120834
$4.95
Reads easily without smacking of the throwntogetherness of
much contemporary political autobiography.   Chapter 15
"Women and their liberation."   Her concerns for abortion,
youth and the war in evidence.   Note many passages where
one could read "women" instead of "blacks" in regard to
type of treatment and the attitude of the majority that is
determined to stay on top.   Chapter 10 "How I view Congress" (a fossil) should be required reading for every
American.   Title is from her Congressional election campaign slogan.   "As a matter of fact, there is as much--it
could even be more--panic among white men confronted by
an able, determined female who refuses to play the sex role
they think is fitting" [p. 53-54].   Susan Brownmiller's
"Shirley Chisholm" (Doubleday, 1970, $3.50) is well suited
for grades 5-9.

(264)   Collette
Earthly paradise; an autobiography.   Tr. by H. Briffault,
      et al., ed. by Robert Phelps.
Farrar Strauss   1966   505p   65-23837
$8.95; $2.65   (pap S2)   1969   Sunburst

(265)   Barth, Edna
I'm nobody!   Who are you?   The story of Emily Dickinson;
      drawings by Richard Cuffari.   HS
Seabury   1971   128p
$4.95
A very good biography that begins with the nine-year old
Emily, smoothly incorporates passages of her writing within
the content of the text, and includes selected poems at the
conclusion of the biographical material.   The writing style
is direct and informal, all of the dialogue based on research,
and the tone is objective.   A bibliography, a list of sources,

an index of poems by first lines, and a general index are
appended.   Grades 5-8.   (Center for Children's Books'
Bulletin.)

(266) Duncan, Isadora, 1878-1927
My life. HS
Liveright   c1955   359p   28-577
$5.95   0-87140-942-9; $1.75/pap   French. S
The autobiography of a woman who was a pioneer in every
sense, who believed that "truth and mutual faith are the
first principles of love."   There is a "young adult" version
on the market--before giving anything in form other than
the author's, read it yourself and compare; if you are a
"young adult," opt for the real thing!

(267) Milford, Nancy
Zelda; a biography [of Zelda Sayre Fitzgerald]
Harper   1970   424p   66-20742
$10   0-06-012991-3
An essay by Sylvia Robinson Corrigan in the fifth issue of
Aphra raises provocative ideas about Zelda and F. Scott
Fitzgerald, and Virginia and Leonard Woolf--the reasons why
Virginia Woolf emerged as a major creative force in our
century while the talented Zelda went under.

(268) Goldman, Emma, 1869-1940
Living my life; the autobiography of Emma Goldman.
Garden City pub. co.   1930   36-27233
$3.50 ea/pap vol. 1, 0-486-22543-7; vol. 2,   0-486-
    22544-5 Dover

(269) Shulman, Alix
To the barricades; the anarchist life of Emma Goldman.
Crowell   1971   255p   bib   index   72-132
$4.50   0-690-83280-X
Anarchist queen of the 1900's espoused same causes as
today's feminists--birth control, pacifism and draft opposi-
tion.   Well written.

(270) Jesus, Carolina Maria de
Child of the dark; the diary of Carolina Maria de Jesus,
    tr. from Portuguese by David St. Clair.   HS
Dutton   1962   190p
$4.50;   75¢/pap   T3565   SigNAL
Unique autobiography by an almost illiterate woman whose
life has been spent in the slums of São Paulo, Brazil (no
tenements, no dirty sidewalks, no fire hydrant on hot days--

instead, shacks put together by the occupant from anything
she can scrounge). Her diary was originally written in
what she had acquired of the Portuguese language, and then
edited by a compassionate journalist, Audalio Dantas, and
published as "Quarto de despejo." A woman's desolation,
oppression, hopelessness crying out in the literal dark,
breeding, scavenging in the trash to feed the by-products of
her sex-life, coping with the Church and fly-by-night
politicos. (Give this to Latin-American friends who deny
Machismo exists!)

(271) McCarthy, Mary Therese, 1912-
Memories of a Catholic girlhood.
Harcourt 1957 245p 57-8842
$4.75 0-15-15885907; 75¢ (pap 0-245-01211-5)
    Medallion, Berkeley.
Autobiography of a brilliant woman who, with her three
brothers, was suddenly orphaned as a child. Her memories
are gathered into several episodes, each accompanied by
subsequent reflections. (Title is not "Memoires..." as it
is sometimes misunderstood to be.) More catholic than
Roman Catholic. About the emergence of a young woman
who was later to write "The group"), the people who
touched and shaped her life (her brother is actor Kevin
McCarthy). This is real writing.

(272) Marshe, Surrey, pseud.
Girl in the centerfold: the uninhibited memoirs of Miss
    January. HS
Dell c1969 181p 72-78793
$4.95 (2913-6); 1970 95¢/pap 2846-1) Dell
Norwegian Solveig Mellomborgen made the big-time as a
Playboy bunny and Playmate-of-the-Month. Jacket pictures
and subtitle may draw an audience who will be disappointed,
and repulse the people who should read this book--a
foreigner's analysis (albeit via male ghost-type writer R.A.
Liston) of the American male society-Playboy-Hefner syn-
drome. (Liston is a skilled writer-by-trade, mainly young
adult books.) The motion picture, "You worm," is worth
mentioning here (see Audio Visual Resources, at the end
of Part IV).

(273) Nin, Anaïs
Diary.
Harcourt Brace v1 The diary of..., 1931-1934. Ed. and
    with an Introd. by Gunther Stuhlmann. c1966 1st ed.
    368p index 66-12917; v2 1934-9 c1967 357p index;

v3   1939-44   c1969
v1 $6.95; $2.85/pap   0-15-626025-5;   v2 $6.95   0-15-
125589-X; $2.85/pap   HB 174;   v3 $7.40;   0-15-
125591; $2.85/pap   HB 199.
An unconventional, sensitive woman.

(274) Sanger, Margaret Higgins, 1883-
Margaret Sanger; an autobiography.
Norton   c1938   38-38018
1970 $25.   0-8277-2000-9   Maxwell Reprint
Also, Emily Taft Douglas' "Margaret Sanger; pioneer of the
future" (Holt, 1970, $7.50) is a new popular biography of
the crusader for family planning and population control.

(275) Stanton, Elizabeth Cady
Eighty years and more (1815-1897)
Source Library   (orig. 1898)   486p
$18.
Reminiscences of one of the most important American suf-
fragettes.   The first volume of "Elizabeth Cady Stanton,"
edited by Theodore Stanton and Harriet Stanton Blatch
(Arno, $25) is a revision of "Eighty years and more."

970 General History of North America

(276) Brown, Dee
The gentle tamers; women of the Old Wild West.
Putnam   c1958   317p   bib   index   58-7164
1968 $1.95   (pap 0-8032-5025-8, 370)   Bison Univ. of
     Nebraska
Bad title and good photographs.   Well documented.   Chapter
16, The male viewpoint:" ... there ain't only about two
occupations fer 'em: Prostitution or runnin' a boardin'
house.   Danged if a feller can tell which on the whole
is worse"; "... no male was willing to hew wood, draw
water, cook meals, or wash clothes for the other males"
[p. 295].

(277) Lerner, Gerda
The Grimke Sisters from South Carolina; rebels against
     slavery.
Atlantic Monthly   c1967   479p   bib   index   67-25218
$6.95   Houghton
This is a history book of women who, circa 1837, lectured
all over New England in behalf of anti-slavery when women
did not speak in public--and there lies the nexus with Women's Liberation.   Angelina and Sarah Grimke were attacked

as Abolitionists and as women. (The Declaration of Women's
Rights at Seneca Falls wasn't until 1848.) The daughters of
a Southern judge, jurist, planter and slave-holder, they found
themselves exiled to the North, where they became agents of
the American Anti-Slavery Society (which in 1836 published
Angelina's "Appeal to the Christian women of the South") and
were the only Southern white women to become Abolition
leaders. They publicly acknowledged their relationship to
two Negro nephews (sons of their brother and a slave) they
discovered. Angelina and Theodore Wald, an anti-slavery
leader, were married, Includes her speeches. Someone
should make a movie! Sarah's "Letters on the equality of
the sexes, and the condition of women" was published in
1838--the first serious discussion of women's rights by an
American woman--and has been reprinted in the Source
Library of the Women's Movement Series ("Letters," $6.75).

FICTION

Novels

(278)   Atwood, Margaret, 1940-
The edible woman.
Little   c1969   181p   79-121421
Canadian Marian MacAlpin, approaching her wedding day,
begins to have the "problems of an unliberated member of
this consumer world who unexpectedly finds herself identifying with the things consumed" (she can't eat). The reviews
convey nothing of the relevance to women of this line of
thought. The "plus" here is great entertainment. There
isn't a page without timely insights on today and the way it
is in woman's daily life--she's got it all down on paper;
e.g., where Ainsley tells Len she's pregnant and his "female" reaction [p. 154f] ... the Christmas party at the
office [p. 164f] ... Peter's party [chap. 27].

(279) Austen, Jane, 1775-1817
Pride and prejudice. HS
Dutton 1961 $3.95; Dell 1970 50¢ (pap 7106). S
Technically probably the most perfect of her novels. Read
aloud. All have significance for women, but "Pride and
prejudice" and "Sense and sensibility" are especially poignant.
"The business of her life was to get her daughters married"
describes Ms. Bennett, mother of the two delightful and
three unattractive sisters. Since she was restricted by late
18th-century conventional respectability and by her impecuni-
ousness, as well as by the narrowness of English country

life in her day, she had a problem that would appear formidable to mothers of any era! Even before the end of the
18th century, forward-looking young woman Jane Austen put
into the mouth of Elizabeth Bennett the sentiment, "Do not
consider me as an elegant female ... but as a rational
creature."

(280)   Austen, Jane
Sense and sensibility.   HS
Heritage press $6.95;   Dell   50¢   (pap 7796)
"Sense and sensibility's" heroines are perhaps less attractive
than "Pride and prejudice's" Elizabeth, but the economic
insecurity of women and their helplessness in running their
own lives come across.   Two sisters: two-timed Marianne
has sensibility and a so-called nervous breakdown; Eleanor
is sensible, which doesn't protect her from being taken in
by a man, although it does preserve her pride.   The step-
brother who also treats women badly--the economic insecurity
of women at a time when young ladies were of course completely helpless in running their own lives.

(281)   Barnes, Margaret Ayer
Years of grace.   HS
Houghton   c1930   581p
1968 $8.98   Berg
A novel which offers, in addition to nostalgia and a well-
developed story line, an "exercise" in identification.   Read
through carefully and attempt to identify snatches here and
there, fragments of dialogue and thought especially ("character development" some might call it), as Jane and her
girlhood friends are drawn into a system the windup of which
produces the title--years of "grace."   What might be a better, more accurate title?   Or did the author mean it
ironically?   Compare your reactions (how would you anno-
tate it?) with descriptions by others, e.g., one well-known
bibliography recommends it for young people--would you
agree, aside from the reading-level?   A writer on women
in literature considers it a "family story," and another
commentary takes off from the title to explain it is "grace
into a woman's middle years."   If you need help, look
closely at chapter four of part one: Andre.

(282)   Boyle, Kay, 1903-
Year before last.
H. Smith   1932   373p
1969   Modern Fiction Series   224p   74-76191 $6.95
      Southern Illinois Univ. Press Cross-currents

0-8093-0390-6
An old time "Love story."

(283) Brontë, Charlotte, 1816-1855
Jane Eyre. HS
50¢ (pap 4186) Dell. S
Probably Charlotte Brontë's most significant work, considered an autobiographical novel--a strong woman who
rebelled. "Villette" expressed her hatred of the whole
system of Roman Catholicism: lonely heroine Lucy Snowe
has to earn her own living and maintain her integrity
(Villette refers to a Belgian city; Harcourt, 1962, $3.95).

(284) Brontë, Emily, 1818-1848
Wuthering Heights. HS
50¢ (pap 9728) Dell. S
Mid-19th-century portrayal of a marriage ... Heathcliff's
love for Cathy.

(285) Cespedes, Alba de
La bambolona; tr. from Italian by Isabel Quigly.
Simon & Schuster   c1967   316p   76-101869
$6.50   671-20377-0
Film version produced in Italy.   This, to go by the jacket,
would be (just) the story of Giulio, Ivana, and rigid 19th-
century sexual taboos and narrow bourgeois ambitions of
her lower-middle-class Italian parents.   But it is also the
portrait of Giulio's attitudes--Latin, male, Roman Catholic--
toward marriage, the female, sexual objects, role, etc. --
all perceived and conveyed so well by the author.   Her
"Between then and now" (Houghton, 1959, $3.) concerns a
cosmopolitan woman journalist--an independent modern
Roman woman in her thirties, and her more conventional
sisters, her lover, her loneliness and her courage.   Cespedes is a contemporary Italian novelist popular in France,
throughout Europe and Latin America.

(286) Chopin, Kate O'Flaherty, 1851-1904
The awakening.
Capricorn 1964 (orig. 1899) 303p 64-7425
$13.50 (pap 105) library binding 0-512-00101-4 Gar-
     rett Press, American Authors Series 1970; 1964
     $1.65 (pap 105) Putnam
A married woman, Edna Pontellier, leaves her husband and
three children to devote herself for several months to
thinking about herself and to painting.   In all of her 29
years, she had never done anything like this!   19th-century
novel still comes across.

(287)   De la Roche, Mazo, 1885-1961
Jalna.   HS
Little   1927   28-17906
$5.95. S
Stolid young woman unprepared for the masculinity of her
husband engulfs her daughter, who repays her by growing up
to prefer her father.   In some other ways, e.g., the generations, like the Forsyte saga.

(288)   Didion, Joan
Play it as it lays.
Farrar, Straus   c1970   213p   79-113779
$5.95
Best-selling contemporary novel of a woman who, in her
thirties, finds herself radically divorced from her husband,
friends, her past and even her own future.   Also read her
'On morality' from "Slouching toward Bethlehem" (Farrar,
1965, $5.95).

(289)   Drexler, Rosalyn
I am the beautiful stranger.
Grossman   c1965   185p   65-16854
$4.50   0-670-38940-4
Three years of growing up in the 1930's in the life of
Selma Silver.

(290)   DuMaurier, Daphne, 1907-
Mary Anne.
1954   Doubleday   351p   54-6254
1970   75¢   (pap 0-671-75469-6)   PB. S
Mary Anne Clark was mistress of Frederick, Duke of York,
son of George III, contemporary of Thackeray's Becky Sharp
("Vanity Fair").   Historical novel.

(291)   Dunn, Nell
Poor cow.   HS
Doubleday   c1966   133p   67-24336
$3.95
A novel of England today, her first, of a 22-year-old
ironically named Joy.   Movie of same title.   Also read
her "Up the junction" (Lippincott, 1966, $3.95).

(292)   Evans, Marion, 1819-1880 [Pseud.:   George Eliot]
Adam Bede.   HS
Great illustrated classics $4.50   0-396-00467-9   Dodd
She divides her novel into a study of three women: Dinah,
Hetty and Ms. Poyser.   "Mill on the floss" (Collier, 95¢)

was written after "Adam Bede"; the author studied womanhood all in one character--the struggles of Maggie Tulliver.

(293)   Farrar, Rowena
A wondrous moment then.   HS
Holt, Rinehart   1968   343p   bib   68-10058
1968 $6.50   0-03-065570-6
Although not great literature, it is a readable, rewarding
historical novel built around the Suffrage Movement, and
undoubtedly the author had access to her facts.   She describes how American women have suffered physical per-
secution for their cause.   Set in Nashville, Tennessee
during and immediately following World War I, the plot is
built around the final stages of the long, bitter struggle women engaged in to gain the since wasted right to vote.
Bigotry, tyranny, injustice faced those brave enough to stand
up for civil rights about which there is so much talk today
--it was a wondrous moment then for women.   Her first
novel, "Bend your heads all" about 18th-century middle-
Tennessee and the women who settled there (Holt, 1965,
$5.95).

(294)   Gould, Lois May, 1906-
Such good friends.
Random   1970   277p   77-10253
$5.95

(295)   Green, Hannah
I never promised you a rose garden; a novel.
Winston   c1964   300p   64-11018
$4.95   0-03-043725-3   Holt
See if you agree with someone who recommended this for
"grade seven and up."   About a girl in "an institution" and
dominating mother.

(296)   Hall, Radclyffe
Well of loneliness.
Covici   1928   506p   OP 1960
1959   75¢   (pap 75020)   BB. S
Famous oldtimer about lesbianism, by a woman novelist.
Jess Stearn's "The grapevine" (Doubleday, 1964, $4.95)
is perhaps better known, but generalized and full of the
male author's point of view re role and assumptions, e.g.,
"While she thinks directly and to the point, like a man,
she has the endurance and resilience of the female" ("Grapevine," p. 10).

(297)   Kaufman, Sue
Diary of a mad housewife.   HS
Random   c1967   311p   67-12721
$7.95
Insufferable husband, but not over-done.   Doesn't ridicule
psychiatry or other females along the way of creating a
witty real book about things as they are: four months in
Tina's life.   Read before seeing the award-winning motion
picture, if possible.   Masterpiece of writing technique without too much sarcasm.   Insights.   Perhaps the single flaw
is the ending, which unfortunately just doesn't happen that
easily or well.

(298)   Lessing, Doris M.
Golden notebook.
Simon & Schuster   1962   567p
$5.95   (28770)   Simon & Schuster;   1970 $1.25/pap
      0-345-01875-3   Ballantine
Autobiographical novel of an English woman alone with her
child in London--her experiences with sex, independence,
as a writer and with The Left.   Lessing is the author of
a number of novels and short stories relevant to women;
this is frequently referred to.   "A man and two women" is
a collection of her stories about marriage, woman's fate
(Simon & Schuster, 1958, $5).

(299)   McCarthy, Mary Therese, 1912-
The group.
Harcourt   c1963   378p   63-15316
95¢   (pa Q2501)   Sig. S
Novel with a collective heroine: eight Vassar women who
"grouped together" at college in the Class of '33.   Sad-
funny; read after her "Memories of a Catholic girlhood."

(300)   McCullers, Carson, 1917-1967
The member of the wedding.   HS
Houghton   c1946   132p   46-20221
$4.95; $1.50   (pap NDP 153)   New Directions. S
Carson McCullers was a contemporary American woman
novelist and playwright whose works speak to the female
heart--she was not afraid of tenderness.   Her writing
nevertheless "makes" Broadway and Hollywood.   "The
member of the wedding" was dramatized for the stage by
the author.   "The heart is a lonely hunter" (Bantam, 1940,
95¢/pap) and "Reflections in a golden eye" (Bantam, 1941,
95¢/pap) are also in-print and recommended.

(301)   Miller, Isabel
A place for us.
Bleecker Street Press   1969
$2.25/pap   (Also McGraw, 1971)
Lesbian novel.   Received First Annual Gay Book Award of
the SRRT Task Force on Gay Liberation at the 1971 Ameri-
can Library Association Conference.

(302)   Oates, Joyce Carol, 1938-
Them.
Vanguard   c1969   508p   74-89660
1970 $1.25   (pap P 1467)   Crest Fawcett World
Re-read 'Author's note' after finishing book.   Note Maureen's
ultimate concern with getting married and having kids--even
within her neuroses, she was indoctrinated as to what was
"normal."   Oates' review-article, "Love on film" (<u>McCalls</u>:
14f, October 1970) is also worth-reading.

(303)   O'Brien, Edna
Casualties of peace.
Simon & Schuster   c1966   175p   67-12920
$4.50;   1970   95¢   (pap 0-345-01977-6)   Ballantine
Sexuality dominates.   Patsy and Beryl--two young women in
a casual friendship which ends in tragedy.   "Girls in their
married bliss" (Simon & Schuster, 1964, $4.95) portrays
sensitive Kate and wisecracking Baba, in her sequel to
"The country girls" (OP).   Her "The lonely girl" (OP)
was filmed as "The girl with green eyes."   Edna O'Brien
is a contemporary Irish novelist who became a central
figure in the London literary world in the sixties.   All of
her books are good examples of the novel supplying sub-
stance for knowing about contemporary woman living in
today's world of misuse and abuse, sexual objects, social
placement, loneliness.

(304)   Petry, Ann Lane, 1911-
The street.
World Houghton   1946   436p   46-1079
$3.50
Petry also writes for young people, e.g., "Tituba of Salem
Village" (Crowell, 1964, $4.50) and "Harriet Tubman, con-
ductor on the underground railroad" (Crowell, 1955, $3.95).

(305)   Plath, Sylvia, 1932-1963 [pseud.:   Victoria Lucas]
The bell jar (with a biographical note by Lois Ames...)
Harper   1971   206p   76-149743
$6.95   0-06-013356-2

Almost all her reviewers emphasize Sylvia Plath's breakdown, madness, suicide, insanity, self-destruction, confes-
sional; some also point up her creativity, readability, wit,
art. Inevitably, some have comdemned her for taking her
own life, almost blocking recognition of her as a person/
writer. This novel, a "scarcely disguised autobiography,
covers six months in a young girl's life, beginning when she
goes to New York to serve on a fashion magazine's college
editorial board. It ends when she emerges from a mental
hospital after a breakdown. . . . It is obvious why Sylvia
Plath's mother is distressed by the novel. The author
remembers every misguided attempt to guide her, every
play to use her, every complacent piece of advice . . . "
[Martha Duffy in Time:87-8, June 21, 1971]. The novel
made the 1971 best-seller list.

(306) Richardson, Dorothy M. , 1873-1957
Pilgrimage.
Knopf 1967/new ed.   (orig. 1919-1938)   4v   66-22423
4v $7. 59 ea, $30 set
The novels of Dorothy Richardson delved honestly into the
feminine psyche and expressed lucidly in a semi-stream-of-
consciousness what it means to be a woman. One reviewer
in 1923 commented that "Revolving lights suffers more than
do some of the other books from Miss R's besetting sin--her
tiresome twist towards feminism. It is the one block upon
her exquisite fairness and detachment" [Spectator:1084-5,
June 30, 1923]. Another wrote that she "has drawn her in-
spiration neither from man-imitating cleverness nor from
narcissistic feminine charm but from the abyss of the
feminine subconsciousness" [John Cowper Powys' "Dorothy
Richardson," 1931, p. 8]. And finally, Graham Greene:
"I should imagine Miss R in her ponderous unwitty way has
had an immense influence on such writers as Mrs. Woolf
and Miss Stein" ["The lost childhood:" 84-5, 1951]. Here
is a new Borzoi edition about the woman who went out into
the world, Miriam Henderson. Vol. 1, Pointed roofs (1915),
Backwater (1916), Honeycomb (1917); Vol. 2, The tunnel
(1919), Interim (1919); Vol. 3, Deadlock (1921), Revolving
lights (1923), The trap (1925); and Vol. 4, Oberland (1927),
Dawn's left hand (1931), Clear horizon (1935), Dimple hill
(1938), March moonlight (previously unpublished).

(307) Richardson, Samuel, 1689-1761
Clarissa Harlowe.
Dutton 1932 4v 37-31202
Everyman $3. 25ea: v1 0-460-00882-X; v2 0-460-00883-8;

v3 0-460-00884-6; v4 0-460-00885-4.
"Pamela" (Norton, 1958, $1.45) is also recommended.

(308)   Roiphe, Anne Richardson
Up the sandbox.
Simon & Schuster   c1970   155p   79-130488
$4.95   671-20704-0
A bestselling novel that Irma Pascal Heldman (Time:74,
Jan. 25, 1971) felt would interest New Yorkers especially.
"Captures the minutiae of matrimony and maternity.   It is
meant for those who dig men and the other two M's and
ask only to be out of the doll's house part of the day."
"Another pregnancy--man's eternal solution to fear of mor-
tality" and "a whole new set of ego-building fantasies."
Another audience might be women who know it's not possible to be a part-time feminist or partly liberated (like a
little bit pregnant).

(309)   Schreiner, Olive, 1855-1920
Story of an African farm.
Orig. 1883
$1.95   (610) W Collins;   1968   60¢   (pap R 374)   Fawcett
   World. S
Olive Schreiner has been called the bravest of all the brave
women feminism has produced, and her Lyndall is a figure
of feminine courage (if courage can be sexed).   Actually,
she had all the stereotyped aspects of today's femininity:
youth, beauty, small stature.   But she wanted merely
knowledge, some distinction, and love.   Schreiner's "Women
and labour" is also influential; see Clark's "Working wife..."

(310)   See, Carolyn
The rest is done with mirrors.
Little   c1970   307p   70-105356
$6.95
The title derives from the author's "there were changes in
their small lives, but the general cast of characters remained the same.   There are only two hundred people in
the world, ... the rest is done with mirrors."   She is a
former graduate student at UCLA (the setting of the novel),
now teaching there.   An observer of life in the 1950's in
veterans' housing.   Don't read the jacket bait--gives no
idea of the intricacy of plot development, style, etc.

(311)   Solomon, Barbara Probst
The beat of life.
Lippincott   1960   222p   60-13579

75¢/pap SigNAL
Unmarrieds--big city--intellectuals--abortion.

(312)   Thackeray, William Makepeace, 1811-1863
Vanity fair; a novel without a hero.
[many editions--see "Books in print"] S
Movie: "Becky Sharp. "

(313)   Undset, Sigrid
Kristin Lavransdatter [a trilogy made up of:] The bridal
     wreath, The mistress of Husaby, The cross. HS
Knopf   c1923-55   1069p
$7.95
Undset is the author of books for children as well as this
monumental historical novel, e. g. , "Happy times in Norway. "
Of "Kristin, " Ruth Suckow wrote, "This trilogy is the first
great story founded upon the normal events of a normal
woman's existence. It is as grand and as rich, as simple
and as profound, as such a story should be. " Interesting
Notes provided in most editions. Only edition now in print
is a so-called "young adult" version. See how it suits you.

(314)   Wertenbaker, Lael Tucker
The afternoon women. HS
Little   c1966   312p   66-10983
1970   95¢   (pap N5469)   Bantam
A novel about abortion (Lucinda Cisler suggests it may be
based in part on abortionist Dr. Robert Spencer of Ashland,
Pa.). Ms. Wertenbaker has an irritating style at times
("then slit open the envelope with a finger slenderer at the
base than at its tip"; "her smudge of a nose and lipstick
renewed on her old-fashioned mouth"; "your eyes are kind";
and a woman who is a researcher and seeing a psychiatrist
regularly in New York City!) But, by page 247 (chapter 19
of original hard cover), an excellent series of interpretive
statements, e. g. , "Are you all right?" means are you con-
tracepted?   The afternoon women are the abortion patients
of physician Hill in rural North Carolina, circa 1959.   How
he came to be an ethical abortionist (i. e. , good work, rea-
sonable rates the patient can afford, concern for the total
patient--in short, the epitomy of the Hypocratic Oath-taker)
and what happens to him and his last three afternoon women
constitute the plot.   The author has "selected" the three
women well: two married (the majority of illegal abortion
operations have been performed on married women); one
unmarried, and in the doctor's opinion, on the verge of instability; one each from Massachusetts, New York City and

locally; one late-menopausal grandmother; one middle-aged
mother of several half-grown children; and one sexually active
young woman who, as it develops, had once been conned into
going through with an illegitimate birth.   Even in this day
and age, some communities, boards of trustees, parents,
teachers, and other friends of the library may influence the
library administrator to restrict (label, censor, segregate)
"The afternoon women" beyond its normal shelving with
adult fiction.   Whether they are successful is entirely up
to you.

(315)   Wharton, Edith Newbold Jones, 1862-1937
Age of Innocence.   HS
Appleton 1920 (orig.)
1968 $5.95 Scribners; Modern library $2.95
Reading this novel may help shake up the older or more
conventional thinker, for it is a classic--by a dead, and
incidentally female, novelist--which portrays the past, when
a man's woman was his helpmate.   Conventionalized presentation of femininity popular in late 19th-century fashion-
able New York City: He marries her, He loves someone
else, she renounces him in fine romantic self-sacrifice.
Pulitzer Prize winner.   See also her "The custom of the
country" (Scribners, 1913, $5.95).

Short Stories (Collections)

(316)   Beauvoir, Simone de, 1908-
Woman destroyed, tr. by Patrick O'Brien.
Putnam c1969 254p 69-15486
$5.95
Ms. Beauvoir is a French contemporary writer in several
genres.   Many of her works are in print.   Only one or two
examples can be considered in this limited collection.
Three stories (The age of discretion, The monologue, and
The woman destroyed) portray the dilemma of the middle-
aged woman whose world is slowly slipping from her grasp.

(317)   Paley, Grace
The little disturbances of man; stories of men and women
    at love.   HS
Viking   c1959   189p   68-17421
$4.50   0-670-43179-6
Eleven stories.   Philip Roth: "An understanding of lone-
liness, lust, selfishness, and ... fatigue that is splendidly
comic and unladylike."   Herbert Gold's viewpoint: "Her

stories are shrewd, funny, and full of feeling; she has a
girl's charm and a woman's strength; she is an exciting
writer. "

(318)   Stein, Gertrude, 1874-1946
Three lives.
Orig. 1909
$2. 29   PBL; $1. 45   (pap V153)   Vin Random. S
Stein uses repetition and common words used by everyone,
the simplest possible, to express complexity.   Three
poignant stories of "The good Anna, " "Melanctha, " and
"The gentle Lena. "

Part IV

NON-BOOK RESOURCES

PAMPHLETS

Reprints of underground press articles and pamphlets are important printed resources in a movement where members are unable to get their works published in regular channels or are exploited by the media. They provide a cheap, albeit transient, medium for communication: publications of unconventional, sometimes underground, publishers, distributors, groups and individuals. They are usually current although sometimes reprinted, possibly of temporary interest but nevertheless timely. Only a sampling of pamphlet subjects, authors and distributors can be included here in an attempt to provide a representation. Addresses appear in the "Directory of Sources" (Part V). Other pamphlets can be located by use of such tools as "Alternative Press Index," "Alternatives in Print," and "Vertical File Index."

Adams, Whitney
How to talk back to your television. (Package) Contact Ms. Whitney at 938 National Press Building, Washington, DC 20004.

Berkeley Rat (Radical Arts Troupe)
Reserve Liberal Training Corps; a play. Suggestions for building a Guerrilla Theatre Group. 5¢ from New England Free Press

Calvert, Carolyn
Sexism on Sesame Street. 21p paper includes statistical tables showing such things as: females appear less than half as often as males. Designed to make parents think twice. 50¢. Contact Ms. Calvert at 11541 Hierra Court, Los Altos, Cal. 94022

Farrell, Warren T.
The resocialization of men's attitudes towards women's role in society. Deals with myths men have about women, the confines of masculinity and areas in which men can benefit from WL; a paper presented to the American Political Science Association, Los Angeles, September 1970. 50¢ from the author.

Feminists on Children's Media
Little Miss Muffett Fights Back; Recommended Non-sexist Books about Girls for Young Readers. Compiled and distributed by FCM, c1971, 48p, 50¢ in coin + 16¢ SASE.

Human Rights for Women
    Job discrimination handbook.   c1971, with new editions
planned for the future.   13p 8 1/2x11" 50¢ and quantity rates.

Joreen
    The 51% minority; a statistical essay.   From the University
Women's Association.   25¢ + SASE.

KNOW
    A guide to female studies.   Compilation of research across
the U.S.A., $2.

Library Service to the Disadvantaged Child Committee
    Libraries and day care.   A kind of fold-out how-to from the
committee which is part of the Children's Services Division of the
American Library Association.   25/$3 and other quantity rates.
0-8389-5362-X

National Organization for women:
    from national N.O.W.:
        Business and industry discrimination kit.   How to file dis-
crimination complaints with the OFCC and EEOC and under the
EPA. $3/members, $5/public.
    from Atlanta N.O.W.:
        Speaker's kit. $5.95.   Box 54045, Civic Center Station,
Atlanta, Ga. 30308.

Partisan Press (An example of an English source)
    Women's Liberation and the new politics.   35¢
    The myth of motherhood.   25¢

Ringo, Miriam K.
    The well-placed wife; what she thinks, what she wants.
1970 study concludes most women would get a more career-oriented
education and pursue a career if they could live their lives over.
16 West 220-97th Street, Hinsdale, IL 60521.

Sojourner Truth Press
    Sleeping beauty, a Lesbian fairy tale.   70¢

Taylor, Kathryn
    Generations of denial; 75 short biographies of women in his-
tory.   1971-2 $1.25 from Times Change Press.   ["A woman re-
sponsible for the strategy that won the Civil War? for the doctrines
of the Methodist faith? for trail blazing the Northwest Territory?
Yes, women were in fact responsible for these and many other significant achievements which male supremacist history has falsely
credited or consigned to oblivion..." (Times Change Press).]

Tinsley, Adrian
    Academic women, sex discrimination and the law: an action
handbook ... prepared for the Women's Caucus for the Modern
Languages and the MLA Commission on Women.   December, 1971.

50¢ (From Ms. Tinsley, University of Maryland, College Park
20742, or Carol Ohmann, Wesleyan Station, Middleton, CT 06457.)

U.S. Dept. of Labor Women's Bureau
    Guide to conducting a consultation on women's employment
with employers and union representatives.   Pam 12   1971   15p
WB72-144

Vidal, Mirta
    Women; new voice of La Raza.   16p   Pathfinder Press.
Chicanas speak out.

Wood, Sally Medora
    Questions I should have answered better; a guide to women
who dare to speak publicly.   12p   KNOW   25¢

MOVEMENT PERIODICALS

An up-to-date and completely accurate listing of serial publications from any contemporary movement would, by its very nature, be impossible to compile. The titles which follow are magazines, newsletters, journals, newspapers and other serials from today's Women's Liberation Movement and some closely allied causes; a few from the past are included.

Because prices and frequency change constantly, they have not been included. "Street" can be assumed. The first line of each entry is the title of the serial. Most organizations and groups publish some type of newsletter; where the type of publication is not stated, it is usually a newsletter. Organization addresses appear in the "Directory of Sources" (Part V).

AAUW
American Assoc. of University
  Women

ALA-SRRT Task Force: Status
  of Women in Librarianship
  Newsletter. Discontinued in
  1972; refer to SRRT Newsletter. See American Library
  Assoc. Being revived.

Abortion Counseling Service
  Newsletter

Action for Children's Television Newsletter

Ain't I A Woman?
WLF Publications Collective

Akamai Sister
PO Box 11042
Honolulu, HI 96814

Alliance Link
Equal Rights Alliance

American Medical Women's
  Journal. See Woman Phy-
  sician

And Ain't I A Woman?
1401 N. E. 106
Seattle, WA 98125

Antioch College Newsletter
Yellow Springs, OH 45307

Aphra; a Feminist Journal
4 Jones
New York, NY 10014

Arena Three
bcm Seahorse
London WC I, England

Asian Women's Journal
3405 Dwinelle Hall, University
  of California
Berkeley, CA 94720

Association for Children Deprived of Support Newsletter

Association for the Study of
  Abortion Newsletter

Association for Women in Psychology Newsletter
189 West End Avenue,
c/o Leigh Marlowe
New York, NY 10023

Association of Women in
Science Newsletter

Association to Repeal Abortion
Laws Newsletter

Awake and Move
Box 93
Penllyn, PA 19422 [Also:
Philadelphia Women's Center]

Battle Acts
YAWF Women, 58 West 25
New York, NY 10010

Bay Area WL Newsletter [de-
funct?]
2237 Pine
San Francisco, CA 94115

Berkeley WL [defunct?]
Berkeley, CA 94701

Beyond the Looking Glass
Associated Students
Univ. of Calif.: Santa
Barbara 93102

Black Maria: Chicago Women
Speak
Box 230
River Forest, IL 60305

Black Women United
c/o Sherrie McKee, Box 421
Wilberforce, OH 45384

Bloomington WL
Bloomington, IN 47401

Body and Soul
Dallas, TX 75221

Bread and Roses
1495 Massachusetts
Cambridge, MA 02138

The Bridge
25 Beacon
Boston, MA 02108

Bristol WL Group
Bristol, England

Broadside [defunct?]. See
New Broadside

A Broom of One's Own
Washington, DC 20013

Bulletin
c/o Cidal, Arteaga #3
Cuernavaca, Morelos, Mexico

Bulletin ... of the Women's
Bureau
Canada Department of Labour

Cassandra [defunct?]
PO Box 1797
Chicago, IL 60690

Catalyst
6 East 82
New York, NY 10028

A Change Is Gonna Come
968 Valencia
San Francisco, CA 94110

Chicago. University. See
UWA News.

Chicago WL News
2875 West Cermak, Room 9
Chicago, IL 60623

Citizens' Advisory Council
on the Status of Women Newsletter

Come Out!
Box 233, Times Square Station
New York, NY 10036

The Common Woman Is the
Revolution [defunct?]
Box 2267, Station A
Berkeley, CA 93312

Concerns
Women's Caucus for the
Modern Languages

Congress to Unite Women Newsletter

Connecticut Valley Newsletter
207 Hampshire House
Amherst, MA 01002

Connections
3109 16
San Francisco, CA 94103

Continuing Education for Adults
Syracuse University

Council for Women's Equality
Newsletter

Dayton WL
Dayton, OH 45401

Denver WL
1452 Pennsylvania
Denver, CO 80203

The Digging Stick
Boston Women United, Box 278
Boston, MA 01432

Do It NOW; Monthly Action
Newsletter of the National
Organization for Women
NOW National Office

Durham North Carolina Newsletter
Durham Women's Association

ERA Newsletter (National Ad
Hoc Committee for ...)

The Eagle's Eye
Local #850, AWPPW, Rt. 1,
Box 1155M
Antioch, OH 94509

Earth's Daughters (journal)
409 Richmond Avenue
Buffalo, NY 14222

East Bay Feminists Newsletter
[defunct?]
Berkeley, CA 94701

East Bay Women for Peace
Berkeley, CA 94701

East Village Other
20 East 12
New York, NY 10003

Elle
1700 Broadway, c/o Irena
Balinska
New York, NY 10019

Employee Press (newspaper)
2483-A Hearst
Berkeley, CA 94709

Enough Is Enough (journal)
Bristol Militant Group, England

Essence
Hollingsworth Group, 102
East 30
New York, NY 10016

Essecondsex Newsletter
58 High
Rockport, MA 01966

Everywoman (newspaper)
6516 West 83
Los Angeles, CA 90045

Explode
c/o Lois Graessle, 27 Albany
Mansions, Albert Bridge Road
London S W 11, England

FEW News & Views
Federally Employed Women

Feelings (journal)
243 Baltic
Brooklyn, NY 11201

Female Liberation Journal
371 Somerville Avenue
Somerville, MA 02143

Female Liberation Newsletter
Box 300, University of California
Eshlemann Hall
Berkeley, CA 94720

Female Liberation Newsletter
Box 303, Kenmore Square
Boston, MA 02215

Female Liberation Newsletter
PO Box 14061, University Station
Minneapolis, MN 55414

Female Liberation Newsletter
Box 954
Chapel Hill, NC 27514

Female Studies Newsletter
Dr. Rae Siporin, Asst. Dean,
College of Arts & Sciences,
University of Pittsburgh, PA
15213

Feminine Focus
420 West 11, c/o Grace Ellen
Rice
Lawrence, KS 66044

A Feminist Journal
c/o Amazon Bookstore

A Feminist Journal
509 East 5
New York, NY 10009

Focas
Box 558, Cathedral Station
New York, NY 10025

Focus
Box 221, Prudential Center
Station
Boston, MA 02199

Forever Amber
1822 West 4
Los Angeles, CA 90057

Four Lights
2006 Walnut
Philadelphia, PA 19103

The Fourth World (newspaper)
Box 8997
Oakland, CA 94608

Free and Proud
Box U 6800, Florida State
University
Tallahassee, FL 32306

Free Kids
Box 4854, Cleveland Park Station
Washington, DC 20008

Free Schools Newsletter [defunct]
PO Box 3511
Santa Barbara, CA 93105

Front Page (newspaper)
515 North Washington
Bloomington, IN 47461

The Furies; A Lesbian/
Feminist monthly newspaper
Box 8843, S E Station
Washington, DC 20003

Getting on Women Collective
(Pissed Off Pink) [defunct?]
358 North Harrison
East Lansing, MI 48823

Goodbye to All That (newspaper)
PO Box 3092
San Diego, CA 92103

El Grito Del Norte
Route 2, Box 5
Española, NM 87532

The Hand That Rocks the Rock
c/o Ronny Howard, Dept. of
English, Slippery Rock State
College, Slippery Rock, PA
16057

Harriet Tubman Brigade Newsletter

Her Own Right
Box 4026 (Also 1608 Milan,
  Apartment 6)
New Orleans, LA 70118

Hertha (Journal--Eng. ed. avail.)
Swedish Information Service

High Point Women's Union News-
  letter
Box 84
High Point, NC 27260

Human Rights for Women
  Newsletter

Hysteria (newspaper)
2 Brookline
Cambridge, MA 02139

Indianapolis WL Newsletter
Indianapolis, IN 46204

It Ain't Me Babe (newspaper)
Box 6323
Albany, CA 94706

Jane
c/o Susan Brownmiller,
61 Jane
New York, NY 10014

Journal of Female Liberation.
See No More Fun And Games

Journal of Female Psychology
32 Washington Square, c/o Alix
  Shulman
New York, NY 10011

Journal of the American Medical Women's Association.
  See Woman Physician

Just Like a Woman
Box 5432, Station E
Atlanta, GA 30307

KNOW News

The Ladder (journal)
Box 5025, Washington Station
Reno, NV 89503

Lavender Vision (newspaper)
Media Collective

The Law and Women Series
Human Rights for Women &
  Today Publications and News
  Service. See Today Publica-
  tions

The Lesbian Tide
1910 South Vermont, DOB
  Center
Los Angeles, CA 90007

Library Bulletin, International
  Planned Parenthood Federation

Lilth (magazine) [defunct?]
2021 East Lynn, Women's Majority Union
Seattle, WA 98102

Los Angeles Women's Liberation Newsletter
1027 South Crenshaw Blvd.
Los Angeles, CA 90019

Louisiana Women Newsletter
Louisiana Commission on the
  Status of Women

Louisville WL Newsletter
Louisville, KY 40202

Lysistrata. See The Hand
  That Rocks the Rock

Ms.
Majority Enterprises, Inc.

Majority Report
PO Box 558, Cathedral Station
New York, NY 10025

Maternal Information Services.
See The Working Mother

Matrix; For the She of the
New Aeon
Box 46067
Los Angeles, CA 90046

Maverick
Box 77, Agnew Station
Santa Clara, CA 93154

Media Women's Monthly
[defunct]
New York, NY

Mejane (newspaper)
67. Glebe Point Road
Glebe, Sydney, Australia
2037

Memo (by Women Strike for
Peace)

Michigan. University. Center
for Continuing Education of
Women Newsletter

Minnesota. University. Women's Continuing Education
Program Quarterly.

Montreal WL Newsletter
3694 Ste. Famille
Montreal, Quebec

Mother (newspaper)
Box 8507
Stanford, CA 94305

Mother Lode
334 Winfield,
San Francisco, CA 94110

Moving Out
679 West Hancock
Detroit, MI 48201

MS. See Ms.

Mutah
2506 Arden Way
Sacramento, CA 95825

NOW. See National Organization for Women

National Constituents for Bella
Abzug

National Council of Women of
Canada Newsletter

National Organization for Women
has many publications--those of
chapters, regions, caucuses,
interest groups and task-forces.
For example:
    Do It NOW, and NOW Acts:
    1957 East 73, Chicago, IL
    60649 (the national NOW).
    NOW York Times, and NOW
    York Woman:
    28 East 56, New York, NY
    10022 (the N.Y. NOW).
    Women in Poverty Newsletter
    "The Directory of Sources"

National Women's Political
Caucus Newsletter

Native Movement
Box 6152
Vancouver 8, British Columbia
Canada

The New Broadside
Box 390, Cooper Station,
Dept. S
New York, NY 10033

New Broom
Prudential Center Station,
Box 341
Boston, MA 02199

New Carolina Woman (newspaper)
Box 368
Knightdale, NC 27545

New Feminist
PO Box 597, Station A
Toronto 116, Ontario, Canada

New Mexico WL
c/o Nancy Adair, 804 Vassar
N.E.
Albuquerque, NM 87106

New University Conference
Newsletter

The New Woman; First Magazine
for the Thinking Woman
Box 24202
Ft. Lauderdale, FL 33307

The New York Woman. See
The NOW York Woman

New York Women Strike for
Peace Newsletter

New Yorkers for Abortion Law
Repeal Newsletter

News and Letters
Detroit Women's Liberation,
415 Brainard
Detroit, MI 48201

News & Views
Federally Employed Women, Inc.

No More Fun and Games; A
Journal of Female Liberation
16 Lexington Ave.
Cambridge, MA 02138

North Dakota WL Newsletter
PO Box 235, Minot Women's
Collective
Minot, ND 58701

Notes from the First Year
799 Broadway, Room 412,
New York Radical Women
New York, NY 10003

Notes from the Second Year
Box 22, Old Chelsea Station,
Radical Feminists
New York, NY 10001

Notes from the Third Year:
Women's Liberation
PO Box AA, Old Chelsea
Station
New York, NY 10011

Notes from the Lower Classes
I and II
The Feminists

Now ... and Then
135 Eastern Parkway, c/o Ann
DiLeo
Brooklyn, NY 11238

The NOW York Times
New York N. O. W.

The NOW York Woman (monthly
suppl. to The Manhattan Tribune
New York N. O. W.

OSU WL Newsletter
Ohio State University
Columbua, OH 43210

Off Our Backs; A Women's
News-Journal
PO Box 4859, Cleveland Park
Station
Washington, DC 20008

Pandora
4224 University Way, N. E.
Seattle, WA 98105

Pandora's Box [defunct?]
PO Box 22094
San Diego, CA 92122

Partisans
3 rue Rottenbourg, c/o Claude
Hennequin-Geindre
Paris 12, France

The Pedestal (newspaper)
Vancouver Women's Caucus

Philadelphia Women's Liberation
Center Newsletter

Pissed Off Pink (newspaper)
1404 East Oakland
Lansing, MI 48906

The Planner
301 Walter Library, University
of Minnesota
Minneapolis, MN 55455

Progressive Woman
WL Movement, Box 510
Middlebury, IN 46540 (Also
Corson Publishing, Inc.)

Pro Se National Law Women's
Newsletter

Purple Star
Student Activities Building,
c/o WL Office, University of
Michigan
Ann Arbor, MI 48104

Rat (newspaper)
Box 375
New York, NY 10009

Reach Out
PO Box 244, Greenfield Station
Dearborn, MI 48126

Real Women
1411 Locust, The Women's
Center
St. Louis, MO 63103

Red Clay Reader 7 (annual)
6366 Sharon Hills Rd.
Charlotte, NC 28210

Red Star [defunct?]
700 East 9
New York, NY 10009

Remember Our Fire; Poetry
by Women
Box 424
San Lorenzo, CA 94580

Restless Eagle
6504 Pardall, The Isla Vista
Women's Center
Goleta, CA 93107

The Revolution, 1868-1872.
See The Source Library
Series

Rising Up Angry
3746 Merchandise Mart
Chicago, IL 60654

Rivolta Femminile
Contact: Maria Pia Cantamessa,
Piazza di Sant' Egidio, 14
Rome, Italy

SIECUS Newsletter

SRRT Task Forces (e.g. Status
of Women in Librarianship)
Newsletters. Contact American Library Association.

Saint Joan's Bulletin
St. Joan's Alliance

San Diego State College. Center
for Women's Studies and Services. See The Second Revolution

San Francisco Bay Area Women
in the Technical Trades [de-
funct?]

San Francisco Women for Peace

San Francisco Women's Liberation [defunct?]
1380 Howard
San Francisco, CA 94103

Scarlet Letter Collective
923 West Dayton
Madison, WI 53703

Second Calling (newspaper).
See Second Coming

Second Coming (newspaper)
Austin Women's Liberation,
Box 8011, U T Station
Austin, TX 78712

Second Revolution
San Diego State College Center
for Women's Studies & Services
San Diego, CA 92115

Second Wave; Magazine of the
New Feminism
Box 303, Kenmore Square Sta-
tion. Female Liberation.
Boston, MA 02215

Sherwood Forest
20372 Birch, c/o Barbara
Connely
Santa Ana, CA 92702

Sheryn's Nifty Newsletter
[defunct?]
1946 El Dorado c/o S. Kalla-
way
Berkeley, CA 94707

The Shrew
12/13 Little Newport, WL
Workshop
London WC 2, England

Sisterhood Songs
WL Front/WL Center, 36
West 22
New York, New York 10010

Sisters
1005 Market, Room 208
San Francisco, CA 94103

Sisters
Box U-6800, Tallahassee WL
Tallahassee, FL 32306

Sisters Unite
4334 Polk, c/o M. Jarin
Houston, TX 77023

Skirting the Capitol (with
Marian Ash)
PO Box 4569
Sacramento, CA 95825

Socialist Woman
182 Pentonville Road
London N. 1, England

Socialist Women
16 Ella Road
West Bridgeford, Nottingham,
England

Society for Humane Abortion,
Inc. Newsletter

Sociologists for Women in
Society Newsletter

Some People's Paper
Women in Publishing

Source Library of the Women's
Movement Series. See Source
Book Press in "The Directory
of Sources" (Part V)

Soviet Woman
Soviet Woman's Committee &
Central Council of Trade
Unions
22 Kuznetsky Most,
Moscow, U. S. S. R.

Spark
6729 North Ashland, c/o Vas-
quez
Chicago, IL 60614

Spazm; Newsletter of the Women's History Library
2325 Oak
Berkeley, CA 94708

Spectre (newspaper)
Box 505
Ann Arbor, MI 48107

The Spokeswoman (newsletter)
Urban Research Corp.

Statues of Liberty
11 West 94, c/o Deborah Biele
New York, NY 10025

Switchbored
Box 694, Stuyvesant Station
New York, NY 10009

Sydney Women's Liberation
 Newsletter
22 Nicholson
Balmain, Australia

Through the Looking Glass
 (newspaper)
Box 1254
Philadelphia, PA 19105

Title VII Report; For Women
 in Business & the Professions
866 3 Ave.
New York, NY 10022

To, For, By, & About Women
1615 Lyndhurst Ave., Charlotte
 Women's Center
Charlotte, NC 28203

Tooth and Nail [defunct?]
Box 4137
Berkeley, CA 94704

Torchon-Brule
11 Rue de l'Eloilez, c/o Michel
 Louie
Toulouse, France

Toronto Women's Liberation

Traffic Jam (Women at AT & T)

Trans-Sister
1307 South Wabash--NCCIJ
Chicago, IL 60605

Transition '70
c/o Women's Center, 36 West 22
New York, NY 10011

Trial
2150 West Halsted
Chicago, IL 60614

True to Life
Box 36003, 80 Butler
Atlanta, GA 30303

Turn of the Screwed (newspaper)
4213 Wycliff Avenue
Dallas, TX 75219

UWA News
University Women's Assoc.

Under the Sign of Pisces
Ohio State University Libraries,
1858 Neil Ave.
Columbus, OH 43201

The Underground Woman
1911 Locust, c/o The Real
 Woman Newspaper
St. Louis, MO 63103

Union Women's Alliance to Gain
 Equality
c/o AFSCME 1695, 2483 A
 Hearst
Berkeley, CA 94709

United Women's Contingent

Untitled Journal #1
Female Liberation

Up from Under
339 Lafayette
New York, NY 10012

Vancouver Women's Conference
 Newsheet
928 West Tennyson Road,
c/o Marie Cardiasmenos
Hayward, CA 94544

Vancouver WL News
Vancouver, British Columbia,
Canada

Vassar Newsletter
718 27 Avenue, The College
 Club
San Francisco, CA 94121

Velvet Fist (newspaper)
188 Adelaide West
Toronto, Ontario, Canada

Velvet Glove
Box 188, Velvet Glove Press
Livermore, CA 94550

Voice for Children
Day Care & Child Develop-
  ment Council of America, Inc.

Voice of the WL [defunct?]
816 East 58, c/o Joreen
Chicago, IL 60637

Voice of Women--La Voix des
  Femmes
1554 Yonge, Room 4
Toronto, Canada

Voice of Women's Liberation
  Movement
816 East 58
Chicago, IL 60637

La Voix des Femmes.   See
  Voice of Women

WEAL Word Watcher

WISE

WL League Newsletter
52 Elgin c/o Peggy Morton
Toronto, Ontario, Canada

Washington Newsletter for
  Women
1730 M Street N.W.,
Suite 510
Washington, DC 20036

Welfare Fighter
1419 H Street N.W.
Washington, DC 20005

Whitebook (journal)
PO Box 4
Atlantic Beach, FL 32233

Whole Woman Catalog
PO Box 1171
Portsmouth, NH 03801

Wildflowers (newspaper)
Box 14308, University of Cali-
  fornia
Santa Barbara, CA 93107

Woman Activist; a National
  Legislative Newsletter
2310 Barbour Road
Falls Church, VA 22043

Woman Physician
1740 Broadway
New York, NY 10019

Woman; the Majority Report
PO Box 347
LaJolla, CA 92037

Woman Worker (newspaper)
PO Box 26605
Los Angeles, CA 90026

Womankind
Chicago WL Union

Womankind (newspaper)
1131 South Brook, #1
Louisville, KY 40203

Womankind
4200 Cass
Detroit, MI 48201

Womanpower; A Monthly Report
  on Fair Employment Practices
  for Women
Betsy Hogan Associates, 221
  Rawson Road
Brookline, MA 02146

Woman's Journal
200 Main, Valley Women's
  Center
Northampton, MA 01060

Woman's Rights Law Reporter
180 University Avenue
Newark, NJ 07102

Woman's World, 1888-1890,
Oscar Wilde, ed. See The
Source Library of the Wo-
men's Movement Series

Woman's World
Box 694, Stuyvesant Station
New York, NY 10009

Women; A Journal of Liberation
3028 Greenmount Avenue
Baltimore, MD 21218

Women and Revolution (news-
paper)
Box 40663
San Francisco, CA 94140

Women; By, For & Of
Box 3488, Ridgeway Station
Stamford, CT 06905

Women in City Government
United [defunct?]

Women in Struggle
Box 324
Winneconne, WI 54986

Women Lawyers' Journal
National Association of Women
Lawyers

Women Now! (newspaper)
85 Rivermead, Wilford Lane--
Nottingham WL Group
West Bridgeford, Nottingham,
England

Women of the Whole World
13 Unter der Linden
108 Berlin, Germany

Women of Viet Nam
Viet Nam Women's Union

Women--Philadelphia Area WL
928 Chestnut, WL Center
Philadelphia, PA 19107

Women Speaking
The Wick, Roundwood Avenue
Hutton Brentwood, Essex,
England

Women Speaking
24 Hatters Lane
Farmington, CT 06032

Women Speaking
KNOW, Inc.

Women Studies Abstracts
PO Box 1
Rush, NY 14543

Women; The Majority Report
PO Box 347
LaJolla, CA 92037

Women: To, By, For and
About
205 East 42
New York, NY 10017

Women Today
1132 National Press Building
Washington, DC 20004

Women West
75 Monterey Road
South Pasadena, CA 91030

Women's Ad-Hoc Abortion
Coalition Newsletter

Women's Caucus for Political
Science

Women's Education Newsletter
University of Wisconsin Exten-
sion, 432 North Lake
Madison, WI 53706

Women's Forum
University of California Wo-
men's Liberation Center
Davis, CA 95616

Women's Liberation Coalition
of Michigan
2230 Witherell, Room 516
Detroit, MI 48201

WL Magazine
The Women's Group, Union of
   South Africa

Women's Liberation Newsletter
67, Glebe Point Road
Glebe, Sydney, Australia 2037

Women's Liberation Newsletter
360 Frank, #105, c/o Valerie
   Angus
Ottawa 4, Ontario, Canada

Women's Liberation Newsletter
[defunct?]
2 Brookline
Cambridge, MA 02138

Women's Liberation Newsletter
3800 McGee, Women's Liberation Union
Kansas City, MO 64132

Women's Liberation Newsletter
PO Box 230, East Side Station
Providence, RI 02906 (or 50
   Olive)

Women's Monthly
GPO Box 1692, Media Women
New York, NY 10001

Women's National Abortion
   Newsletter

Women's Newspaper
12/13 Little Newport
London WC 2, England

Women's Newspaper
37 Warriner Avenue,
c/o Zaft
Springfield, MA 01109

Women's Page (newspaper)
1227 37 Avenue
San Francisco, CA 94122

Women's Press (newspaper)
PO Box 3306
Eugene, OR 97403

Women's Rights Law Reporter
180 University Ave.
Newark, NJ 07102

Women's Struggle; Bulletin of
   the Women's National Coordinating Committee
3 Rona Road
London, N. W. 3, England

Working Mother, the Voice of
   Mothers' & Children's Libera-
   tion
Maternal Information Services

YWCA Magazine
600 Lexington Ave.
New York, NY 10022

Yale Break
Yale University
New Haven, CT 06519

You
261 5 Ave., c/o Diane Silver
New York, NY 10016

SPECIAL ISSUES ON THE WOMAN

     Included are references to some special issues and features from periodicals outside the Woman's Movement about women today or of vital interest to them. The magazines themselves range from scholarly journals to popular titles such as are indexed in "Readers' Guide"; newspapers are occasionally cited. Addresses of the less well known titles are provided; addresses for others can be obtained from "Readers' Guide" or "Ulrichs' International Periodicals Directory."

AAUP BULLETIN. Summer 1970
Harris, A. S. "Second sex in academe" (293-95). And subsequent issues.

AMERICAN LIBRARIES.
Schiller, Anita R. "Aware" column.

ANNALS of the American Academy of Political & Social Science. Various issues: e.g.
    Sept. 1943   "Women in industry"
    Jan. 1968   "Women around the world"
    March 1968   "Sex and the contemporary American scene"

ANNALS of The New York Academy of Sciences. October 30, 1970
Milner, Esther. "The impact of fertility limitation on women's life-career and personality" (v175:781-1065).

ART NEWS. Jan. 1971
"Women's liberation, woman artists and art history; symposium, with editorial comment."

ATLANTIC. March 1970
"Women against men--a special issue" (with discussion in May 1970).

BARNARD ALUMNAE. Spring 1970
"Feminism" issue (v59, no3).

CHICAGO JOURNALISM REVIEW. July 1971
"Women and the media" (v4, no7).

CHILDHOOD EDUCATION. Jan. 1972

Herzog, Elizabeth & Cecelia E. Sudia.   "Families without fathers,"
and other articles in a Symposium (v48, no4).

CHRONICLE OF HIGHER EDUCATION.   v5, no10, Nov 30, 1970 &
others.

COLLEGE ENGLISH.   May 1971
"Women in the colleges; status, teaching, feminist criticism."

COLLOQUY.   July-Aug. 1970   (1505 Race, Philadelphia, PA 19102).

COMMON CAUSE REPORT FROM WASHINGTON (newsletter).
Extra edition v2, no4, March 1972 re Equal Rights Amendment
(2100 M Street, N. W. , Washington, D. C. 20037).

CONCERN.   Special issue during 1971
"Women's liberation in a biblical perspective," 6-session study-
guide by Letty Mandeville Russell.   Also other issues.   (United
Presbyterian Women, 475 Riverside Dr. , New York, NY 10027.)

CONGRESSIONAL RECORD.   (92nd Congress, 2nd session v118,
no21.)   Summary Report of the EEOC on the Bell System entitled
"A unique competence; a study of equal employment opportunity in
the Bell System. "   pE1243-E1272:   "How Ma Bell discriminates,"
Hon. Shirley Chisholm, Thursday, Feb. 17, 1972.   (Obtain from
EEOC, Washington, DC 20506.)

CONTACT MAGAZINE
Has monthly NOW column reaching 100, 000 black readers (Pat
Adams, 1270 6th Avenue, New York, NY 10020).

CONTEMPORARY EDUCATION.   Feb. 1972
"Women in education" issue (118 North 6 St. , Terre Haute, IN
47809).

DAEDALUS.   Spring 1964
"The woman in America" issue.   (Proceedings of the American
Academy of Arts & Sciences).   See Basic Book Collection, no76.)

DUKE LAW JOURNAL.   Aug. 1968
"Sex discrimination in employment; an attempt to interpret Title
VII of the Civil Rights Act of 1964. "

EBONY.   Aug. 1966
"Negro woman; symposium, with Introduction by J. H. Johnson" (v21:
25+).

EDITORIAL RESEARCH REPORTS.   Aug. 5, 1970
Shaffer, Helen B.   "Status of women" v2, no5 (Congressional Quarterly, 1735 K Street, N. W. , Washington, DC 20006).

FORTUNE. Sept. 1946
Roper, Elmo. "Women in America. Fortune Survey, Part II, "
p. 5-6.

GREAT CONTEMPORARY ISSUES. 1972 v4.
"Women; their changing roles." A New York Times Resources
Series.

HARPERS. March 1971
Mailer, Norman. "The prisoner of sex." v242, no1450: 41f.

ILLINOIS LIBRARIES. Sept. 1971.
"The right to read, view and listen" issue. Included here as an
example of thematic issues coming from the profession, often having
relevance to the contemporary Feminist movement.

IMPACT OF SCIENCE ON SOCIETY. Jan.-March 1970
"Women in the age of science and technology" issue. v20, no1;
105p.

INTERNATIONAL LABOUR REVIEW. Articles in various issues,
e.g., "Women's employment and conditions of work in Switzerland, "
Sept. 1967.

INTERNATIONAL SOCIAL SCIENCE JOURNAL. V14, no1, 1962,
pt I "Images of women in society" (UNESCO; Canadian Government
Printing Bureau).

JOURNAL OF SOCIAL ISSUES. April 1966
"The sexual Renaissance in America" v22:2.

LADIES HOME JOURNAL. July 1967:
"California woman; symposium" v84:61-81; June 1964: "Woman:
the fourth dimension, " special issue, v81, no5; Aug. 1970: special
suppl. , "The new feminism; a special section prepared for The
Ladies' Home Journal by the Women's Liberation Movement. "

LEVIATHAN. May 1970.
Issue devoted to Women's Liberation. 50¢, available from New
University Conference, and Leviathan, 968 Valencia, San Francisco,
CA 94110.

LIBERATION. April 1966 and Dec. 1967
Hayden, Casey, et al. , "Sex and caste" (5 Beekman Pl. , New York,
NY 10038).

LIBRARY JOURNAL. Sept. 1, 1971
Cover photo, editorial, several features and bibliography. v96, no15.

LIFE.   3-part-series beginning Aug. 13, 1971
"The woman problem--then and now" v71, no7, pt1.

MBA.   March 1971
A kind of WL issue, v5, no6 (373 6 Avenue, New York, NY 10016).

MC CALLS.   Beginning and throughout 1971.
"Right now; a monthly newsletter for women."

MADEMOISELLE.   Feb. 1970
" Women re women; symposium" v70:159-63.

MANHATTAN TRIBUNE.   See NOW York Woman, in "Movement
Periodicals" section.

MILITANT.   June 25, 1971
Preview of abortion conference and article answering Norman
Mailer's article re Kate Millett.

MONTHLY LABOR REVIEW.   June 1970
"Women at work; a symposium," v93:3-44.   Also other issues, e.g.,
Feb. 1968, "Women of the labor force."   See Women's Bureau Pub-
lications List and "Readers' Guide."

MONTHLY REVIEW.   Sept. 1969
Benston, Margaret.   "The political economy of Women's Liberation."

MOTIVE.   March-April 1969
"On the liberation of women" special issue.   See "A Basic Book
Collection" (Part III), item 46.

BULLETIN of the National Association of Secondary School Principals.
Summer 1970.   Not a special issue, but article by Helen M. Mor-
sink, "Leader behavior of men and women principals," somehow
crept through.   v54:80-7.

NEW LEFT NOTES.
"International Women's Day" special issue available from Radical
Education Project, 5¢.

PERSONNEL POLICIES FORUM.   Dec. 1967
"Sex and Title VII" (Survey no. 82.)

PRESBYTERIAN LIFE.   Feb. 1, 1971
(Witherspoon Building, Philadelphia, PA 19107.)

PSYCHOLOGY TODAY.
Frequent coverage of subject-matter relevant to woman as a being,
e.g., May 1970 "Abortion is no man's business."   CRM, Inc., Del
Mar, CA 92014.

PUBLIC AFFAIRS PAMPHLET. no. 469
Flexner, Eleanor. "Women's rights--unfinished business" 1971
25¢.

PUNCH. Nov. 16, 1971
"Punch Goes Playboy" issue

RADICAL AMERICA. Feb. 1970
Issue devoted to WLM (1237 Spaight, Madison, WI 43703).

RADICAL TEACHER. no. 2.
Florence Howe, editor.

RADICAL THERAPIST. v1, no3, 1970.
Issue devoted to WL (PO Box 1215, Minot, ND 85701).

RADIX. v1, no3, p2/pt I: Faculty, n.d. (Circa July 1971)
"A report on discrimination against women at TC." Teachers
College, Columbia University, Student Senate.

RAMPARTS. Sept. 1971
Griffin, Susan. "Forcible rape is the most frequently committed
violent crime in America today."

REDBOOK. Oct. 1971
Rolfs, Mary Jane. "The sisterhood," a short novel.

REFERENCE SHELF. Jan. 1972
Reische, Diana, ed. "Women and society" v43, no6 (H.W. Wilson
Co., 950 University Avenue, Bronx, NY 10452).

REVOLUTIONARY AGE.
Special issue devoted to American women. v1, no3 (3117 East
Thomas, Seattle, WA 98102, 60¢).

SATURDAY REVIEW. May 18, 1963:
Special issue on women's education. Oct. 16, 1971: cover story:
"Educating women--no more sugar and spice."

SCHOLASTIC TEACHER. Nov. 1971

SCHOOL LIBRARY JOURNAL. Jan. 1971
Issue contains 2 relevant articles re sexism in children's literature.

SCHOOL REVIEW. Feb. 1972
Issue re education and socialization of women. v80, no2.

SYNERGY. December 1969
WL issue. Other issues of relevance as well e.g., no35, Winter
1971 on "The family" (Bay Area Reference Center, Civic Center,
San Francisco, CA 94102).

TEMPO.   Oct. 1, 1970
(National Council of Churches, 475 Riverside Dr., New York, NY 10027).

THIS MAGAZINE IS ABOUT SCHOOLS.   Summer 1969:
Spinks, Sarah. "Sugar 'n spice"; Spring 1969: Limpus, Laurel.
"Liberation of women; sexual repression and the family" (PO Box 876, Terminal A, Toronto 1, Ontario, Canada).

TIME.   Aug. 31, 1970:
Not a WL issue but has cover story, "Kate Millett of Women's Lib" and several articles. v96. March 20, 1972: special issue: "The American woman," v99, no12.

THE TOWER.   Spring 1971
Special issue "Do women belong in the church?" (Union Theological Seminary, 3041 Broadway, New York, NY 10027).

TRANSACTION.   Nov. 1970
Special issue on women (Rutgers University, pub.).

TRENDS.   Oct. 1970
(Witherspoon Building, Philadelphia, PA 19107).

UNITED NATIONS MONTHLY CHRONICLE.   March 1968
Jiagge, Annie R.   "Introduction to the Declaration on Elimination of Discrimination Against Women."

VALPARAISO LAW REVIEW.   v5, no2, 1971
Symposium issue: "Women and the Law."

VOCATIONS FOR SOCIAL CHANGE.
(PO Box 13, Canyon, CA 94516.)

VOGUE.   June 1970:
"The life and looks of the American woman"; May 1967: "American woman 1967," v149:159-67.

WILSON LIBRARY BULLETIN.   Oct. 1971.
"Sex and the single child."

WIN MAGAZINE.   Jan. 1, 1970
Special issue (War Resister's League, New York, N.Y.).

YWCA MAGAZINE.   Feb. 1972
Issue devoted to women and justice (40¢, Communications, Room 605, National Board, YWCA, 600 Lexington Avenue, New York, NY 10022).

AUDIO-VISUAL RESOURCES*

This section is intended to guide in locating and utilizing all relevant media in such other types of resources as motion pictures, tapes, kinescopes, filmstrips, recordings, posters and other graphics. Audiovisual media are listed alphabetically by title, with an indication of the medium, followed (when known) by the producer, date of production, length, and distributor(s) if different from the producer, and cost of rental and/or purchase. In the case of originally-commercial productions, e.g., "Adam's Rib," rental fees usually vary according to size/type audience. All motion pictures are 16mm black-and-white sound unless otherwise stated.

The source of information on motion pictures and filmstrips wherever possible has been the Library of Congress because its information is generally more accurate and complete, and its annotations are descriptive rather than evaluative; they can be identified by inclusion of the unique LC catalog-card-number which appears after the data and before the annotation. In other cases, information has been obtained from the distributor's catalog; occasionally, comments by the author will appear at the conclusion of an entry.

Standard abbreviations are used: BW = black and white, C = color, fr = frames, mm = millimeters, min = minutes, R = rent, S = sale, etc. Fuller information regarding the distributors is provided in Part V, "Directory of Sources." Inclusion here does not necessarily imply recommendation, especially of motion pictures. "Murder in the Family," for example, opposes abortion, while "Psychological Differences Between the Sexes" is a "loaded" film used in "family-life" courses. They might, however, be utilized in consciousness-raising and group discussions. Some titles on children's and young people's levels have been included.

Abortion (mo pic)
American Documentary 30min R$30 S$200
Produced by a women's collective in Boston. 1971.

Abortion (tapes)
James Clapp.

Abortion and the law (mo pic)
CBS News 1965 54min
Available from: Carousel; American Doc R$40 S$250
FiA66-709: Televised on CBS TV documentary show, CBS Reports."
Producer/writer David Low, narrator Walter Cronkite.
A documentary which focuses on legal, moral, social and psychological aspects of abortion in the U.S. Presents clergymen, lawyers

See p. 333 for late additions to this list.

and physicians who hold diametrically opposed views and tells of
specific cases of abortion.   Includes a summary of the problems,
attitudes and legal aspects in England, Sweden, Poland, Chile,
Mexico and Japan.

Abortion: London's dilemma   (mo pic)
NBC News (30 Rockefeller Plaza, New York, NY 10020)   circa
1970   22min   C
74-709031:   Televised as part of the NBC "First Tuesday" series.
Producer Eliot Frankel.
Portrays the big business aspects of abortion in London, which is
rapidly becoming the world's abortion capital, to present the essential dilemma of abortion as a social practice.

Abortion without cervical dilation   (mo pic)
Lalor Foundation   July 1971   C   By Alan J. Margolis, M. D. and
Sadja Goldsmith, M. D. of University of California: San Francisco
Medical Center.   For professional use only.   Without cost.
Shows methods and results of latest techniques for very early
termination on an outpatient basis utilizing 4mm and 6mm curettes.

Adam's rib   (mo pic)
MGM   1949   101min
Available from: Films Inc   R
Spencer Tracy, Katharine Hepburn, Judy Holliday, Tom Ewell.
Director George Cukor.   Original play and screenplay by Ruth
Gordon and Garson Kanan.
The courtroom combat of a female lawyer and her husband, the
assistant DA, intrudes into their domestic life when he prosecutes
and she defends a woman who has shot her two-timing husband.
An adult comedy treatment of the "battle of the sexes."

Advocates; on abortion at will in the first twelve weeks   (mo pic)
Public Broadcast Lab.   ETS   57min
Available from: Indiana University   R$12.25   S$265.   CS2128
Advocates and opponents of legalized abortion argue whether or not
a woman has the right of self-determination in having her own
pregnancy terminated during the first three months.   One view
asserts that ready accessibility to abortion would reduce the number of unwanted children.   Studies cited show that these children
run a greater risk of being socially maladjusted or mentally ill.
The opposing side believes that the embryo is a human being, even
though it is not able to sustain life independently and that women
often only "think" they want an abortion.   It is emphasized that
most abortions are sought by married women.

"Ain't I A Woman?" See "And God Created Woman..."

All kinds of babies   (mo pic)
Carousel   1968   9min   C   S$125
For younger children; re family relationships

All my babies (mo pic)
Medical AV Institute of the Association of American Medical Colleges
1953   55min
Available from: Center for Mass Communication of Columbia University Press   S$330   R 1 day=10%S   Spanish-language version
available.   Restricted to use by professional audiences and cinema
courses.
Director George C. Stoney
Shows simply and clearly the methods a midwife should follow from
the time she takes a case until the baby is taken to its first Well
Baby Clinic.   Photographed in Georgia and features a certified midwife, her patients and the doctors and nurses who supervise the
local midwife training program.   (Restriction is unfortunate as this
is a film about women, with many insights possibly unrecognized by
the producer-distributor.)

Amazon   "Women Unite and Resist"   (poster)
The Feminists   23 x 29" $2.

An American tragedy (mo pic)
Universal/16   87min   R$85   #23831
Director Josef Von Sternberg.   Sylvia Sidney, Frances Dee.
Theodore Dreiser's novel of a young man reared in poverty who
tries to get rid of his factory-girl sweetheart when he meets a
beautiful and wealthy girl.   See also "A place in the sun."

The American woman   (FS)
Coronet 195-?   21fr   35min
Released by Society for Visual Education (1345 Diversey Parkway,
Chicago, IL 60614)
FiA68-5252
Explains that the American woman, with her dignity, strength and
faith in life, is the symbol in which American traditions, progress
and vitality are rooted.

The American woman in the twentieth century   (mo pic)
Wolper   1964   58min
Released by United Artists TV; also available from Films Inc.
S$250
FiA64-650.
Producer Mel Stuart.   Narrator Richard Basehart
Surveys the changing role of the American woman in the 20th cen-
tury from Gibson girl, through flapper, through Rosie the riveter to
the woman of the 60's.   Explains how the American woman has both
shaped and reflected the sexual and social mores of our time.   See
also "Social change and the American woman."

"And God Created Woman..."   (poster)   (cards/note-paper)
Greyfalcon House.   Add 50¢ for postage-handling:

design/title	poster	cards/note-paper
"And God created woman..." (Michelangelo)	$2 ea or 3/$5 BW 20 x 28"	small or large quantities, with
"Ain't I A Woman? (Sojourner Truth)	$3 ea or 3/$7.50 2-color 23 x 34"	envelopes; cream or white

Angela: like it is (mo pic)
WABC-TV 1970 60min
American Documentary S$250 R$65
Angela Davis speaks from the New York Women's House of Detention
shortly after her arrest in December 1970 on charges of conspiracy
to commit murder, in a conversation taped with her lawyer, Margaret Burnham; televised panel-discussion follows, includes Burnham
and Charlene Mitchell, a leader of the Angela Davis Defense Committee and former presidential candidate for the Communist Party.

The artillery women of LonVan (mo pic)
American Documentary 15 min S$100 R$25 English soundtrack.
Socialist women organize to defend their homeland against U.S. air-
attack.

L'Avventura (mo pic)
Janus 16mm R BW Italy 1960 Subtitled.
Director, scenario and dialogue Michelangelo Antonioni.
Penelope Huston in "The contemporary cinema": The recurring
themes of the impermanence of love, the difficulty of communica-
tion, the ease of betrayal of one's self or someone else preoccupy
Antonioni...."

Beginning (mo pic) see "Sex education for young children" Series.

Bernadette Devlin (mo pic)
American Documentary In production August 1971
The outspoken and militant member of the British Parliament speaks
on the movement for self-determination of Ireland.

Betta splendens (A love story) (mo pic)
Grove Press film division
19min C R$25 S$175 #258
Director John Steinberg
Mating ritual of Siamese Fighting Fish--sensual and subtle--2 weeks'
process: mating to family break-up. No words, just piano.

Beyond conception (mo pic)
Newenhouse
35min C S$275
Producer George C. Denniston, M.D. with Martha K. Willing.

Birth (mo pic)
1968 45min BW Verite Productions
Available from: Film-makers Library
R$7.25 from University of Michigan.
Birth of the first child of a young artist and his wife. Couple is
followed through natural childbirth classes and last prenatal examination; labor and delivery sequence emphasizes husband's role as
coach; actual delivery of child; how the birth of a baby fits into the
total life experience of the parents. (Or, pregnant wife supporting
husband takes off 6 months ... knitting ... selecting a boy's name

... "relax" yells husband "helping" her.)   See also " Sex education
for young children" Series.

Birth control   (mo pic)
Indiana University   60min   BW   CS-1699   S$200   R$12 NET
This film provides a comprehensive look at the legal, medical,
moral, and social aspects of the birth control issue in the U.S.
Experienced reporters are shown as they conduct interviews with
people who use the services of birth control clinics, with administrators of private clinics, with federal and state officials, and with
public health administrators.   The interviews cover such topics as
the reasons for the success of these clinics in some places and
not in others, the legislative hurdles that continue to plague state
governments and their agencies, the opposition to using public funds
to control population, and some of the unresolved problems facing
over-populated cities.

Birth of the baby   (mo pic)
Indiana University   29min   BW   hs-642   S$125   R$6.75   WQED
Discusses the process of birth from the onset of labor pains,
through the stages of labor, to the actual birth itself.   Follows an
expectant mother from her admittance to the hospital until the delivery of her baby.   A film from The Months Before Birth Series.
Other titles:
    Physiology of reproduction   Nutrition and dental care in preg-
    Beginning of pregnancy   nancy
    First visit to the doctor   Middle months of pregnancy
    Weeks after birth   Birth of the baby
                          Last months of pregnancy

Birthday--through the eyes of the mother   (mo pic)
Made and released by Lawren Productions   1970   30min   C   With
teacher's guide.   Producer-director Lawrence A. Williams
77-708643
Pictures various aspects involved in the birth of a baby from the
time the mother is admitted to the hospital until the baby is given
to the mother.   Discusses labor, the use of epidural anesthesia and
the delivery, including views of the birth of the baby as seen by the
mother in the delivery room mirror.

Black girl   (mo pic)
New Yorker Films   1965   60min   R
Producer-director Ousmane Sembene had been a writer and Mar-
seilles dockworker, is a native of Senegal.   First black African
feature-length film tells the story of a young girl from Dakar who
is hoodwinked into working as a domestic for a French middle-class
family in Antibes.   Once in France, where she is virtually im-
prisoned as a housemaid, she despairs and commits suicide.

Breakdown   (mo pic)
Produced for the Mental Health authorities of the provinces of
Canada by the National Film Board of Canada   40min
McGraw   S$270

The story of a young woman's schizophrenic breakdown, and of her recovery in a modern mental hospital. Inherent is an appeal for greater public understanding of mental illness and for the removal of the stigma that now surrounds it.

British women's film (mo pic)
Newsreel 6min R$10
No other information available.

BUTTONS. Available from such sources as:
The Feminists
New Feminist Bookstore
New Yorkers for Abortion Law Repeal
Society for Individual Rights
University Women's Association
Zero Population Growth
Inquire also at local women's center, NOW chapter office, etc.

CALENDARS and ALMANACS. Available from such sources as:
Feminist Book Mart
Minot Woman's Collective
Women's Heritage Series
Inquire also at local women's center, NOW chapter office, etc.

Changes in sex behavior; where are we headed? (mo pic)
Focus education C 12min S$130
Participants: Mary S. Calderone, M.D., SIECUS; Lester A. Kirkendall, Oregon State University; Dr. John Money, Johns Hopkins University; Ira Reiss, Iowa University; Dr. Morton Schillinger, Lincoln Institute for Psychotherapy, New York.
Employs question-and-answer format to present leading social scientists' conclusions about past, present and future patterns of sexual behavior and attitudes.

Changing role of women in the Soviet Union (tape)
American Documentary $4/reel service charge

Chicago Women's Liberation Rock Band
PO Box 1574, Evanston, IL 62204. Tape of the band $3. Film made but not yet edited.

Childbirth; a family experience (mo pic)
Association for Childhood Education 195-? 22min C
For use with expectant parents; shows actual labor and delivery. (Rather awkward, home-made-type film.)

Childcare--people's liberation (mo pic)
Newsreel 1971? 20min R$20 NR56
From San Francisco Newsreel catalog: Reviews how mothers and children in this society tie each other down; shows through examples, how community-run childcare centers are a step toward liberation. Also presents special problems of working mothers, and the pitfalls of corporate childcare.

La chinoise (mo pic)
New Yorker Films (France) 1967 95min C
Jean Luc Godard director.
Perceived by some critics as a film criticizing the mistakes of five
young people engaged in the process of becoming revolutionaries.

Chisholm, Shirley. See "Shirley Chisholm."

Choice: Challenge for modern woman (kinescopes)
Originally filmed in 1965 to be shown on local educational station
by UCLA Extension. Discussion-syllabus and other materials also
prepared then are no longer available. Series purchased for distri-
bution outside California by NET, which produced a new Syllabus.
12 films 30min each Daily R$10 each S$150
Explores the question of what should be the place of women in
mid-20th-century America. 1. And who are you? (Hubert S. Coffey,
Marya Mannes). 2. What is a woman? (Keith Berwick, Margaret
Mead). 3. The principle that counts (Ethel Alpenfels, Herbert
Fingarette, Joan Lasko). 4. Marriage or mirage? (Alexander C.
Rosen, Gertrude Sackheim). 5. The family affair (Joan Lasko,
Edgar V. Winans). 6. The unlonely woman (Richard Farson, Eve
Merriam). 7. Where does all the money go? (Frances Feldman,
Bruce McKim). 8. Wages of work (Mary Keyserling). 9. The
time of your life (Eva Schindler, Paul Sheats Rainman). 10. Who
wants freedom? (Elisabeth Mann Borgese, Richard Lichtman). 11.
Is personal growth selfish? (Sr. Mary Corita, Anne Steinmann).
12. What is the shape of tomorrow? (Jeanne Noble, Rabbi Alfred
Gottschalk). Series moderator, Rosalind K. Loring. National
Educational Television, 10 Columbus Circle, New York, NY 10019.

Consenting adults; a study of homosexuality (mo pic)
BBC-TV 40min Time-Life R$30 S$300
Homosexuality exists all over the world and cannot be ignored.
This film presents the subject in a tasteful, direct manner, giving
the viewer intelligent insights into both the homosexual man and
woman. It provides a sound basis for understanding and discussion.
Many questions are answered through interviews with practicing
homosexuals. Wide-ranging points of view are offered.

Courtship and marriage (mo pic)
National Film Board of Canada 1962 60min (2 parts, 30min each)
McGraw S$250
Contemporary customs of Sicilian, Iranian, Canadian and Indian
couples.

Cycles of life. See "Starting tomorrow."

Dare to be different (FS & Rec.)
Guidance Associates 2 parts E100-956 $40 Cassette or recording
Explores pressures to conform in our society and styles of non-
conformity; suggests criteria for drawing the line between destructive and constructive reactions to group and social norms. American Film Festival Honors.

Davis, Angela.   See "Angela; like it is."

A day of plane hunting (mo pic)
Newsreel 1971?   20min   R$20   #126
The film portrays the crucial role that women play in the defense,
education and economic development of Vietnam.

Devlin, Bernadette.   See "Bernadette Devlin."

Diary of a mad housewife (mo pic)
Universal/16   1970   90min   C   R$
From the c1967 novel by Sue Kaufman.   Richard Benjamin, Carrie
Snodgrass.   Producer-director Frank Perry.
Judith Crist: "The Perrys have captured a life of quiet desperation
so many young New Yorkers live in the rat race of upward mobility."
(Read the book first!)

The divorce dilemma (mo pic)
CBS 1966   60min
Fi68:123   Telecast on the CBS-TV documentary "CBS Reports."
Producers Burton Benjamin, Isaac Kleinerman; writer Warren
Wallace; commentators Walter Kronkite, Warren Wallace; pho-
tographers William Wagner, Robert J. Clemens; film editors Tom
Spain, Maurice Murad.
Describes personal and legal difficulties surrounding divorce pro-
cedures in the U.S.   Discusses neglect in dealing with basic mar-
riage difficulties and in providing for the interests of the children.
Analyzes two beneficial programs which exist in Milwaukee and
Detroit.   (Nary a female policy-maker involved.)

Dixon, Marlene.   See "Marlene Dixon on Women's Liberation."

Duncan, Isadora.   See "Loves of Isadora."

Egg and sperm (mo pic)
Sterling 1968   10min   C
University of Michigan   R$4
In successive sequences, younger students see that when the male
sperm fertilizes the female egg, new life begins.   Process in the
sea gull, chicken, and house cat.   Comparison of litter-bearing
animals with human mother.

Eleanor Roosevelt (mo pic)
NBC   30min   filmed in 1960
Films Inc S$150 33-006-; Univ. of Calif. Extension Media Center.
A warm and human woman, who was a part of so many important
events of this century, comes alive in this interview with William
Atwood.   She comments candidly on what in her opinion were the
most important of her husband's accomplishments, and some of his
mistakes.

Eleanor Roosevelt story (mo pic)
CCM 90min R$35 7-year lease $750 #9-4000-028-8
Producer Sidney Glazier; director Richard Kaplan; writer Archibald
MacLeish; narrators MacLeish, Eric Sevareid, Frances Cole.
Loving tribute to a great lady who became a national and interna-
tional institution. Academy Award for Best Documentary Feature.

Electra Rewired (radio program)
WBAI-FM 99.5 New York City Monday midnight to around dawn.
A combination of studio discussion, telephone calls, tapes and
music.

Equalitarianism and male dominance; a Catholic-Protestant dialogue
on changing religious concepts (tape)
Perennial $10
Discussion between David R. Mace, Ph.D., and the Rev. George
Hagmaier, a Paulist priest, concerning the situation of male domi-
nance in Western tradition as it is reinforced by Christian culture.

Equality-for-Women (postcards)
Local NOW chapters. (Usually printed with the equality-for-women
symbol in 6 colors standard size 10¢ each 12/$1
Use for quick notes, to post public announcements, place cards,
etc.

Esther (mo pic)
Fishtail Sky Films 1968 3min C Made by Robert Johnson
Available from Pyramid Films (PO Box 1048, Santa Monica, CA
90406) 74-709827: reveals the character and independence of a
black woman through a photographic study which captures her individual beauty.

EXHIBITIONS
c/o Biblioteket Dronningensgade 14, 1420 Copenhagen K, Denmark.
Public exhibition of WL literature and graphics from all over the
world.

The eye of the beholder (mo pic)
Stuart Reynolds 25min C 1 week:R$25 BW, $400C per week;
S$250 BW (English only) $300 C English, Spanish, French.
Discussion leader's guide by Gilbert Brighouse, Prof. of Psychology,
Occidental College. The basics of perception.

A fable (mo pic)
Audio Brandon/Ideal (Bulgaria) 7min R$7.50 Director Radka
Buchvarova
A cartoon about women's liberation. In this short film, the war
between men and women is expressed as a parable about a rooster
who expects everyone to do his bidding and a tiny hen who refuses
to be his servant. This is a charming film with an especially up-
to-date theme.

Families   (mo pic)
E C Brown Trust   Made by Wexler Film Productions   1970   10min
C
Available from Churchill, Newenhouse, Perennial With guide
78-70930:   Producer-director Sy Wexler; basic text Curtis E. Avery;
script Carol Ledner; animation Maggie Bowen.
An animated film depicts the interdependence of all human beings,
touches on heredity, introduces and stresses sociological concepts
of the extended family.   Primary grades.

Family planning   (mo pic)
The Population Council in cooperation with Walt Disney Productions
(800 Sonora Avenue, Glendale, CA 91201)   1967   10min   C
An elementary film for adults.

Farewell to Birdie McKeever   (mo pics)
Stuart Reynolds   25min   Discussion-leader's guide   R$25 minimum
S$195
Magnetic half-stripe sound track for redubbing in another language,
i. e., other than English, can be added for $30. per print + $15.
for English script.
... a light and entertaining story about a receptionist and her employers.   Underneath the humor, however, is a provocative situation which raises significant questions about employer-employee relationships and the whole area of understanding (and misunderstanding)
between people.   (Be sure to get the Discussion-leader's guide!)

Felicia   (mo pic)
Stuart Roe   1965   13min   BW; Univ. of Calif. Extension Media.
A black high school student in Watts--her reflections, hopes, aims.

The female rebellion   (mo pic)
Hearst Metronome News (4 West 58, New York, NY 10019)   1963
53min
Fi67-903:   telecast on the documentary program "Perspective on
greatness"
Producer-director Robert Foster, writer John O'Toole, narrator
Luis Van Rooten, hostess Joan Fontaine.
Discusses the attempts of American women to rebel against their
traditional feminine role in a masculine dominated society.   Includes
scenes of suffragettes during wartime.   Points out the influence of
motion pictures in determining the sexual role of women.

Fertilization and birth   (mo pic)
E C Brown Trust   1967   10min   C
Available from: Churchill, Newenhouse, Perennial S$135
Designed for lower and upper primary grades, to be used after
"Human and animal beginnings" has been shown and discussed.   In-
cludes scenes of birth of animals in live action and of human beings
in animation.

Flora   (mo pic)
New Line Cinema   6min   16/35mm   R$10   S$50

Director Benjamin Hayeem
Thin, untidy girl tries to arrange her one-room apartment and dress
for a date; her efforts to stuff her bureau drawers and tease her
hair are frenetic and sloppy ... her date merely arrives to undress
her anyway. Edinburgh Film Festival.

Focus on children (mo pic)
National Association for Nursery Education (now the National Association for the Education of Young Children) 1961 16min Made by
Film Production Unit of Iowa State University
FiA63-326: shows that a child's learning to satisfy his curiosity,
to use his body, to apply himself, to cope with his own feeling and
emotions, and to get along with other people is basic learning,
wherever it happens. Explains that parents assume the chief responsibility for their children, but that this responsibility may be
shared by thoughtful communities through the establishment of nursery education programs.

Four families (mo pic)
National Film Board of Canada 1960 90min
Contemporary/McGraw S$145
Different modes of mothering in different cultures.

Freedom from pregnancy (mo pic)
Allend'or Productions 11min C S$125 Also available in 8mm or
Super 8. In English and/or Spanish.
International Planned Parenthood Federation Library Bulletin v. 7:
designed to explain to men and women in straightforward, simple
manner, facts and procedures of two modern, medically-approved
methods of contraception--tubal ligation and vasectomy.
Use "Planned families" first

Fuck housework (poster)
Shirley Boccaccio, 468 Belvedere, San Francisco, CA 94117.
17 x 22" BW Parchment $2 (wholesale $12/dz.) Has broken
all San Francisco records. Original copyrighted poster by Virtue
Hathaway.

Full circle see "Sex education for young children" series

The future of the family (FS and Record)
Guidance Associates 1971 C 2 parts E-101-566 S$35 Recording
or cassette available. Study guide.
Historical survey of family structure; analyzes traditional concept of
the immediate family as an economic, cultural entity; examines isolated, highly-mobile family units of contemporary American society
and influences on these units--employment conditions, society's emphasis on "independence" from parents, recent birth control developments.

The game (mo pic)
National Film Board of Canada 1967 28min

McGraw; University of Michigan R$5.50 Teacher's guide
FiA67-277: problems of relationship; high school student provoked
by his friends to prove his claimed ability as a seducer, seeks to
demonstrate his masculinity by winning over a girl in his class.
He succeeds, feels guilty because he has come to like her, and
drops her. (Especially good for relationships of people to people,
boys to boys, boys to girls.)

Gaslight (mo pic)
MGM 114min
Films Inc R
Charles Boyer, Ingrid Bergman, Joseph Cotton. Film based on
Broadway play, "Angel Street."

Gay Liberation (poster)
Times Change Press c1970 17 x 22" TCP-7 $1 Designed by
Su Negrin using a photograph by Peter Hujar and mandala by Suz-
anne BeVier. Red-orange and purple on soft gold.

Girl to women (mo pic)
Churchill 1962 16min C S$210
For girls, dealing with human growth and development; describes
male and female reproductive systems. Produced under medical
and psychiatric supervision. Animation used. (Companion film is
"Boy to man")

God bless God--she needs it (musical play)
Play and lyrics by Patricia Horan; score by Victoria Vidal. Being
produced by T.C.B. Productions (December 1971). The play's controlling theme is women's liberation; for information about shares in
the production, backers' auditions, etc., contact the producers.

Goodall, Jane See "Miss Goodall and the Wild Chimpanzees."

A graphic notebook on feminism (graphics)
Times Change Press c1970 64p SBN 87810-004-0 $1.25 By
Su Negrin

The group (mo Pic)
United Artists/16 1966 150min C R
Director Sidney Lumet, producers Sidney Buchman and Charles K.
Feldman; screenplay by Buchman based on Mary McCarthy's novel;
photographer Boris Kaufman.

Growing into womanhood/manhood; a middle school approach, rev.
(FS & Rec.)
Guidance Associates 1971 C S$40 2 parts G101 939 With cas-
sette or recording.
A program combining study of male and female reproductive systems.

Growing up female (mo pic)
Newsreel (not available from New York Newsreel) 1971 60min R$70
NR#147; American Documentary R$70, S$375

... examines the social forces that shape women's self-conception
as they grow up. "I was much moved by this film and its genuine
picture of ordinary American women" (Elizabeth Hardwich in New
York Review of Books). "I wish every high school kid in America
could see this film" (Susan Sontag).

Henry 9 to 5 (mo pic)
Audio Brandon/Ideal 1970 (Great Britain) 8min R$12.50 Di-
rector Bob Godfrey's cartoon was a hit at the 1970 New York Film
Festival. This is hilarious fun, an extremely imaginative adult
short about a mild-mannered businessman who relieves the boredom
of his work day by thinking about sex. Godfrey provides glimpses
into his hero's many unusual sexual fantasies, which become especially humorous when accompanied by the man's matter-of-fact
narration. As with other cartoons by this unpredictable artist,
there is an unforgettable surprise ending. A perfect short for almost any program but leave the children home!

Her name was Ellie; his name was Lyle (mo pic)
Louis de Rochemont 1965 29min S$75
Gives symptoms of VD.

Herstory (mo pic)
Newsreel 1971 9min C R$10 NR#61
San Francisco Women's Street Theatre presents a short history of
women's struggles from prehistory to the present.

The herstory of the Women's movement (slide/FS)
Produced by Tony Carabillo (1126 Hipoint Street, Los Angeles,
CA 90035) 1972
S$60 R also
From Mary Wollstonecraft to NOW.

"Hey, Doc" (mo pic)
WCAU-TV 1971 26 min C
Carousel S$300
A day in the life of Ms. E.D. Allen, M.D. and Negro.

The homosexuals (mo pic)
CBS-TV 1967 45min
Available from: American Documentary; Perennial; Carousel
S$250. R$25
Psychological and sociological aspects of homosexuality.

How life begins (mo pic)
ABC News 1968 46min C
Available from McGraw/Contemporary S$530

Human and animal beginnings (mo pic)
E C Brown Trust 1966 13min C
Available from: Churchill, Newenhouse, Perennial. S$175.
For primary grades. Photography of animals lays foundation for

more advanced study of human biology, reproduction and sexuality.
Gold Plaque for best children's film, 1967 International Film Festival, Venice.

Human growth, 2nd ed. (mo pic)
E C Brown Trust 1962 20min C
Available from: Churchill, Newenhouse, Perennial. S$225.
Possibly the best known of Brown Trust Foundation's films. Illus-
trates growth of human beings as well as their biological beginnings.

Ida Brayman (poster)
Times Change Press c1970 17 x 22" TCP-8 $1 Rose on beige.
A memorial, apparently by her co-workers, to the 17-year-old Ida,
who was killed in February 1913 during the great garment workers'
struggle in Rochester, New York.

Illegal abortion (mo pic)
National Film Board of Canada 1968 (made in 1966) 25min
McGraw
72-700877: producer Guy Glover, script and direction by Robin
Spry, photographer Robert Nichol, editor Roy Ayton.
Dramatizes the social and emotional problems of a couple faced
with an unwanted pregnancy; follows them as they seek a way to
terminate it, and includes the backroom scene where the abortion
finally takes place.

Importance of mother (mo pic)
Animal Secrets, Inc. 1968 24min C
Distributed by Graphic Curriculum S$300
For children and adults; describes research that has been done
with monkeys exploring mother-child relationships.

In the company of men (mo pic)
William Greaves (254 West 54, New York, NY 10019) 1971?
52min S$150
Sensitivity training and role-playing utilized to enhance communication between black and white men. (Sisterhood is possible.)

Inside LADIES' HOME JOURNAL (mo pic)
American Documentary 15min R$20 S$150
Representatives of WL occupy the offices of The LHJ to confront
the male editor-in-chief about the degrading images and exploitation
of women ... "We demand an end to the basic orientation of the
Journal toward the concept of "children, kitchen and church," and a
re-orientation around the concept that both sexes are equally responsible for their own humanity."

The invader (mo pic)
Center for Mass Communication of Columbia University Press
29min S$174 Teacher's guide
... introduction to the subject of venereal disease for young people
and adults ... man's efforts since the 15th century to cope with

syphillis. The medical advances, changes in public attitude ...
woodcuts, engravings, paintings and drawings by such artists as
Durer, Breughel, Hogarth and Daumier; later years reconstructed
with photographs of Ehrlich, Hata, etc.; motion pictures of Fleming
and Mahoney. Direction by George C. Stoney. Award-winner.

Is the American woman losing her femininity? (mo pic)
CBS News 1959 60min
Fi68-323 Telecast in the CBS-TV special program "Woman!"
Producer-writer James Fleming, photography by Julian Townsend
and Richard Miller, director Al de Caprio, narrator Esther Williams, editor Dena Burner.
Discusses the confusion and unrest of the modern world. Presents
differing opinions of men and women, including a discussion by
anthropologist Margaret Mead, who talks to and answers the questions of college students. (Now old.)

It's all the same (play)
Available from Caren Cronk (21250 Almar Drive, Shaker Heights,
OH 44122) $25-35. In 1970 a small group in Cleveland performed
their own guerilla theatre-type production involving short statements
by different "types" of women (teenager, housewife, secretary, etc.)
about what they have to put up with, their goals, what they expected
and what they got.

Jane Eyre (mo pic)
20th C Fox 96min
Films Inc R
Novel by Charlotte Bronte. Orson Welles, Joan Fontaine, Margaret
O'Brien, Peggy Ann Garner, Agnes Moorehead.

Janie's Jane (mo pic)
Newsreel 1971? 40min
A poor white sister who married at 15, had 5 children, and then
threw her husband out after 12 years, raps about her family, her
past, and the changes she's been going through now that she's on
her own.

Jeanette Rankin Brigade (mo pic)
Newsreel 8min R$10 #4
10,000 women led an orderly march against the War in Washington
in 1968. It left its more politically-active members frustrated.
Their discovery reflects the opinions of more and more Americans
--that such actions are politically ineffective.

Jobs and gender (FS & Recs.)
Guidance Associates C 2 FS's and 2 12" LP recordings = $35;
2 FS's and 2 cassettes = $30.
Program challenging stereotypes about "woman's work" and "man's
work" by introducing students to a female carpenter, a female newspaper reporter, a male nurse, and two male teachers; indicates
trend is toward more realistic job classification based on individual
interest and ability.

Jobs for women; where are you going, Virginia? (mo pic)
Vision Associates   circa 1969   11min   C
McGraw   Teacher's guide
70-702727:   a vocational guidance film for junior and senior high
school students, using dramatized situations in discussing jobs for
women.   (McGraw/Vision also have "Jobs for men; where am I
going?"   It is in the "World of work series.")

Johnny Belinda (mo pic)
Warner Brothers - UAA   103min
Films Inc   R
Jane Wyman, Lew Ayres, Agnes Moorehead, Jan Sterling.   Delicate
and intelligent story of a deaf-mute girl.   Jean Negulesco director.

Johnson, Virginia E.   see "Masters and Johnson explore six myths
about sex"

Juliet of the spirits (mo pic)
Audio Brandon/Ideal   1965   (Italy)   137min   R
Federico Fellini director.   Italian dialog with English subtitles.
Has been called "the female '8 1/2'."   It seems almost that Fellini,
having explored his own subconscious, decided to do the same for
his wife, Giulietta Masina.   JULIET is about a more universal
problem: the role of a woman in marriage.

KMPX Special on Women's Liberation (tape)
American Documentary $4/reel service charge.   May be dupli-
cated.

KSAN Special on Women's Liberation (tape)
American Documentary $4/reel service charge.   May be dupli-
cated.

Kathy (mo pic)
Charles Cahill & Associates   1969   19min   C
Aims Association   S$240
Kathy discovers she has gonorrhea.

Kisses for my president (mo pic)
Ideal   113min   R$30
Fred MacMurray, Polly Bergen, Arlene Dahl, Eli Wallach
Non-partisan, non-political and non-serious, this good-natured
comedy explores the possibilities of what COULD happen were a
glamorous and brainy woman elected President of the U.S. and her
business tycoon husband became the first male "First Lady" in
American history!   There are gags galore ... laugh-filled entertainment for the whole family.   (Comedy!)

The knack ... and how to get it.   (mo pic)
United Artists/16   1965   84min
Richard Lester director, Oscar Lewenstein producer, Charles Wood
screenplay; based on the play by Ann Jellicoe.   Rita Tushingham.

Best picture at 1965 Cannes Film Festival.
The fine art of "la seduction," as the French put it, or "the knack,"
as the British prefer it.

The L-shaped room (mo pic)
Columbia Cinematheque 124min R
Director Bryan Forbes also write, James Woolf and Richard Atten-
borough co-produced. Leslie Caron as a lonely, frightened woman
who finds romance while awaiting the birth of a baby conceived in
a loveless weekend affair. Best-actress-of-the-year, British Academy.

La chinoise. See Chinoise.

L'avventura. See Avventura.

LABELS. See STICKERS and LABELS

Look out girlie, Women's Liberation's gonna get your Mama (Film
& Slide)
Nancy Hancock, 5084 McKean Avenue, Philadelphia, PA 19144
No other information available.

The lottery (mo pic)
Encyclopaedia Britannica circa 1971 18min C S$265.
Shirley Jackson's story of suspense and terror in a small American
town, filmed as a statement about society and the individual.

Lovemaking (mo pic)
Grove 1968 40min C Silent R$60 By Stan Brakhage.
An American Karma Sutra--Love's answer to filmic pornography.
Four visions of sexual loving which exist in an aesthetic balance of
feeling the wry opposite of the striptease as usually encountered in
both Hollywood movies and the foreign so-called "Art Film."

Loves of Isadora (mo pic)
Universal/16 131min C R Production #26960
Vanessa Redgrave, Jason Robards. 12-year old Isadora Duncan
bows to a bedroom shrine, pledging herself to an eternal pursuit
of art and truth. To seal the act, she piously burns her parents' wedding certificate. Thus begins the passionate biography of
a free spirit who conquered the turn-of-the-century art world by
defying society and its conventions.

Loving (FS Program)
Media Plus 1971 C 4 FS's + 4 LP recordings + teacher's
guide = $60; with cassettes instead of recordings = $68. Each
FS 50+ frames; running time 10-15 min each. Sound Part 1
Nature; part 2 Animals; part 3 Loving families; part 4 Love. Ele-
mentary grades.
About Kenny. Musical score includes rarely-heard Javanese instru-
ment, the gamelan.

Lucy Stone   (poster)
Times Change Press   c1970   17 x 22"   TCP-2 $1   Black on white.
Illustrated quote from the dynamic abolitionist and suffragist--orator
of the 19th century Woman's Movement.   Designed by Su Negrin.

Make out   (mo pic)
Newsreel   5min   R$10   NR#49
The oppressive experience of making-out in a car ... from the woman's point of view.   Short and sweet.   Good with discussion and/
or other women's films.

Malawi: the women   (mo pic)
Churchill   20min   C   S$230
This southeastern country of Africa exemplifies the contrasting cultures of a society in transition.   It focuses first on the women of a
village where Westernization has already left its mark, then on a
secretary in a city office and finally on a housewife who retains
village customs in her suburban tract house.   ("Malawi: two young
men" become "entrepreneurs, " however.)

Margaret Mead   (mo pic)
NBC   30min
Films Inc   S$150   33-0052.   Univ. of Calif. , Extension Media.
Discussion includes marriage and morality, the place of women in
modern life, the education of young people, the role of the individual
in a democratic society.

Marlene Dixon on Women's Liberation   (tape)
American Documentary   1971 $4/reel service charge.   May be
duplicated.

The married woman   (mo pic)
Columbia Cinematheque   94min   R$125
Jean-Luc Godard director.
The story of a young wife and mother in love with both her husband
and her lover, and finding much the same satisfactions from each.

Masculine feminine   (mo pic)
Columbia Cinematheque   103min   R$125
Jean-Luc Godard director.   Based on a story by Guy de Maupas-
sant updated to portray youthful Paris.   The story of an impulsive
callow young man and a comely, freewheeling young woman, who
have their problems with each other and with the world around
them--but their relationship is their own thing.   Jean-Pierre Leaud,
best-actor-of-the-year, Berlin Film Festival.

Masculine or feminine; your role in society (mo pic)
Coronet 19min C S$245 BW S$122.50
Collaborator Fred McKinney, Ph.D., Prof. of Psychology, University of Missouri.
In-depth study of today's changing attitudes asks what is the man's role in the home? What about the woman in business?

Masculinity and femininity (FS & Recs.)
Guidance Associates 1969 2 parts G103-000 $40 with cassette or recording. 10 and 11min Author Richard Hettlinger, Prof. of Religion, Kenyon College.
Students learn traditional stereotypes of male and female roles are changing.

Masters and Johnson explore six myths about sex (mo pic)
Focus education 1970 14min C S$130
Interview with William Masters, M.D. and Virginia Johnson, pioneers in laboratory research into the nature of human sexuality and authors of the study, "Human sexual response."

Mead, Margaret. See "Margaret Mead"

Merry go round (mo pic)
National Film Board of Canada 1966 26min
McGraw/Contemporary S$60
Young people, pre-marital sex.

Miss America. See "Up against the wall Miss America."

Miss Goodall and the wild chimpanzees, edited version (mo pic)
National Geographic Society & Metromedia Producers Corp.
Films Inc 28min C 083-0016 S$327.50 (Original version = 083-0001 51min C S$500.)
The story of a 26-year old English woman and her advantures in the jungles of East Africa. (Her name is Jane Goodall.)

Modern women; the uneasy life (mo pic)
NET Released by Indiana University 1967 60min
Available from Indiana University CS1750 R$12 S$200; Mass media associates; University of Michigan.
Fi68-2499: explores the feelings of college-educated women about the various roles open to them and examines the attitudes of married and unmarried men toward the educated woman.

Months before birth series. See "Birth of the baby"

Mothers and daughters (mo pic)
CBS 27min
American Documentary R$35 S$150
An exchange of ideas--differences between generations in a world of changing values.

Mothers--what they do (mo pic)
Aims 11min C S$130 #3915
Primary and middle grades.
Mothers take care of their families in many different ways. Visual-
ized in this film is the work of three mothers--a full time housewife, a full time working mother, and a part time working mother.
The general atmosphere created throughout the film is that each
mother is helping provide for HER family in the best way suited to
the family's needs. (A counterpart seems to be "Fathers--what
they do"; both are "guidance films, " but "Fathers..." is also an
"economics film. ")

Murder in the family (mo pic)
Paulist Productions (17576 Pacific Coast Highway, Pacific Pali-
sades, CA 90272.) 1965 28min "Insight series" Discussion guide.
75-705429: producer John Furia, director Jack Shea, writer Harry
Fink, cast includes Guy Stockwell.
Dramatization about the marital difficulties of a young couple after
the wife becomes pregnant and agrees unwittingly to an abortion.
(Insight from John, Jack and Harry.)

My little chickadee (mo pic)
Swank 83min R$75
Mae West and W. C. Fields both wrote their own material and tried
to outdo each other; wedding-night sequence a classic.

A new human life (mo pic)
Sterling 1968 10min C
Available from University of Michigan R$4
Development of human baby during final 5 months of pregnancy.
The maternity hospital routine. How the new-born is welcomed
into the family. A boy is born and this leads to a basic introduc-
tion of male/female differences at birth. For young children.

No handouts for Mrs. Hedgepeth (mo pic)
North Carolina Fund 1968 27min C
Newenhouse S$275
Study of the touch, feel and sight of poverty; the thoughts, opinions,
dreams of a Negro domestic worker as she moves back and forth
between the shack she lives in and the home of her affluent woman-
employer.

Normal birth (mo pic)
Medical Arts Productions 1951 11min Education for Childbirth
Series
Newenhouse S$100
Carefully details the actual birth of a baby from first labor pains
to the completed birth. (Male narrator's constant "you ... " is tire-
some; does not show incision but at least includes episiotomy.
Usual assumption of the "he" baby ... do most mothers get this
much support?)

Not me alone (mo pic)
For information, American Society for Psychoprophylaxis. Circa
1970. A "short."
Shows labor and delivery of a child by a couple trained in the Lemaze Method of Prepared Childbirth; while it is meant to show the
advantage of this method over others, it also strongly stresses the
need for a couple to limit the number of children they have. (New
York NOW Newsletter, October 1970)

The nun (La religieuse) (mo pic)
Audio Brandon/Ideal 1965 (France) 130min C
Based on the novel by Denis Diderot. French dialog with English
subtitles; banned for two years by the French government; finally
released in the U.S. in 1971, when it was acclaimed as one of the
best films of the year. Rivette is concerned not only with an in-
dictment of repressive Church institutions, but with the concept of
freedom for women in general.

The nun's story (mo pic)
Ideal 151min R$50
Audrey Hepburn, Peter Finch, Dame Edith Evans, Mildred Dunnock.
Based on Kathryn Hulme's novel. Records the training and ritual in
the formation of Sister Luke.

Our brother's children (mo pic)
Dan Productions, Ltd., for International Planned Parenthood Federation and Family Planning Council of Nigeria. 45min C In Yoruba,
with English narration S$200
For Nigerian audiences: family planning needed for times are
changing ... now that most children live and are healthy, and it is
important to have only as many children as one can educate. Methods of contraception not discussed. Nigerian Village and family
life. English and Spanish annotations of this film in greater detail
appear in v. 7:66, 7 of IPPF Library Bulletin.

Phoebe; story of a premarital pregnancy (mo pic)
National Film Board of Canada 1965 28min
McGraw R$17.50 Teacher's guide prepared by Dr. Lillian Bilkey
Redcay, Associate Professor of Psychology, State University of
New York College, Plattsburgh.
A day in the life of teenaged Phoebe just after she has realized she
is pregnant. Not a sociological "lesson," however. Reveals her
thoughts as she recollects and imagines the various reactions to her
situation.

Phyllis and Terry (mo pic)
Center for Mass Communication of Columbia University Press 36min
S$126. R$15 from Univ. of Calif. Extension, Berkeley.
Improvised film which lets two black teen-aged girls display their
wit and outspoken friendship against the background of New York tenements, stark schoolyards and crowded streets. Directed by Eugene
and Carole Marner.

A place in the sun (mo pic)
Paramount 120min
Films Inc R
Montgomery Clift, Elizabeth Taylor, Shelley Winters. Producer-
director George Stevens. Based on the novel, "An American
tragedy," by Theodore Dreiser. See also "An American tragedy."

Planned families (mo pic)
Allend'or 20min C $200 16mm, also in 8mm Available in sev-
eral languages including Spanish "Familias planeadas." Segments
will be added; purchase entire film program or those methods-
segments meeting "your specific needs" (rhythm, condom, sponge,
diaphragm, spermicides, pill, IUD). Animation and filmed
troduction give background for someone not knowing reproductive
organs, conception, etc. Relate to "Freedom from pregnancy" and
"Unwanted pregnancy."

Poor cow (mo pic)
National Gen circa 1967 104min C
Films Inc R
Director Kenneth Leach. From the novel by Nell Dunn.
Sadness and futility. Character study of a lower-class girl in Lon-
don forced into a loveless early marriage by pregnancy.

POSTERS Available from such sources as:
        Boccaccio, Shirley (see "Fuck housework")
        New Feminist Bookstore
        Society for Individual Rights
        Women's Center--New York City
        Women's Heritage Series
        Zero Population Growth
Inquire also at local women's center, NOW chapter office, etc.

Pregnancy and birth (mo pic)
Institut fur Film und Bilt 1969 12min C
Available from Films Inc and University of Michigan R$4.50
Animation shows complete process including female sex organs,
fertilization of egg by a single sperm, division of cell and attach-
ment to uterus membrane, function of the mother's blood in the development of embryo and fetus; actual birth sequence.

Pride and prejudice (mo pic)
MGM 118min
Films Inc R
Greer Garson, Laurence Olivier, Mary Boland, Maureen O'Sullivan,
Ann Rutherford, Heather Angel, Marsha Hunt, Edna May Oliver.
Screen play by Aldous Huxley and Jan Murfin from the novel by
Jane Austen.
The captivating Bennett family of five sisters in quest of a husband,
their frankly scheming mother, and wisely retiring father is thrown
into a dither at the approach of any eligible male, but especially
one like the elegant, arrogant, rich Mr. Darcy. His felicitous fall
for Elizabeth, the eldest daughter, and her recovery from her initial

prejudice against him, develop through many amusing clashes of temperament. A comedy of manners which captures Jane Austen's provincial England in the 18th century. (Read the book!)

Proud years (mo pic)
Center for Mass Communication of Columbia University Press 28min S$168
Director George C. Stoney
Practical steps that can be taken to help old people lead useful active lives.

Psychological differences between the sexes (mo pic)
McGraw 1964 19min Study guide R$12.50 S:C$160 S:BW$180
Correlated with the book, "Your marriage and family living," by Paul Henry Landis. (Seeing is believing.)

The pumpkin eater (mo pic)
Swank 110min R$35
From the novel by Penelope Mortimer. Anne Bancroft as the woman plagued and tormented by the knowledge that the husband she adores is a flagrant adulterer.

Quarter million teenagers (mo pic)
Churchill 1964 16min C
Uses animation to explain the physiological aspects of VD, including syphillis and gonorrhea. Uses some photography.

Radcliffe blues (film soundtrack)
American Documentary $4/reel service charge (edited)

Radcliffe blues (mo pic)
American Documentary 23min R$30 S$175
Claudia Weill director. A young woman speaks on alienation and radicalization in college, consciousness of women's oppression.

Rankin, Jeanette. See "Jeanette Rankin Brigade."

Red desert (mo pic)
Audio Brandon/Ideal 1964 (Italy) 116min C
Director Michelangelo Antonioni. Italian dialog with English subtitles. Time: Never has so bleak a vision of contemporary life been projected with such intensity, from craven yellow and life-brimming green to violet, passionate crimson and the grey of total despair.

Reproduction and birth. See "Starting tomorrow."

Rock a bye baby (mo pic)
Time-Life 30min C R$30 S$300 Life around us Series.
In the years from birth to three, the mother-child relationship is paramount in human development. The stimulation of all senses is

a basic requirement for the development of healthy children. ...
Examines some of the techniques psychologists use to weigh and
measure mothering practices around the world.   Based on Life
Science Library--"Primates."

Roosevelt, Eleanor.   See "Eleanor Roosevelt Story" and "Eleanor
Roosevelt."

Salt of the earth   (mo pic)
American Documentary   1954   94min   R$55-$100 scale
Director Herbert Biberman.
Women's struggle for unity and equality midst a Mexican-American
miners' strike for better working conditions.

The savage eye   (mo pic)
City Film Corp.   1959   67min   35min
Released by Trans Lux Distributing Corp.
Fi68-1570: production, direction and writing by Ben Maddow, Sid-
ney Meyers and Joseph Strick; music Leonard Roseman; photography
Helen Levitt, Haskell Wesler and Jack Couffer.
Cast includes Barbara Baxley, Gary Merrill, Herschel Bernardi.
A dramatized semi-documentary film describing a year in the life
and thoughts of a young divorcee in Los Angeles.   Picture the
emptiness of her search for happiness as a commentary on the dis-
illusioned, hopeless and lost people of contemporary society.

Self-defense for girls   (mo pic)
Bailey Film Associates
1969   17min   C
78-705660: utilizes dramatized episodes of threatened attack to introduce fundamental self-defense tactics and to prepare girls and
women to meet attack without panic.

Sex education for young children   (mo pic series)
BBC-TV   3 films/20 min each
Time-Life   R$25 each   3/$60   S$250 each   3/$600.
   1. Beginning (no details of conception)
   2. Birth (shows human emerging)
   3. Full circle over (intercourse described, not shown)
For elementary school children and teacher-training.   No discussion
of morality or behavior, just answers to the three questions young
children most often ask: where do babies come from?   how do
they get out?   what makes them grow?

Sex in today's world   (mo pic)
ABC-TV   1966   52min   C
Available from Focus Education   S$500   (BW$250.)   Specially-
edited 28min version S$300   (BW$150.)   Also available from Uni-
versity of Michigan R$10.
Originally produced for ABC TV as documentary, "Sex in the sixties."
Examines social forces which have changed public treatment of sex.

Sexism (game)
Carolyn Houger, Seattle NOW, 600 N.W. 126th Place, Seattle, WA 98177.
$5 ($3.50 to NOW chapters)
A woman who wants to be liberated follows a tortuous path across the board from the Doll House to the White House, while male-chauvinists gleefully put her down whenever they can. 144 cards put one in hilarious, thought-provoking predicaments calling for role-playing and discussion.

Sexism in children's books (tape/slide presentation)
Feminists on Children's media 1970
Program is not available for rent or purchase. For information re possibility of representatives of Feminists on Children's Media giving the program (travelling expenses and honorarium), contact them at PO Box 4315, Grand Central Station, New York, NY 10017.

Shaw and women (mo pic)
BBC-TV 45min
Time-Life R$35 S$350
"I shall never be able to begin a new play until I fall in love with somebody else," said George Bernard Shaw (1866-1950). Film recreates his story through his relationships with ten women.

She's beautiful when she's angry (mo pic)
Newsreel 17min R$20 #48
Skit presented at a New York City abortion rally by some angry women.

Shirley Chisholm (mo pic)
Mert Kopkin-Charles Grinker Production 4min C
Time-Life #9 Black view on race Series. R$15 for any 3 in the Series (note: only other woman--out of 20--is Coretta Scott King, #12.)
"There comes a time when we can no longer think in terms of business as usual if the Democratic Party is really going to reflect the composition of all kinds of people in this city.... The whole question of business as usual is the reason for the downfall of our Democratic Party...."

The silenced majority; a Women's Liberation multimedia kit.
Media Plus 1971 C Narration by Arlene Francis

FS format with LP recordings	108 FR	$ 75.
FS format with tape cassettes	108 FC	85.
Slide format with LP recordings	108 SR	340.
Slide format with tape cassettes	108 SC	350.

Part 1: Liberation now
Part 2: Women, jobs, and the law
Part 3: Women and education
Part 4: This ad insults women
Part 5: Rapping with The Feminists (Millett, Kennedy, Megan Terry, Ceballos.)
Discussion guide, script, bibliography, posters, buttons.

Raises questions: what do the feminists want? Are American women really unliberated? Are feminists man-haters? What does the
movement mean in the light of the precepts of the U. S. Constitution,
the viability of the institution of marriage and the needs of the family
unit? Utilizes variety of graphic techniques: photos, cartoons, col-
lages, comic strips, ads. Music, sound effects, narration.

Sisterhood feels good (poster)
Times ChangePress 1971 16 x 22" TCP-12 $1 Photo by Donna
Gottschalk. Light blue on yellow.
"Lesbians Unite!" is the sign on the wall in this morning sun-lit
room where two women are asleep.

Smouldering fires (mo pic)
Film images/Radim 1924 85min Silent R
Clarence Brown's drama about the unhappiness of a woman of forty
who falls in love with a young man of twenty-five; revealing sociological portrayal of a woman's role in business in the early Twenties.

Social change and the American woman, edited version (mo pic)
Metromedia 1964 motion picture "The American woman in the
20th century" 19min Wolper Productions
Released by Encyclopaedia Britannica (1967) Teacher's guide.
Also available from Films Inc. S$119 96-0043
FiA68-565: surveys changes in the American woman from the in-
nocent years of the Gibson Girl to her often-puzzling role today.
Focuses on the American woman, to examine changes occurring in
the larger fabric of American life including legal emancipation,
widening economic opportunities, changing social conditions, expan-
sion of education and technological advances.

Some of my best friends are bottomless dancers (mo pic)
Universal/16 18min C R$30 S$200 Production #2122
Directed by Barry Pollack, Department of Communications, Stanford University.
A cinema-verite study of Roman (Bert) Balladine, ex-choreographer
for the Folies-Bergère. He now teaches belly-dancing and exotic
strip-tease to aspiring women and curious housewives in San Francisco. Visits to actual classes and professional performances are
accompanied by interesting and witty remarks by the teacher. (Catalog also calls it "mature.")

Songs for Women's Liberation; reviving a dream (Rec.)
Sung by Ruth Batchelor and Voices of Liberation. Femme Records
#82671 Stereo copyright RAB Music Publishing Co.
Photography Bettye Lane. Written and produced by Ms. Batchelor.
$5. Side 1: 1. reviving a dream, 2. stand and be counted, 3. to
keep his love, 4. equal rights, 5. drop the mop, 6. reprises.
Side 2: 1. we need to know more, 2. the princess, 3. what's
gonna happen, 4. barefoot and pregnant, 5. progress, 6. reprises.

Sparrows can't sing (mo pic)
Janus 1963 93min R

Direction and screen play by Joan Littlewood; production by Donald
Taylor. Based on stageplay by Stephan Lewis.
This British comedy is about the sailor home from the sea who
finds his bird has flown the domestic cage. The big mister is
ready to tear London apart to find his blond and buxom missus.
More than just a funny film, this steamy look at the problems of
human passions comes from Joan Littlewood's talented East End
London crew that produced "A taste of honey."

Splendor in the grass (mo pic)
Swank 124min C R$75
Natalie Wood, Warren Beatty, Audrey Christie; producer-director
Elia Kazan; written by William Inge.
Young lovers in a small town facing the choice of containing their
passion or falsifying the illusion of purity within their consciences.

Standing room only (mo pic)
CBS News 1967 25min C
Contemporary/McGraw S$325
Worldwide population control.

Starting tomorrow series (multi-media)
Ealing Corp. (2225 Mass. Ave., Cambridge, MA 02140) 1969 C
An inservice program for elementary school teachers.
Participating teachers' guide; workshop leader's guide. Two 28min
films: "Cycles of life," "Reproduction and birth." Sex education is
purpose. Other materials include bibliographies, diagrams, charts.

STICKERS and LABELS. Available from such sources as:
     New Feminist Bookstore   Media Plus, Inc.
     Zero Population Growth
     Inquire also at local women's center and NOW chapter office, etc.

The string bean (mo pic)
Claudon Capac Productions (France) 1964 17min BW with C sequences.
McGraw/Contemporary S$175
An elderly Parisian seamstress seeks to have beauty in her room by
planting a string bean. The ultimate fate of the plant and the opti-
mism of its guardian form the narrative.

Sugar and spice ... (mo pic)
King (320 Aurora Avenue N., Seattle, WA 98109) 1972
... and everything nice. That's what little girls are made of. Or
is it? This film tells the story of Alicia, one little girl who is
made of other things as well.

Tales (mo pic)
New Line Cinema 70min R
Cassandra Gerstein, director; Andrea Loomis, camera; Jill God-
millow, editor; W. Snyder, producer.
About sex although not especially sexy. A group of more or less

young New Yorkers is asked to describe their most exceptional
sexual experiences. The men with one exception, cast themselves
as the heroes of ribald fantasy, while the women scarcely cast
themselves at all!

TAPES. Available from such sources as:
    American Documentary
    California Committee for Legalized Abortion
    Information Center on the Mature Woman
    Perennial
    Radio Free People
    WBAI
    Zero Population Growth
Inquire also at local women's center, NOW Chapter office, etc.

Termination of pregnancy by vacuum aspiration (mo pic)
Lalor Foundation 20min C By Dorothea M. Kerslake 1966
English and/or Spanish. soundtrack For professional use only.
Pioneer film made in 1966; in 1968 British Medical Association
awarded certificate commending film for use in medical education.
See also "Termination with safety."

Termination with safety (mo pic)
Lalor Foundation September 1969 See "Termination of pregnancy
by vacuum aspiration." C For professional use only.
Summation of Ms. Kerslake's three years of additional experience
under the Abortion Act of 1967 of Great Britain and her wider
scope as Consultant in Obstetrics to the Newcastle Regional Hospital Board.

The now (mo pic)
National Sex & Drug Forum with a grant from Glide Foundation
1970 14min C
Film images/Radim R$40 S$200 non-commercial
Film by Constance Beeson; Laird Sutton consultant; music by
Patrick Gleason.
A relationship film with the theme of the freeing of self and the
liberation of people from habitual distinctions of color which separate. An experimental film taking the form of a dream in which
a black girl re-experiences a life when she was black and when she
was white, and when her loves were white and when they were black.
All of the characters in the dream are yourself, as well, in past
and future lives.

They need these days--day care for children (mo pic)
University of Minnesota for Department of Public Welfare (University of Minnesota, AV Education Service, Minneapolis 55455) 1965
25min C
FiA67-1836rev: presents the work and play program of the day-care
plan for children of working parents. Outlines advantages of this
program through opinions ranging from that of a child psychologist
to the Minnesota State Department of Public Welfare. Emphasizes
that the day-care plan is not a substitute for home life.

Third World women speak on Women's Liberation   (tape)
Militant Labor Forum   1971
American Documentary $4/reel service charge   May be duplicated.

This is no time for romance   (mo pic)
National Film Board of Canada   28min   C
Available from Newenhouse S$300;   Perennial #787;   McGraw R$17
Idle hours at a summer cottage, when the husband is at work and
the children busy at play, give a wife time to dream a little and
reflect on her life and her marriage.   Is it enough?   What else
might she have made of herself?   But then her husband returns and
she opts for things as they are.

Three lives   (mo pic)
A Women's Liberation Cinema Production   1971   75min   C & BW
Impact (144 Bleecker, New York, NY 10012)   R$135 vs 50% of gross
By Kate Millett
Mallory, Lillian and Robin are three women talking of their lives
as women today.

The times they are changing   (FS)
Warren Schloat (Palmer Lane West, Pleasantville, NY 10570)   1970
35mm   91fr   C   13min   Human birth, growth and development:
facts and feelings #11.   With teacher's guide.   Barbara Martinsons,
author
75-736359:   reconsiders traditional role playing.   Discusses the
need for images and masculinity and femininity before one can
establish one's own sex role.

To be a man.   See "To be a woman"

To be a woman   (mo pic)
Billy Budd Films   1970   14min   C
"Circle of life" Series
74-705694:   a Verite sound track of live interviews forms the basis
for a study of girlhood, personhood, femininity, anti-stereotypes,
sexuality and idealism.   ("To be a man" = 78-705695)

To plan your family   (mo pic)
Churchill   1967   14min   C   16mm and 8mm   R$17   S$180
Frank description of woman's reproductive system and of the most
common methods of contraception, stressing The Pill and I. U. D.
Side effects and irrational fears are discussed.   Animation and interviews with women using contraceptives are geared to be understood by persons with all levels of education.

A total program for sound family planning   (mo pic)
Focus Education   1971?   24min   C   Free loan for professional
personnel
Contact Focus Education, Inc. Medical Division.   Consultant Edward
Tyler, M. D. (Ob-Gyn); filmed at the Family Planning Centers of
Greater Los Angeles.

Triology   (mo pic)
Universal/16   University of Southern California Cinema Picture
Production #21251   21min   R$15   S$100
Directed by Sargon Tamimi.   Probing study of personal relationships
set in a beach house shared by two attractive girls.   A male stranger
approaches one of the girls.   There is then a sudden change in their
personal relationships as the character of the man is revealed.

Two or three things I know about her   (mo pic)
New Yorker Films   1966   84min   C   16mm and 35mm   R
Jean-Luc Godard director.
About the quality of life in modern French society.   The "her" of
the title and the knowledge thereof in the film refer both to Paris
and to a housewife living in a low-cost high-rise housing project,
who, like many other women in similar circumstances, takes up
prostitution on a daily but strictly amateur basis to make ends
meet.   Prostitution as a way of life under capitalism and woman-
as-object in the consumer society are subjected to a political
analysis.

Two women   (mo pic)
Audio Brandon/Ideal   1961   (Italy)   105min
Director Vittorio De Sica; producer Carlo Ponto; based on novel by
Alberto Moravia.   Sophia Loren, Jean-Paul Belmondo.   Italian dia-
log with English subtitles.   Also available in English dubbed version.
Story of a mother and daughter struggling to survive in Italy during
World War II.   Loren won the Cannes Film Festival Award and the
Oscar as Best Actress, the only time an Academy Award has been
given for a foreign language performance.

Understanding human reproduction   (FS)
Guidance Associates   1968   18 and 19min   C   2 FS's with 2
33 1/3 rpm recordings   S$45
Fertilization and conception.   Frank.

Unfolding   (mo pic)
Produced by National Sex & Drug Forum with grant from Glide
Foundation
Film Images/Radim   1969   17min
Available from Film Images   R$40   S$200   non commercial; also
American Documentary
Director Constance Beeson.   Laird Sutton, consultant.
An aesthetic expression of human sexuality from a woman's point
of view.

Unmarried mothers   (mo pic)
Granada   (British)   25min
Perennial   R$15
This film on unmarried mothers considers such questions as inter-
course outside of marriage, the responsibility of the father, adop-
tion, the effect of illegitimacy on the child.

Unwanted pregnancy (mo pic)
Allend'or 9min C $125 Available in Spanish. 8mm or Super
8 also available.
The idea of choice by the woman. Show "Planned families" first,
"Freedom from pregnancy" second, then "Unwanted pregnancy."

Up against the wall Miss America (mo pic)
Newsreel 1971? 7min R$10 #22
WL groups attempt to disrupt the 1968 Miss America Pageant and
make boardwalk and contestant spectators more aware of the in-
sidious contest that perpetuates the image of "mindless womanhood."
Includes footage from inside the Convention Hall which TV camera-
men were forbidden to show.

VD prevent it! (mo pic)
Alfred Higgins Productions (9100 Sunset, Los Angeles, CA 90069)
11min C S$145
Available from Syracuse University, Perennial, University of
Southern California R
Soap and water used immediately after sexual contact may wash
85% of the germs from the male; males may also flush germs from
the urethra by urinating after contact. Females may destroy VD
germs by using a bacteria-killing douche.

Veronica (mo pic)
Jason Films (2621 Palisade Avenue, Riverdale, NY 10463) 1970?
27min C S$300
An attractive, articulate black teenage young woman in a middle-
class environment is a leader in her predominantly white high
school, but she has personal problems related to her position between black and white.

Wedding day (mo pic)
National Film Board of Canada 29min
McGraw S$175
The "I do's" may differ, but everywhere in the world there are
tribal customs to observe before a bride and groom may consider
their wedding knot officially tied. Filmed at village weddings in
Canada, Brazil and Nigeria, it makes interesting and illuminating
comparisons of wedding customs.

Weekend (mo pic)
Audio Brandon/Ideal 1963 (Denmark) 85min C
Danish dialog with English subtitles
Kjaerulff-Schmidt's film is a portrait of three young married
couples and a bachelor who spend an orgiastic weekend together
in a cottage. The director explores the fragile illusions on which
social status and respectability are often based. He exposes the
hollowness and absence of love which characterize the central characters' marriages, and the deep-seated fears which prevent them
from seeking divorce.

Welfare rights (mo pic)
American Documentary 30min R$30 S$200
Over 85% of welfare recipients are women and children. This film
documents the actions taken by the first welfare group in Oakland,
California to demand their rights and their dignity, the movement
that later became the National Welfare Rights Organization.

What do fathers do? (mo pic)
Churchill 1min S:C$120/BW$65 Children's film
On a special day Toby learns about some of the kinds of work that
fathers do--on a construction job, besides watching his father, he
meets the architect and different workmen. Toby begins to understand how a father's earnings buy the things his whole family wants
and needs. Toby discovers that fathers like their work. (No
"What do mothers do?")

What do girls want from boys? (mo pic)
Churchill 9min C S$120
"The searching years; a series of open-ended films" by Dimension
Films. Why do girls often prefer to date older boys? Why do
some boys resent girls their own age? What does a girl mean
when she asks to be "treated like a woman"?

What is marriage? (FS & Rec.)
Guidance Associates 1971 C 2 parts G106 292 S$35 with cas-
sette or recording
Explores changing aspects of marriage as a traditional institution:
examines alternative contemporary arrangements, including "free
union," group marriage; analyzes successful, creative marriages;
invites discussion of the nature and meaning of marriage.

What's the panic? Paul Ehrlich on pollution and birth control (tape)
American Documentary $4/reel service charge. Also available
from Zero Population Growth.

Where Mrs. Whalley lives (mo pic)
National Film Board of Canada 27min
McGraw S$175
A study of the conflict between generations that can arise despite
the best efforts of everyone to avoid it. Ms. Whalley is an aging
grandmother who lives with her son's family, and sometimes it
becomes a strain to hide hurt and loneliness for the sake of har-
mony in her son's home.

Woman doctor in Vietnam (mo pic)
CBS News 1966 28min
CCM (866 3 Avenue, New York, NY 10022) #BS-941 R$10 S$150
71-702040: sponsored by Prudential Insurance Company of America
and telecast on the CBS-TV documentary, "The 20th Century," on
March 20, 1966. Producer Isaac Kleinerman; director-writer Earle
Luby; reporters Walter Cronkite, Peter Kalischer, Morley Safer;
photographer Jerry Sims; film-editor Harold Silver.
Presents Pat Smith, M.D., of Seattle, born 1926, who runs a

hospital for Montagnards near Knotum, Vietnam, treating patients
and performing surgery.

Woman is (mo pic)
American Standard 1969 27min C
Made by Fred A. Niles (1058 West Washington Blvd., Chicago IL
60607)
71-70524: examines the personal philosophy of a woman in today's
world, and shows her in some of her many roles--as an enigma,
a philosopher, and a romantic. (Roles!)

A woman rebels (mo pic)
Films Inc 1936 88min R
Producer Pandro S. Berman; director Mark Sandrick; script by
Anthony Veiller and Ernest Vajda; editor Jane Loring. Cast
Katharine Hepburn, Herbert Marshall. Based on the novel, "Portrait of a rebel," by Netta Syrett.
A strong-willed young lady straining at parental ties yearns to try
her wings ... in 19th century England. She does so by fighting for
sex without marriage and by editing a trail-blazing crusader-type
woman's magazine. Her drive for freedom and independence de-
lights and distresses her judge-father.

Womankind (radio program)
WBAI 99.5 FM, New York City

The woman's film (mo pic)
Newsreel 1971? 40min R$50 NR 55
Winner, First Prize, Inter-film Festival, Berlin.
"... [S]peaks in clear and unmistakable words from real people
about what's wrong with the system and how women are especially
victimized by the class, racial, and sexual inequality. The anger
of "The Woman's film" is positive, even optimistic. These beautiful, strong sisters are ready to struggle for a better world for
themselves and their children...." (Ruth McCormick, Cineaste).
Made up of the conversation of working women discussing careers,
politics, love affairs, the women's movement--including some history.

Women (mo pic)
Newsreel No other information available.
Examines how the ability to bear children is used to oppress women and how women have begun to recognize the importance of
fighting together for their liberation.

Women (mo pic)
Grove 1971? 12min C S$100
A profile of Toulouse-Lautrec, focusing on his paintings and litho-
graphs of the women in his life.

Women in Africa (FS)
BFA Educational Media 1970 36fr 35mm & phonodisc C 12"
33 1/3 rpm 5min "Africa; focus on culture" series.

70-73;7825: contrasts the African woman's conventional role--child-bearing, preparing food, working in the fields--with the changing status and new life-style of the contemporary African woman who enters businesses and professions.

Women in revolt (kit)
Viking "Jackdaws" 1971 Junior Books $3.95 each packet 9 x 13 1/2"
Primary source materials that make historical events, persons, etc. come alive--each title contains a wealth of facsimile documents (letters, posters, charts, proclamations, etc.) chosen by experts in field to give relevancy to the subject.   Guide and topic sheets provide perspective. (Be specific ...)

Women of Russia (mo pic)
International Film Foundation (474 5 Ave., New York, NY 10017)
1968 12min C "Russia today" Series.   Producer Julien Bryan, music Stephen M. Gould, editing Yehuda Yaniv.
78-701846: shows the role of the Russian woman in Soviet life.

Women of telecommunication center Number Six (mo pic)
Newsreel 1971? 20min R$20 NR#136 English soundtrack
Even in the middle of an air attack, North Vietnamese women are able to keep open the crucial lines of communication that make the defense of their country possible.   Made by the North Vietnamese.

Women of the Reformation; in Germany and Italy (phonograph recording)
Augsburg Publishing House 1971? 12" LP $4.95 Coordinate with Roland Bainton's book of same title.

Women on the march; the struggle for equal rights (mo pic)
National Film Board of Canada 1959 29min each/2 parts
McGraw S$202 each $350/both
The struggle for equal rights that characterized the suffragette movement, spearheaded by resolute women such as Emmeline Pankhurst, imprisonment, martyrdom, exile.   First part deals with the fight for the franchise; the second with the status of women today.

"Women unite and resist" see "Amazon..." (poster).

Women win voting rights (mo pic)
Anargyros Film Library (1813 Fairburn Avenue, Los Angeles, CA 90025)
1966 4min Silent 8mm loop film issued in standard 8 and super 8mm
79-700352: documentary about the movement to get women the right to vote, with emphasis on the suffragette campaign in America.

Women's Liberation (mo pic)
ABC Media Concepts (1001 North Poinsettia Plaza, Hollywood, CA 90046)
1972 23min C $270
ABC News correspondent Marlene Sanders, writer/producer, inter-

viewed representative groups covering a wide range of Women's
Liberation activities to provide an accurate and thoughtful examination of ideologies, programs and objectives endorsed by most female
activists.

Women's Liberation   (poster)
DC   WL $1

Women's Rock Band
Contact Jennifer Abod, 23 Beers Street, New Haven, CT 06511.
No other information available.

Women's Song Book
Judy Busch and Laura X, composers.   23 songs, old and original.
For women $2.   For others $3.   From: Women's History Research Center. $5 subscription brings the first two books and in-
cludes postage.

The yellow leaf   (mo pic)
National Film Board of Canada   28min   S$175
Sympathetic study of the problem of an elderly widow who is forced
to leave her daughter's household to live in a home for the aged.
Shocked and disappointed at first, she finds that her new home
offers congenial friends, new interests and a measure of independence she did not have before.

You don't have to buy war, Mrs. Smith   (mo pic)
American Documentary   30min   R$15   S$200
New York City's Commissioner of Consumer Affairs, Bess Myer-
son Grant, addresses the World Mother's Day Assembly of Another
Mother for Peace, exhorting women to use consumer pressure to
end war-profiteering by makers of Pentagon "anti-people" products.

You don't have to buy war, Mrs. Smith   (film soundtrack)
American Documentary   Edited   With Bess Myerson Grant $4/
reel service charge

You worm   (mo pic)
Raymond D. Collins (6110 N. Kenmore, Chicago, IL 60026)
1967   10min   8mm
FiA68-770:   satire on Hugh Hefner's philosophy.   Young man invites young lady to his apartment for dinner, and after wining and
dining her, kills her and feeds her to his pet worms.

Part V

DIRECTORY OF SOURCES

Because most women's groups publish more or less regular news bulletins and often produce and/or distribute media, a directory of sources of media about women and for their use includes women's centers, collectives, caucuses and Women's Liberation organizations. Some women's groups are mere auxiliaries, but their declared support for the Equal Rights Amendment, for example, indicates some strength. Hopefully it is movement in the direction of independence of or equality with the dominant male group. A number, notably girl-talk and religious, have evidenced interest in improving the status of women, although their full involvement may not have been declared, and their efforts are not up to those of feminists, who themselves range from relatively conservative to radical. (There is no such thing as "moderate equality.")

In addition to organizations, sources include library programs and subject-collections; foundations and philanthropies; publishers, distributors and booksellers; unincorporated and informal groups of people doing their thing; academic centers and Women's Studies programs; specialized information centers, speakers, and theater groups; writers and producers of media; and a number of others. Thus, this "Directory" provides information about sources of information as well as of materials. At the end of the main sequence in this directory are two special sections: "Women's Liberation Groups and Centers" and "Women's Studies."

Much but not all of the information has been verified; descriptive material is also based on such standard sources as The Encyclopedia of Associations, 6th ed., The 1969 Handbook on Women Workers of the U.S. Dept. of Labor's Women's Bureau, and Subject Collections: A Guide to Special Book Collections in Libraries, 3 ed. In the addresses provided here, "street" can be assumed. Inclusion of an item does not necessarily imply recommendation of it. A few names have been included only for identification purposes, e.g., the Pussycat League. If in doubt about an organization, seek out the advice of your local Women's Center or NOW Chapter--always assume sisterhood!

It is hoped that individuals and groups will keep the author informed of changes and developments so that a future edition can be "bigger and better." When contacting WL groups, remember that they usually cannot obtain support from government or philanthropy. A SASE (self-addressed stamped-envelope) should be enclosed; a contribution is often tax-deductible.

255

Abortion Counseling Service
PO Box 9199
San Diego, CA 92109
    For San Diego residents only.   Has newsletter available to
    others for contribution.   Located at 1369 B Street.

Abortion Project.   See Women's Abortion Project.

Abortion Referral & Sex Information Service
133 East 73
New York, NY 10021
    NOTE   The New York City telephone directory contains a num-
    ber of entries beginning with the word Abortion; each can and
    should be checked out at the local women's center.

Action for Children's Television
46 Austin
Newtonville, MA 02160
    Has newsletter.   Membership organization.   Paperback book by
    Evelyn Sarson, "Action for children's television" (Avon W295
    $1. 25)

Aims Instructional Materials
PO Box 1010
Hollywood, CA 90028

Allend'or Productions, Inc.
4321 Woodman Avenue
Sherman Oaks, CA 91403

Alternate Media Center
New York University, 144 Bleeker
New York, NY 10010

Alternatives
PO Drawer A, Diamond Heights Station
San Francisco, CA 94131
    Directories of communes, free schools, social change.

Amazon Bookstore
2418 26 Avenue
South Minneapolis, MN 55406
    A Feminist Journal

American Anthropological Association
Committee on the Status of Women in Anthropology formed Feb. 1970
Prof. Shirley Gorenstein, Chairperson
    Dept. of Anthropology, Columbia University, New York, NY 10027

American Association for the Advancement of Science
Women's Caucus of the AAAS formed December 1971
Virginia Walbot, Chairperson
    Dept. of Biology, Yale University, New Haven, CT 06520

American Association of University Professors
1785 Massachusetts Avenue NW
Washington, DC 20036
    Committee "W" on the Status of Women in the Academic Pro-
    fession established in 1918, discontinued in 1928, voted reacti-
    vated at Spring 1970 meeting.   Chairperson is Alice Rossi (So-
    ciology Dept., Goucher College, Towson, MD 21204)   AAUP
    contact is Margaret Rumbarger, Associate Secretary.   Has
    "Bibliography of studies on the status of women."

American Association of University Women
2401 Virginia Avenue NW
Washington, DC 20037
    Dr. Ruth M. Oltman, staff associate--Higher education, for in-
    formation re caucuses, task forces, etc.   Journal.

American Civil Liberties Union
156 5 Avenue
New York, NY 10010
    Publications list

American College Personnel Association
Women's Task Force formed December 1970
    Dr. Jane E. McCormick, chairperson.   Assistant to Vice Presi-
    dent of Student Affairs, Pennsylvania State University, University
    Park, PA 16802

American Council on Education
1 Dupont Circle
Washington, DC 20036
    Commission on Academic Affairs is developing a roster of wo-
    men in the various disciplines.

American Documentary Films
336 West 84
New York, NY 10024
    A non-profit educational organization renting and selling films.
    Has tapes, posters, fliers, etc.   Also San Francisco: 379 Bay,
    94133

American Economic Association
    Carolyn Shaw Bell, Professor of Economics.   Wellesley College,
    Wellesley, MA 02181

American Historical Association
Committee on Women Historians, January 1970.
    Professor Patricia A. Graham, Chairperson.   Barnard College,
    New York, NY 10027.   Possibility of Roster.
Coordinating Committee on Women in the History Profession, Dec.
    1969.
    Dean Adele Simmons and Dr. Sandi Cooper, chairpersons.
    Simmons: Jackson College, Tufts University, Medford, MA 02155
    Cooper: Richmond College, CUNY, Staten Island, NY 10301

American Library Association
50 East Huron
Chicago, IL 60611
Task Force on the Status of Women in Librarianship, June 1970.
   Michelle Rudy, chairperson/"Coordinator." 1403 LeGore Lane,
   Manhattan, KS 66502.
Roster. Contact Margaret Myers, Graduate School of Library
   Service, Rutgers University, New Brunswick, NJ 08903.
Task Force newsletter discontinued; now utilizing SRRT (Social Re-
   sponsibilities Round Table) Newsletter; for information: Eliza-
   beth Futas, SRRT Clearinghouse, 105 East 24, New York, NY
   10010. $3./year.
For a lucid explanation of the origin of sexism in librarianship--
   one which conveys its unique sociological phenomena--See Anita
   R. Schiller's "Aware" column, American Libraries:427, April
   1972 ... the first seven paragraphs!

American Mathematical Society. See Association for Women in
   Mathematics

American Medical Women's Association
1740 Broadway
New York, NY 10019
   Former Journal now published as Woman Physician.

American Philosophical Association
Subcommittee on Status of Women in the Profession, Dec. 1969.
   Chairperson Dr. Margaret D. Wilson, Dept. of Philosophy,
   1879 Hall, Princeton University, Princeton, NJ 08540

American Physical Society
Committee on Women in Physics, April 1971
Dr. Vera Kistiakowsky, chairperson. Nuclear Physics Laboratory,
   Massachusetts Institute of Technology, Cambridge, MA 02139

American Political Science Association
Committee on the Status of Women in the Profession, March 1969.
   Chairperson, Dr. Josephine E. Milburn, University of Rhode
   Island, Kingston, RI 02881
Women's Caucus for Political Science, Sept. 1969.
   Chairperson, Dr. Evelyn P. Stevens, 14609 South Woodland
   Road, Shaker Heights, OH 44120. Mail to WCPS, Box 9099,
   Pittsburgh, PA 15224

American Psychological Association
Task Force on the Status of Women in Psychology, Sept. 1969.
   Chairperson, Dr. Helen Astin, Director of Research, University
   Research Corp., 4301 Connecticut Avenue NW, Washington, DC
   20008
   Staff liaison, Dr. Tena Cummings, APA, 1200 17 St., NW,
   Washington, DC 20036
   Association for Women in Psychology is an independent group
   initially a caucus within APA, Sept. 1969.

American Society for Microbiology
Committee on the Status of Women Microbiologists
  Chairperson, Dr. Mary Louise Robbins, Medical School, 1339 H
  Street, George Washington University, Washington, DC 20005

American Society for Psychoprophylaxis in Obstetrics
7 West 96
New York, NY 10025
  Professionals and others interested in Lemaze method of painless
  childbirth. Has literature, sponsors courses in the method.

American Society for Public Administration
Task Force on Women in Public Administration
  Chairperson, Joan Fiss Bishop, Director of Career Services,
  Wellesley College, Wellesley, MA 02181

American Society of Training and Development
Women's Caucus, May 1970
Steering committee: Dr. Shirley McCune and Ms. Althea Simmons.
  McCune: Center for Human Relations, National Education Assoc.,
  1601 16 Street NW, Washington, DC 20036
  Simmons: Director of training, NAACP, 200 East 27, New York,
  NY 10016

American Sociological Association
Ad Hoc Committee on the Status of Women in Sociology, Dec. 1970
Chairperson, Dr. Elise Boulding, Behavioral Science Institute,
  University of Colorado, Boulder, CO 80302
Sociologists for Women in Society is an independent group, formerly
  an ASA caucus.

American Speech and Hearing Association
Subcommittee on the Status of Women
  Chairperson, Dorothy K. Marge, 8011 Longbrook Road, Spring-
  field, VA 22152
Caucus on Status of Women in ASHA, August 1970. Same contact.

Anargyros Film Library
1813 Fairburn Avenue
Los Angeles, CA 90025

Art Shop
232 Madison Avenue
New York, NY 10016
  Graphics Collection. WL packet.

Association for Childhood Education International
3615 Wisconsin Avenue NW
Washington, DC 20016

Association for Children Deprived of Support
8622 Wystone Avenue, apt. 7
Northridge, CA 91324

Association for the Study of Abortion
120 West 57
New York, NY 10019
   Bibliography, newsletter.

Association for Women in Mathematics, January 1971
Professor Mary Gray, Chairperson.   Dept. of Mathematics, American University, Washington, DC 20016

Association for Women in Psychology, Sept. 1969
An independent group, initially a caucus within APA.
   Policy Council to be announced.
   Editor, Dr. Leigh Marlowe, Manhattan Community College, 180
   West End Avenue, New York, NY 10023
   PR, Dr. Jo-Ann Evans Gardner, 726 St. James, Pittsburgh,
   PA 15232

Association of American Law Schools
Women in the Legal Profession
   Chairperson, Prof. Ruth B. Ginsburg.   School of Law, Rutgers
   University, Newark, NJ 07104

Association of Asian Studies
Committee on the Status of Women
Chairperson, Prof. Joyce K. Kallgren.   Center for Chinese Studies,
   2168 Shattuck Avenue, Berkeley, CA 94705

Association of Women in Psychology
c/o Polly Elliott, 324 East 13, New York, NY 10003

Association of Women in Science
Co-presidents: Dr. Judith G. Pool, Dr. Neena B. Schwartz
   Pool: Stanford Medical School, Stanford University, Stanford,
   CA 94305
   Schwartz: Dept. of Psychiatry, College of Medicine, University
   of Illinois Medical Center, PO Box 6998, Chicago, IL 60680
Editor of newsletter is Dr. Anne M. Briscoe, Dept. of Medicine,
   Harlen Hospital Center, New York, NY 10037

Association of Women Sociologists.   See Sociologists for Women...

Association--Sterling Films
600 Madison Avenue
New York, NY 10022

Association to Repeal Abortion Laws
PO Box 6083
San Francisco, CA 94101
   Has newsletter; contributions requested for helpful lists, reprints,
   etc.   Post-abortion care center, classes and other activities.

BFA Educational Media
2211 Michigan Avenue
Santa Monica, CA 90404

Bailey Film Associates
11559 Santa Monica Blvd.
Los Angeles, CA 90025

Baird, Bill.   See Parents' Aid Society

Barnard College.   Wollman Library
New York, NY 10027
> The Overbury Collection consists of some 1900 volumes and
> some manuscripts and autographed letters written by/about Amer-
> ican women.   It was given to Barnard by Bertha VanRiper Over-
> bury ('96) in 1950, and is basically historical/literary.   Repre-
> sented are Hannah Mather Crocker, Catharine Beecher, Lydia
> Francis Child, Helen Hunt Jackson, Sara Buell Hale, Anne Royall,
> Harriet Farley, Margaret Fuller, Elizabeth Peabody, Louisa May
> Alcott, Harriet Beecher Stowe, Marie Sandoz, Amy Lowell,
> Marianne Moore, Emily Dickinson, Gertrude Stein, Edna St. Vin-
> cent Millay, Lucy Larcom, Kate Chopin, Charlotte Perkins Gil-
> man and others.   Robert B. Palmer, Librarian.

Barnard College.   Women's Center
606 West 120
New York, NY 10027
> Income from bequest of Helen Rogers Reid ('03), life-long cru-
> sader for women's rights, is being used to launch the Center's
> first programs (1971).   Plans include: permanent series of
> seminars on Women and Society that will systematically bring
> women of varied experience, alumnae and others to talk to under-
> graduates; committee of Barnard alumnae-lawyers to explore
> cases of discrimination; Women's Studies courses (no major at
> present); encouragement of career conferences.   A Roster of
> Women Scholars is planned.

Bay Area Radical Education Project
491 Guerrero
San Francisco, CA 94110
> Media source; WL literature list.

Bennett College.   Thomas F. Holgate Library
Greensboro, NC 27420
> Small collection of manuscripts, pictures, clippings; Afro-Ameri-
> can women subject-area.

Berkeley WL Basement Press
PO Box 6323
Albany, CA 94706
> Distributes papers from West Coast women's movements.

Bleecker Street Press
Box 625, Old Chelsea Station
New York, NY 10011

Boston Public Library
Copley Square
Boston, MA 02117
   The Galatea Collection: 5,000 volumes including manuscripts.
   Formed by Thomas Wentworth Higginson, relating to women's
   place in history and the Suffragette Movement. Printed book
   catalog as of 1898. Use restricted to qualified scholars.

Boston Women's Health Collective. "Women and their bodies; a course
   by...." 75¢ 193p c1970. See New England Free Press.

Brooklyn Print Shop
573 Metropolitan Ave.
Brooklyn, NY 11211
   Wants original works by women; prints and publishes.

Fredrika Bremer Assoc.
Biblioteksgatan 12 3tr.
11146 Stockholm, Sweden
   Publishes journal, Hertha--special English-language edition
   available; contact Swedish Information Service also.

Brown, E.C. Trust Foundation
3179 South West 87 Ave., PO Box 251130
Portland, OR 97225
   Curtis E. Avery, Director and Prof. of Education, University of
   Oregon. Ruth R. Wolfe, Executive Secretary and assistant to
   the Director. E.C. Brown family-life education films are distributed by Newenhouse and Perennial. The E.C. Brown Center
   for Family Studies is at 1902 Moss, Eugene, Oregon 97401.

Billy Budd Films
235 East 57
New York, NY 10022

Business & Professional Women's Foundation
2012 Mass. Avenue NW
Washington, DC 20036
   Library responsible for compilation of excellent bibliographies.
   Books, manuscripts, research studies, pamphlets, clippings de-
   voted to women and their contribution to the development of the
   U.S. and their role in the evolution of contemporary society.

Business & Professional Women's Clubs, Inc. Same address.
National Business Woman magazine.

Talent Bank. Same address. Dr. Phyllis O'Callaghan.

CBS: Columbia Broadcasting System
485 Madison Avenue
New York, NY 10022

CCM Films, Inc.
866 3 Avenue
New York, NY 10022
   A subsidiary of Crowell, Collier & Macmillan distributing films
   from Association, Brandon, Fleetwood.

California Committee for Legalized Abortion
Box 101
Kentfield, CA 94904
   Has recordings and tapes of women describing their own experi-
   ences; write for list of publications.

California. University: University of California Asian Women
3405 Dwinelle Hall
Berkeley, CA 94720
   Asian Women's Journal

Canada Dept. of Labour
Women's Bureau
Ottawa 4, Canada
   Has Bulletin and other publications.   Director of Women's Bureau
   (1971), Sylvia M. Gelber.

Caravan Theatre
1555 Mass.
Cambridge, MA 02138
   Has play, "How to Make a Woman."

Carousel
1501 Broadway
New York, NY 10036

Center for California Public Affairs
Box 505
Claremont, CA 91711
   "The California Handbook"--directory of sources of information
   and action on California problems.

Center for Mass Communication of Columbia University Press
562 West 113
New York, NY 10025

Chicago. University. See University Women's Association.

Child Welfare League of America, Inc.
44 East 23
New York, NY 10010
   Publications include day-care center guidelines.

Children's Book Council
175 5 Ave.
New York, NY 10010

Churchill Films
662 North Robertson Blvd.
Los Angeles, CA 90069

Citizens' Advisory Council on the Status of Women
U. S. Dept. of Labor
Washington, DC 20210
    Has irregular Newsletter; single copy gratis.

Citizens' Communication Center
1816 Jefferson Place N. W.
Washington, DC 20036
    Established to provide citizens with free legal assistance on se-
    lected communications matters; free materials.

Clapp, James
607 East 12
New York, NY 10009
    Abortion reformer.   Has tapes and other literature.

Clergy Consultation Service (On Abortion/Problem Pregnancies, etc.)
Contact: National Clergy Consultation Service on Abortion
           55 Washington Square South
           New York, NY 10012   Phone 212-254-6314

                           and

           Clergy Counselling Service for Problem Pregnancies
           3150 West Olympic Blvd.
           Los Angeles, CA 90006   Phone 213-737-7988

Also check local telephone directory and ask "Information."   The
following are some phone numbers:
    Arizona   602-967-4234
    California   213-737-7988
    California: Los Angeles   212-666-7600
    Colorado   303-757-4442
    Connecticut   203-624-8646
    Illinois   312-667-6015
    Iowa   515-282-1738
    Louisiana   504-888-9881
    Massachusetts   617-527-7188
    Michigan   313-964-0838
    Nebraska   402-453-5314
    New Jersey   201-933-2937
    New York: City & suburbs   212-477-0034, 254-6314
       "   " :   State   607-272-7172
    North Carolina   919-942-2050
    Ohio   216-229-4723
    Pennsylvania   215-923-5141
    Tennessee   615-256-3441

College Press Service
1779 Church N. W.
Washington, DC 20036

Columbia Cinematheque, a Division of Columbia Pictures.
711 5 Ave.
New York, NY 10022

Committee of Concern for Homosexuals, Inc.
c/o Gay Switchboard, PO Box 4089
Berkeley, CA 94704
    Media source.

Community Sex Information & Education Service
P. O. Box 4246
New Orleans, LA 70118
    Abortion referral.   Phone 504-866-3671

Concern, Inc.
PO Box 19287
Washington, DC 20036
    Information on consumer products, pollution.

Congress to Unite Women
Box 114
New York, NY 10025

Connections: Women in Prison
3109 16
San Francisco, CA 94103
    Guidance at 330 Ellis, 94102.   Publications.

Consumers' Education & Protective Assoc.
6048 Orontz Ave.
Philadelphia, PA 19141

Contact Books
7813 Beverly Blvd.
Los Angeles, CA 91606
    Publisher.

Contemporary. See McGraw-Hill.

Coronet
65 East South Water
Chicago, IL 60601

Corson Publishing, Inc.
Box 510
Middlebury, IN 46540
    Publishes Progressive Woman magazine.

Council for Christian & Social Action
289 Park Ave. South
New York, NY 10010
    United Church of Christ.   Media source: inter-racial marriage,
    homosexuality, responsible parenthood, population problem.

Council for Women's Equality
PO Box 8186
Portland, OR 97209

Council on Religion & the Homosexual
330 Ellis
San Francisco, CA 94102
    Has literature.

D. C. Women's Liberation
Box 13098, T Street Station
Washington, DC 20009
    Has excellent literature including health materials, posters, Birth
    Control Handbook.

Danforth Foundation
222 South Central Ave.
St. Louis, MO 63105
    Provides scholarships for women who want to teach, especially
    those out of school a while.   See "Foundation Handbook."

Daughters of Bilitis (DOB)
Chapters throughout the U.S.A., e.g.
    New York: 141 Prince, 10012
    San Francisco: 1105 Market, Room 208, 94103.   Sisters.
    Dearborn, MI: The New Detroit DOB, PO Box 244, Greenfield
       Station, 48120.   Reach Out.
    Boston: Box 221 Prudential Center Station, 02199.   Focus.
The Ladder, national bi-monthly magazine, called The Voice of
    Lesbianism in America.   Founded in 1955 by eight women.   DOB
    first chartered as nonprofit organization in California, was in-
    strumental in founding The Council on Religion & The Homosexual.
    Encourages new members, including non-homosexuals.

Day Care & Child Development Council, Inc.
1426 H N. W.
Washington, DC 20005
    Voice for Children.   Founded in 1959 as the Inter-City Committee
    for Day Care of Children, Inc.; name changed in 1960 to National
    Committee for the Day Care of Children, until 1968.

DeRochemont, Louis Associates
1600 Broadway
New York, NY 10019

Diana Press
1854 Wyoming Ave., N.W.
Washington, DC 20009
    Wants poetry, photography, art work.

Disney, Walt Productions
800 Sonora Avenue
Glendale, CA 91201

Drexel, Mary J. Library
Lutheran Deaconess School, 801 Merion Square Rd.
Gladwyne, PA 19035
    Complete Minutes of Lutheran Deaconess Conference of America;
    books on deaconess work now OP. Reference use only.

Eagleton Center for the American Woman and Politics
Eagleton Institute of Politics
Wood Lawn, Neilson Campus, Rutgers University
New Brunswick, NJ 08901
    Ruth B. Mandel, Director of Educational Programs and Adminis-
    tration. "research and educational institute dedicated to the study of
    American women and politics and to promoting the full and active
    involvement of women in American public life." Established
    1971.

East Bay Women for Peace
2495 Shattuck
Berkeley, CA 94704

Encyclopaedia Britannica Educational Corp.
425 North Michigan Avenue
Chicago, IL 60611

Equal Rights Alliance
2140 North Magnolia Avenue
Chicago, IL 60614
    Working on programs to change the nature of women's jails and
    prisons in Illinois. Alliance Link newsletter.

Everywoman Bookstore
1043 West Washington Blvd.
Venice, CA 90291
    Send for free catalog. Varda One's "Image of women in homo-
    phile novels" available ($1.15); her "Dictionary of Sexism" an-
    nounced. "World's oldest women's liberation newspaper" is
    Everywoman, sample copies 25¢; graphics design, prints, pub-
    lishes.

Family Planning Information Service, Inc.
300 Park Avenue South
New York, NY 20010
    Has abortion information.

Fanny
c/o Roy Silver, Manager
Burbank, CA 91505
    All-woman rock group that writes own material.   See <u>McCalls</u>
    (November 1971); <u>New York Times</u> Woman's Page, May 15,
    1971.   (Reprise Records, 4000 Warner Blvd.)

Farrell, Warren T.
100 Bleecker, apt. 3B
New York, NY 10012
    Member of Board of Directors of New York NOW Chapter (1971).
    "Beyond masculinity" to be published (1972) by W. W. Norton.
    Author of materials for and active in men's consciousness-raising.

Features and News, Inc. (FAN)
6449 Benvenue, c/o Susan Berman
Oakland, CA 94618
    National news service serving women's pages of approximately
    35 newspapers.

Federally Employed Women (FEW)
487 National Press Building
Washington, DC 20004
    <u>News and Views</u>

Female Liberation
1126 Boylston, Room 200
Boston, MA 02115

Feminist Book Mart
162-11 9 Ave.
Whitestone, NY 11357
    Sells by mail--10% savings.

Feminist Forums
102 East 22
New York, NY 10010
    Director, Jo Hazelton

Feminist Interart Theatre
Contact: Pauline Hahn, c/o New York NOW

Feminist Press
10920 Battersea Lane
Columbia, MD 21043
    Also Box 334, Old Westbury, NY 11568.   SUNY at Old Westbury.
    Interested in contributing to the reconstruction of feminist history
    and in changing the character of children's books.   Has in print
    "The dragon and the doctor" ($1) for younger children, and
    "Challenge to become a doctor; the story of Elizabeth Blackwell"
    ($1.50) for older children.   Annual subscriptions also available.

Feminist Repertory Theater.   See New Feminists Repertory Theater.

Feminist Studies
294 Riverside Drive
New York, NY 10025
   Ann Calderwood, editor

The Feminists
120 Liberty
New York, NY 10006
   Media source: buttons, postal/note cards, literature packets,
   pamphlets.   Men must pay service charge.

Feminists in The Arts.   Contact New York NOW.

Feminists on Children's Media
PO Box 4315, Grand Central Station
New York, NY 10017
   Collective formed in 1970 by women concerned about the stereotyped female image found in children's books--membership a
   cross-section of WL groups and others--many employed in fields
   relevant to children's literature and many are mothers.   The
   group feels that the rigid sex roles depicted in children's books
   are detrimental to the development of young readers of both
   sexes, and are reaching those publishers, writers, teachers,
   librarians and parents who are unaware.   Send for literature
   list; See School Library Journal (1/71), Redbook (3/71), and
   Woman's Day (3/71).

Femme Records
PO Box 548, FDR Station
New York, NY 10022

Film Images, a Division of Radim
1034 Lake
Oak Park, IL 60301
   Also: 17 West 60, New York, NY 10023.

Film Makers Library--Cooperative
175 Lexington Ave.
New York, NY 10016

Films Incorporated, a Subsidiary of Encyclopaedia Britannica Educational Corp.
425 North Michigan Ave.
Chicago, IL 60611

First Women's Bank of Florida
4620 Pine Tree Drive
Miami Beach, FL 33839
   Besides regular banking function, will inform women about
   handling money and act as a training ground for women in
   finance.

Focus Education, Inc.
3 East 54
New York, NY 10022

Four Swords, Inc.
PO Box 431, Old Chelsea Station
New York, NY 10011
    Gay and other publications.

The Fourth World
Box 8997
Oakland, CA 94608
    Fourth World publications, including newsletter-type.

Frances Delafield Family Planning Clinic
99 Fort Washington Ave.
New York, NY 10032
    Teenagers can receive counseling on contraception, pregnancy
    tests, and abortion referrals here and at the Health Clinic, 90-
    37 Parsons Blvd., Jamaica, Queens (Village Voice, May 20,
    1971).

Freedom Socialist Publications
3117 East Thomas
Seattle, WA 98102
    List of women's literature.

Friends Committee on National Legislation
245 2 N.E.
Washington, DC 20002
    FCNL Washington Newsletter. Area offices also. "How to
    write a letter to the editor," "How to visit your Congressman"
    (5¢ each).

Gittings, Barbara
PO Box 2383
Philadelphia, PA 19103
    For reliable information on Gay publications; also has OP titles
    available.

Graphic Curriculum, Inc.
PO Box 565, Lenox Hill Station
New York, NY 10021

Graphics Collective
2 Bank, c/o Eileen Whalen
New York, NY 10014

Greenwich Public Library
Greenwich, CN 06830
    Has "Woman; ad astra ad lib" (1970).

Greyfalcon House
60 Riverside Dr.
New York, NY 10024
   Ann Grifalconi, President.   Graphics.   Discounts.   See also
   Media Plus, Inc.

Grove Press Film Division
214 Mercer
New York, NY 10012

Guerrilla-type Theatre.   See Caravan Theater, New England Free
   Press, and other likely-sounding groups.

Guidance Associates
Pleasantville, NY 10570
   A subsidiary of Harcourt Brace Jovanovich, Inc.

Harriet Tubman Brigade
1217 Wichita, c/o Space City News
Houston, TX 77004

Hastings College of Law Library
198 McAllister
San Francisco, CA 94102
   Legal and economics aspects of employment of women.   See also
   Hughes, Marija Matich.

Hogtown Press
Box 6300, Station A
Toronto 1, Ontario
   Media source, including birth control pamphlet.   Alternate ad-
   dress: 11 Olive Ave., Toronto 174.

Holden Collection
Contact: Ms. Miriam Y. Holden, 57 East 78, New York, NY 10021
   Extensive and remarkable feminist collection; those doing inten-
   sive historical research on women may contact Ms. Holden.

Homosexual Information Center
3773 1/2 Cahuenga Blvd.
Hollywood, CA 90068
   Speakers' bureau, short courses, consultation, special library,
   counseling/referral service, Committee to Fight Exclusion of
   Homosexuals from the Armed Forces.   Publications include newsletters, Homosexual National Classified Directory, selected reading materials.

Hughes, Marija Matich
2422 Fox Plaza
San Francisco, CA 94102
   Reference Law Librarian at Hastings College of Law.   Has
   bibliographic support-type publications re legal and economic

aspects of women's employment; in-print and professionally done.

Human Rights for Women, Inc.
1128 National Press Building
Washington, DC 20004
    HRW newsletter. National non-profit corporation organized to
    provide legal assistance for women seeking to invoke their rights
    under the law; to undertake research, studies and surveys on
    issues relating to sex prejudice; and to help educate the public
    and the women's movement itself concerning the causes and
    effects of denial of human and civil rights to women.

Ideal Pictures. 5 offices in U.S.
    34 MacQueston Parkway South, Mount Vernon, NY 10550
    1619 North Cherokee, Los Angeles, CA 90028

Indiana University
Audio-Visual Center
Bloomington, IN 47401

Information Center on the Mature Woman
3 West 57
New York, NY 10019
    Furnishes tapes, etc. to news media. A clearinghouse founded
    in 1969, not membership organization.

Institute of Labor and Industrial Relations
PO Box 1567
Ann Arbor, MI 48106

Intercollegiate Association of Women Students
Casey Eike, President. 222 Strong, University of Kansas, Law-
    rence 66044

International Anti-Women's Liberation League
Betty Jarboe, founder and president
    Received "Barefoot and pregnant" award (March 1972) from the
    Baton Rouge, LA NOWletter. "Women are simply not as clever
    as men," says Betty Jarboe, and provides ten commandments
    which include "loving your man."

International Archive. See Women's History Research Center.

International Planned Parenthood Federation. Western Hemisphere
    Region, Inc.
111 4 Avenue
New York, NY 10003
    Has films. Quarterly Library Bulletin (Boletín de la biblioteca)
    in both English and Spanish includes reviews of media in fields
    of population, family planning and sex education. See also
    Planned Parenthood.

Janus Films
745 5 Avenue
New York, NY 10022

Joint Committee of Organizations Concerned About the Status of
    Women in The Catholic Church
6825 North Sheridan Road
Chicago, IL 60626
    Elizabeth Farians

Kansas University. Library
Lawrence, KS 55044
    Gerritsen Collection of "La Femme et la Feminisme" includes
    books, pamphlets, etc. purchased from John Crerar Library
    (Chicago) in 1954. Strong only in late 19th and early 20th cen-
    tury materials.

Know, Inc.
PO Box 10197
Pittsburgh, PA 15232
    Distributes materials for women's studies; prints and publishes.
    KNOW Mailing Service. Women's Free Press. Know news.
    Motto: Freedom of the press belongs to those who own the
    Press. We KNOW this.

Lalor Foundation
4400 Lancaster Pike
Wilmington, DE 19805
    Distributes films for professional audiences only; cost-free cir-
    culation to medical schools, hospitals, research institutions,
    medical and para-medical organizations. "Blue book, 6th edi-
    tion" is compendium of information, technical and clinical aspects
    of vacuum aspiration.

League of Women Voters of the United States
1200 17 Street NW
Washington, DC 20036
    Provides voter-information in many languages and in Braille.
    Chapters throughout U. S. A. Purpose to promote political re-
    sponsibility through informed and active participation of citizens
    in government. Not a WL organization specifically.

Lemaze Method of Prepared Childbirth. See American Society of
    Psychoprophylaxis in Obstetrics

Liberation News Service: Women's Graphic Collective
160 Claremont Avenue.
New York, NY 10027

Library of Congress. See U. S. Library of Congress

Loercher, Donna.   See Feminist Book Mart

Lollipop Power
PO Box 1171
Chapel Hill, NC 27514
    A WL collective of people who write, illustrate and publish books
    for the liberation of young children from sex-stereotyped behavior
    and role-models.   Picture books and beginning-readers.   In
    Canada: PO Box 207, Ancaster, Ontario.

Loretto Heights College
Loretto, Denver, CO 80236
    Also Loretto Heights College Research Center on Woman

Los Angeles Public Library
630 5
Los Angeles, CA 90017
    Social Sciences Department has relevant books; manuscripts and
    pictures were turned over to the Henry E. Huntington Library
    (San Marino, CA 91108)

Louisiana Citizens for Abortion Law Reform
Box 16073
Baton Rouge, LA 70803

Louisiana Commission on the Status of Women
State Department of Labor, PO Box 44063
Baton Rouge, LA 70804
    Susan Holton, Administrator and editor of newsletter.

Lucy Stone League
133 East 58
New York, NY 10022
    Center for research and information on the status of women.
    Founded in 1921.   Non-political, non-partisan.   Open to men
    and women.

MG Tours
15 East 40
New York, NY 10016
    Eva

MLA Commission on the Status of Women in the Profession.   See
    Modern Languages Association

MM Production Center
320 East 52
New York, NY 10022
    "In spite of the Governor's Advisory Service for Small Business'
    attempts to discourage her, Ms. Margiotta 'finally got things to-
    gether, by asking around.' "   (NOW York Woman, July 1971.)
    Women's projects, brochures, layouts, pasteups, offset-dupli-
    cating.

MacFadden-Bartell
205 East 42
New York, NY 10017
    Distributors of national newsletter, Women: to, by, for and
    about.

McGraw-Hill
330 West 42
New York, NY 10036
    Rents (and sells) National Film Board of Canada motion pictures
    in the U.S.A.

Majority Enterprises, Inc.
370 Lexington Ave.
New York, NY 10017
    Corporation formed in 1971 to provide products and services to
    women; produces new serial, Ms.

Mass Media Associates/Ministries
2116 North Charles
Baltimore, MD 21218
    Protestant, Catholic, Jewish (only?).

Maternal Information Services, Inc.
46 West 96, suite 1E
New York, NY 10025
    Mrs. Helen Borel, Executive Editor of newsletter, The Working
    Mother. Other services and publications include "New York
    State Abortion Directory."

Media Collective
2 Brookline
Cambridge, MA 02139
    Lavender Vision, newspaper.

Media Plus, Inc.
60 Riverside Dr., suite 11D
New York, NY 10024
    Unique media source.

Media Women
GPO Box 1692
New York, NY 10001
    Media Women's Monthly (defunct?)

Merit. see Pathfinder Press.

Michigan.   University.   AV Education Center
416 4
Ann Arbor, MI 48103

Michigan.   University.   Center for Continuing Education of Women.
330 Thompson
Ann Arbor, MI 48108
    Maintains mailing-list.   Newsletter.   Special programs and
    events, publications.

Minnesota.   University
Minneapolis, MN 55455
    Council for University Women's Progress
        An organization of University of Minnesota women--faculty, stu-
        dents and civil service--whose purpose is to "gather and dis-
        seminate information about the status of women at the University
        and to take appropriate action" toward the improvement of that
        status ... its guidelines for the recruitment, promotion and
        hiring of women faculty members were adopted in the Spring
        1971 University Senate.   Chairman (January 1972):   Prof. Mabel
        K. Powers, 225 Johnson Hall.   No publication; monthly meetings;
        work carried on in active committees.
    Women's Continuing Education Program.
    Has quarterly publication re The Minnesota Plan.

Minot Woman's Collective
PO Box 235
Minot, ND 58701

Mixed Media Women
2325 Oak
Berkeley, CA 94708
    Spazm newsletter

Modern Languages Association
MLA Commission on the Status of Women in the Profession, Dec.
    1968.
    Chairperson, Dr. Carol Ohmann.   Wesleyan University, Middle-
    town, CT 06457
    Women's Caucus of the MLA
        President, Dr. Verna Wittrock, Dept. of English, Eastern Illi-
        nois University, Charleston, IL 61920

Movement Speakers Bureau
365 West 42
New York, NY 10036
    Media source--free catalog.   See also Speakers.

Mushroom Effect
1730 10
Berkeley, CA 92010
    Directory of WL groups, 3rd edition/1972.

NOW.   See National Organization for Women.

National Abortion Council for Therapeutic Abortions & Family
  Planning
7046 Hollywood Blvd., suite 718
Hollywood, CA 90028
  A non-profit, tax-exempt corporation chartered by the state of
  California and registered with the Los Angeles County Dept. of
  Health, which refers matters related to birth control and prob-
  lem-pregnancies to the Council. Composed of counselors,
  psychologists, physicians, social workers and concerned citizens.
  Abortion counseling, pregnancy testing, and other services pro-
  vided without charge by qualified volunteers. Contributions not
  solicited.

National Ad Hoc Committee for ERA
2310 Barbour Rd.
Falls Church, VA 22043
  Newsletter. Flora Crater.

National Assoc. for Nursery Education. See National Assoc. for
  the Education of Young Children.

National Assoc. for Repeal of Abortion Laws
250 West 57, room 2428
New York, NY 10019

National Assoc. for the Education of Young Children
1834 Conn. Ave. N.W.
Washington, DC 20009
  National non-profit association of 17,000+ persons representing
  educational occupations and related disciplines. Founded in
  1926. Publishes Young Children, professional journal devoted
  to children from infancy to age eight. Conferences. Publications include pamphlets, "A beginner's bibliography," "Benefits
  of a good nursery school," "Some ways of distinguishing a good
  school or center for young children."

National Association of Laymen Women Rights Committee
Noreen Dowling, 1340 East 72
Chicago, IL 60619

National Association of Women Artists, Inc.
156 5 Avenue
New York, NY 10010

National Association of Women Lawyers
1155 East 60
Chicago, IL 60637
  Women Lawyers' Journal

National Constituents for Bella Abzug
1829 Phelps Place NW, #2
Washington, DC 20008

National Council of Women
345 East 46
New York, NY 10017
   Publishes international directory of women's organizations, now
   out of print, with plans for updated edition.

National Council of Women (of Canada)
270 MacLaren, Ottawa 4, Canada
   The Council contracted with the Canadian Association for Adult
   Education for preparation of a study guide based on The Report
   of the Royal Commission on the Status of Women in Canada.
   Has newsletter.

National Council on Family Relations
Task Force on Women's Rights & Responsibilities
   Chairperson, Dr. Rose Somerville, Sociology Department, San
   Diego State College, San Diego, CA 92115

National Education Assoc.
1201 16 Street NW
Washington, DC 20036
   Women's Caucus. Chairperson, Helen Bain.

National Federation of Business & Professional Women's Clubs, Inc.
   of the U.S.A. See Business & Professional Women's Foundation

National Film Board of Canada
680 5 Avenue
New York, NY 10019
   NFBC films are rented and sold in the U.S. by Contemporary/
   McGraw-Hill. A list of sources for purchase in the U.S. is
   contained in the NFBC catalog, "16mm films available for pur-
   chase and rental in U.S." latest edition. Benchmark, Pyramid,
   Xerox, Perennial also distribute NFBC films.

National Law Women
1616 Longfellow Street NW
Washington, DC 20011
   Publishes PRO SE newsletter, with law school service rate, i.e.
   includes a copy for each woman student. ($25.)

National Organization for Women (NOW)
   Founded in 1966, NOW's purpose is to work actively for full
   equality for all women in America, in truly equal partnership
   with men. It campaigns for full income-tax deductions for
   child-care costs of working parents, for a nationwide network
   of child-care centers to enable more women to work while raising
   a family, for greatly expanded job-training programs for women,
   and for re-examination of marriage-divorce laws/customs that
   discriminate against women and men alike. Supported passage
   of the Equal Rights Amendment. Betty Friedan was a founder
   and first president, and is currently a member of the national
   advisory committee. Membership, including officers, includes
   men.

National office: 1957 East 73, Chicago, IL 60649.   NOW Acts.
Do it NOW.
New York Chapter Office: 28 East 56, New York 10022.   NOW
York Woman.
Most chapters have literature and other media, e.g. stickers and
labels, for sale.   Chapters throughout the USA; also Task Forces
--Women in Poverty; Religion; Equal Employment Opportunity;
Abortion; Reproduction and its Control; Women and Volunteerism;
Education; and Marriage, Divorce & Family Relations.

National Vocational Guidance Association
NVGA Commission on the Occupational Status of Women, Nov. 1968
Chairperson, Thelma C. Lennon, Director, Pupil Personnel Ser-
  vices, Department of Public Instruction, Raleigh, NC 27602.

National Volunteer Attorney Reserve Corps.   See Human Rights for
  Women, Inc.

National Welfare Rights Organization
1419 H Street NW
Washington, DC 20005
  The Welfare Fighter

National Woman's Liberation Front for Libraries.   See American
  Library Assoc.   Task Force on the Status of Women in Librarianship.

National Woman's Party
144 Constitution Ave., N.E.
Washington, DC 20002
  Kept Equal Rights for Women before the Congress fifty years!
  Established in 1913 for suffrage for women through the adoption
  of the Federal Suffrage Amendment; reorganized in 1921 for equal
  rights for women in all fields.   Its immediate purpose is to se-
  cure adoption of the Equal Rights Amendment.   See "Up hill with
  banners flying--the story of the Woman's Party" by Inez Irwin.
  Affiliated with the World Woman's Party and with the International
  Council of Women.
Library: Florence Bayard Hills Library--manuscripts, maps,
  clippings 1909-22.

National Women's Political Caucus
707 Warner Building, 13 and E N.W.
Washington, DC 20004
  Elected members of Policy Council include Bella Abzug, Shana
  Alexander, Shirley Chisholm, Betty Friedan, Fannie Lou Hamer,
  LaDonna Harris, Wilma Scott Heide, Gloria Steinem.

New England Free Press
791 Tremont
Boston, MA 02118
  Media source.   Catalog includes some articles re women; will
  also train women for printing.

New Feminist Bookstore
1525 East 53
Chicago, IL 60615
  Media: stickers, labels, books, buttons, pamphlets, banners,
  posters and other artifacts relevant to the Women's Movement.
  Mail-order; plans for storefront. Quantity rates.

New Feminist Talent Collective
148 West 68
New York, NY 10023
  Speakers' Bureau and talent agency for presentations before all
  types of groups.

New Feminists Repertory Theater
43 West 54
New York, NY 10019
  Founder: Anselma Del'Olio

New Line Cinema
121 University Place
New York, NY 10003

New University Conference
622 West Diversey Parkway
Chicago, IL 60614
  Founded 1968. Florence Howe active. Newsletter. "How
  Harvard rules women" (77p, 75¢) written and produced by a
  group of Harvard women affiliated with NUC.

New Women Lawyers.
Carol Bellamy. Room 414
93 Worth
New York, NY 10013

New University Conference Women's Caucus
928 Meadowlark Lane
Laguna Beach, CA 93651

New York Media Project
PO Box 266, Village Station
New York, NY 10014
  Free information on the media.

New York Public Library
5th Avenue & 42
New York, NY 10018
  Economics Division has relevant materials.

New York Radical Feminists
Box 621, Old Chelsea Station
New York, NY 10011
  Shulamith Firestone a founder. Publications include "Notes..."
  Sponsors conferences, e.g., Rape Conference, 1971.

New York University
40 Washington Square South, School of Law
New York, NY 10012
   Women and the Law Clinical Program; Women and the Law Research Seminar.   All courses open only to students who have
   applied and been accepted as full-time candidates for the Juris
   Doctor degree.

New York Women Strike for Peace
799 Broadway
New York, NY 10003
   Peaceletter

New Yorker Films
2409 Broadway
New York, NY 10024

New Yorkers for Abortion Law Repeal (NYALR); a Statewide Group.
PO Box 240, Planetarium Station
New York, NY 10024
   Newsletter.   Buttons, kits, literature.   Inquiries welcomed from
   all states.   Aim: help all U.S. get rid of laws and practices
   against abortion/contraception.

Newenhouse, Henk, Inc.
1825 Willow Rd.
Northfield, IL 60093

News & Letters
415 Brainard
Detroit, MI 48201
   Literature source.   "Notes on WL" (50¢)

Newsreel
322 7 Ave.
New York, NY 10001
   Outlets throughout USA, e.g. 968 Valencia, San Francisco, CA
   94110.

Northwestern University.   Special Collections.
Evanston, IL 60201
   Roxanna Siefer, Reference Librarian.   Collects NOW chapter
   newsletters.

O.M. Collective
   Producers of "The Organizer's Manual" available (1971) from
   Bantam (666 5 Ave., New York, NY 10019).   Includes a chapter
   on women as a special constituency.

Old Mole
Brookline, Cambridge, MA 02139
   Pamphlets, reprints.

Ontario Dept. of Labour
Women's Bureau
Toronto, Canada
   "Career selector."

Oscar Wilde Memorial Bookshop
291 Mercer
New York, NY 10003
   Mail-order catalog. Opened 1967. Gay periodicals, fiction,
   non-fiction, counseling. "We exist to serve the Homosexual
   community in an open, forthright and dignified manner."

Parents' Aid Society
107 Main
Hempstead, NY 11550
   Birth-control clinic. Contact by phoning Bill Baird person-to-
   person: 516-538-2626 or 516-437-2828. Birth control and abortion counseling. Abortion and vasectomy clinics planned.

Partisan Press
45 Gamble
Forest Road West
Nottingham NG7 4ET England

Pathfinder Press (Formerly Merit Publishers)
410 West
New York, NY 10014
   Media source.

Perennial Education
1825 Willow
Northfield, IL 60893
   Distributes National Film Board of Canada and E. C. Brown
   Trust Foundation films in U. S. A. Has tapes.

Philosophy of Education Society
Women's caucus, April 1971.
Chairperson, Dr. Elizabeth Steiner Maccia. Dept. of History &
   Philosophy of Education, Indiana University, Bloomington, IN
   47401.

Pine Manor Junior College
400 Heath
 Chestnut Hill, MA 02167
   Library has first editions of distinguished American women
   writers 1822-1932.

Planned Parenthood: Abortion numbers:
   New York   212-777-4504, 212-777-2015
   Colorado   303-388-4125

Planned Parenthood Federation of America, Inc.
    Executive Office: 810 7 Ave., New York, NY 10019
    Margaret Sanger Research Bureau: 17 West 16, New York,
    NY 10011

Planned Parenthood of New York City, Inc.
    Executive Office and Family Planning Information Service: 300
    Park Ave. South, New York, NY 10010
    Family Planning Resources: 44 Court, Brooklyn, NY 11201
    Centers throughout the City.

Planned Parenthood-World Population
    Center for Family Planning Program Development: 515 Madison
    Ave., New York, NY 10022
    See also International Planned Parenthood Federation.

Population Assoc. of America.
Women's Caucus, April 1970.
Chairperson, Prof. Ruth B. Dixon, Dept. of Sociology, University
    of California, Davis, CA 95616

Population Council
245 Park Ave.
New York, NY 10017

Pride and Prejudice
3322 North Halsted
Chicago, IL 60657
    Bookstore

PROBE into the Status of Women at the University of Michigan
PO Box 317
Ann Arbor, MI 48107

Professional Women's Caucus
Radio City Station, Box 1057
New York, NY 10019
    President, Sheila Tobias, Assistant Provost, Wesleyan Univer-
    sity, Middletown, CT 06457

Professionals Organized for Women's Equal Rights (POWER). See
    Professional Women's Caucus.

Project WIL: Women in Leadership
730 Witherspoon Building
Philadelphia, PA 19107
    Offers help to groups of women in local communities who are
    seeking to effect change; assistance would include planning,
    written materials, possibly money.

Public Affairs Committee, Inc.
381 Park Avenue South
New York, NY 10016

Public Library: Telephone Reference Service

Pussycat League
c/o Women's News Service, 1501 Broadway
New York, NY 10036
    Mrs. Lucianne Goldberg, co-founder and national chairman, says
    "It's a man's world" and opposes "Women's Lib." Motto: "Purr,
    baby, purr."

Radcliffe College
10 Garden
Cambridge, MA 02138
    The Women's Archives.   History and contributions of American
        women in all phases of public and private life.   Manuscripts
        and books document history and contributions of American
        women, especially in areas of woman suffrage, education, law,
        family, medicine, and organizations.   Pamphlets and periodicals
        also.
    Arthur & Elizabeth Schlesinger Library on the History of Women
        in America (3 James).   Black history; women's rights; women
        in politics, medicine, nursing, philanthropy, social service.
    Radcliffe Institute.   Established by Radcliffe College in 1960 as
        an integral part of the College, but separately administered
        and funded.   A guidance laboratory, research program, adult
        education-type courses called Radcliffe Seminars (3 James).
        The Institute seeks to expand the choices open to women in
        scholarship, the creative arts, and the professions.   Scholar-
        ships awarded to seniors and advanced training students, and
        for part-time graduate study.

Radical Education Project
Box 561-A
Detroit, MI 48232
    Literature list includes a number of WL publications, e.g. the
    Bread and Roses Statement, and "I am furious female."

Radical Research Center, renamed Alternative Press Centre
Bag Service 2500, Postal Station E
Toronto, Canada
    For "Alternative Press Index.," begun in 1969, when the Center
    was at Carleton College.   Quarterly: $30/year, $6 to move-
    ment groups and individuals.

Radio Free People
160 Prospect Place
Brooklyn, NY 11238
    WL tapes.

Resist
763 Mass. Ave., #4
Cambridge, MA 02139
    Media source.

Resource Center on Women.   See Y. W. C. A.

Reynolds, Stuart Productions
8465 Wilshire Blvd.
Beverly Hills, CA 90212

Roe, Stuart
Box 24569
Westwood Village, Los Angeles, CA 90024

Rosen, Ruth
3024 Fulton B.
Berkeley, CA 94705
    Photographer to the Women's Movement.

SIECUS.   See Sex Information & Education Council of the U. S.

SRRT: Social Responsibilities Round Table Task Force on Status
    of Women in Librarianship.   See American Library Association
    Task Force....

Saint Catherine College.   Library
2004 Randolph Ave.
St. Paul, MN 55116
    Clippings, letters, pictures, slides, manuscripts; emphasis on
    psychological liberation of woman in 20th century includes
    feminist movement.

Saint Joan's (Catholic) Alliance
1941 North 36
Milwaukee, WI 53208
    Saint Joan's Bulletin.   Supports Equal Rights Amendment.

San Francisco Bay Area Women in the Technical Trades
3021 Dana #1
Berkeley, CA 94705
    Newsletter (defunct?).

San Francisco Women for Peace
50 Oak, Room 503
San Francisco, CA 94102

Scripps College
Ella Strong Denison Library
Claremont, CA 91711
    The status, interests and humanistic accomplishments of woman.
    Collection includes manuscripts.

Sex Information & Education Council of the U. S. (SIECUS)
1855 Broadway
New York, NY 10023
    Newsletter is for subscribers, i. e. does not maintain mailing-

list.   Publications office: 1825 Willow Road, Northfield, IL
60093.   Mary S. Calderone, M.D., Director.   SIECUS publications include Study Guide series.   Educational & Research Services.

Smith College
William Allan Neilson Library
Northampton, MA 01060
   Sophia Smith Collection includes manuscripts, pictures.   Social
   and intellectual history of women, with emphasis on women in
   the U.S.; organizational activities of women; and social history
   of women throughout the world.   Large personal collection of
   family papers.   Manuscripts are listed in the U.S. Library of
   Congress' "National Union Catalog" of Manuscript Collections.

Society for Cell Biology
Women in cell biology, Nov. 1971.
Chairperson, Virginia Walbot, Dept. of Biology, Yale University,
   New Haven, CT 06520

Society for Humane Abortion
PO Box 1862
San Francisco, CA 94101
   Has newsletter, reprint list, and "The abortees' songbook" ($1.).

Society for Individual Rights
83 6
San Francisco, CA 94103
   Media source: posters, buttons, pamphlets.

Sociologists for Women in Society, June 1969.
Chairperson, Dr. Alice Rossi.   Department of Sociology, Goucher
   College, Towson, MD 21204

Sojourner Truth Press
432 Moreland Avenue NE
Atlanta, GA 30307

Sons of Thunder
   A very militant anti-abortion group based in Washington, D.C.,
   formed by L. Brent Bozell, William Buckley's brother-in-law.
   Bozell broke with Buckley because he considers Buckley far too
   liberal!

Source Book Press, a Division of Collector's Editions, Ltd.
185 Madison Avenue   [Order from: Van Nostrand Reinhold,
New York, NY 10016   300 Pike, Cincinnati, OH 45202]
   Ann Calderwood, Executive Editor of "The Source Library of The
   Women's Movement" Series begun in 1970; Advisory Board includes Kate Millett, Pauli Murray and Alice Rossi.   40 titles/
   63 volumes of reprints concerning the history of the women's
   rights movement. $950.

SPEAKERS
Contact local women's center and NOW Chapter office; the following
are a few suggestions:
> Bassin, Amelia. 1970's "Advertising Woman of the Year" and
> President of Bassinova, Inc., 12 West 55, New York, NY
> 10019.
>
> Cisler, Lucinda. 102 West 80, New York, NY 10024.
>
> Freeman, Jo. 6031 South Kimbark Avenue, Chicago, IL 60637.
>
> Howard, Carin. 3263 Bramson, San Diego, CA 92104.
>
> Movement Speakers Bureau
>
> New Feminist Talent Collective
>
> Trobec, Maureen. 4752 Tupello, Baton Rouge, LA 70808.

Sterling Educational Films, Division of Walter Reede
241 East 34
New York, NY 10016

Stone, Lucy. See Lucy Stone.

Suzy Creamcheese Collective
2551 North Halsted
Chicago, IL 60614
> Media collective and radio program.

Swank Motion Pictures
201 South Jefferson Ave.
St. Louis, MO 63166

Swarthmore College
Friends Historical Library and Peace Collection
Swarthmore, PA 19081
> Material on women who have contributed to women's rights and
> the advancement of womanhood, e.g. Lucretia Mott, Jane Ad-
> dams, Emily Greene Balch; has brochure available by mail.

Swedish Information Service
825 3 Ave.
New York, NY 10022
> Supplies free materials re all aspects of Swedish life except
> trade and tourist. Contact Information Officer.

The Swedish Institute
PO Box 7072
S-103-82 Stockholm, Sweden
> Relevant publications include Anna-Greta Leijon's "Swedish wo-
> men--Swedish men."

TCB Productions, Ltd.
185 Claremont Ave.
New York, NY 10027
> Producers of musical play, "God Bless God--She Needs It!" by
> Patricia Horan and Vicki Vidall.

Talent Bank
2012 Mass. Ave. N. W.
Washington, DC 20036
      Collecting names of and information on women for appointment
      to high-level Federal Government positions.

Tandem Books
33 Beauchamp Place
London SW 3, England
      Media source.

Task Force on Women in Librarianship.   See American Library
      Assoc.

Theater for Women's Liberation
148 West 68, c/o Jacqui Ceballos
New York, NY 10023

Time-Life Films
43 West 16
New York, NY 10011
      Distributor for BBC-TV in U. S. A.

Times Change Press
1023 6 Ave.
New York, NY 10018
      Media source: posters, pamphlets.   Wants articles by women.

Today Publications
1132 National Press Building
Washington, DC 20004
      Publishes Women Today newsletter.

Trans Lux Distribution Corp.
625 Madison Ave.
New York, NY 10022

Tubman, Harriet. Brigade. See Harriet Tubman Brigade.

Unitarian Universalist Women's Federation
25 Beacon
Boston, MA 02108
      The Bridge

United Nations
UN Plaza
New York, NY 10017
      Commission on the Status of Women.   UN Monthly Chronicle
      indexed in "Readers' Guide."   Publications in print include:
         Civil and political education of women.
         Convention on the Nationality of Married Women: Historical

background and commentary.
Convention on the Political Rights of Women: History and
commentary.
Legal status of married women.
Nationality of married women, rev.
The UN and the status of women, 3 ed.
Study of discrimination against persons born out of wedlock.

United Nations Educational, Scientific & Cultural Organization
  (UNESCO)
UNESCO House: Place de Fontenoy
Paris 7e, France
  General information: UNESCO Liaison Office, UN, New York,
  NY 10017.   Numerous statistical documents re women around
  the world.

United Presbyterian Church of the USA
Task Force on Women, Sept. 1969
Co-chairpersons: Patricia Doyle, Elaine Homrighouse
  Board of Christian Education, United Presbyterian Church,
  Witherspoon Building, Philadelphia, PA 19107

U. S. Council of Commissions on the Status of Women
432 North Lake
Madison, WI 53706
  Founded 1969.   Dr. Kathryn F. Clarenbach, Chairman.

U. S. Department of Labor
Women's Bureau
Washington, DC 20210
  Regional Offices:
  1700-E Federal Building, Boston, MA 02203
  1317 Filbert, Philadelphia, PA 19107
  1371 Peachtree NE, Atlanta, GA 30309
  219 South Dearborn, Chicago, IL 60604
  721 19, Denver, CO 80202
  450 Golden Gate Ave., Box 36017, San Francisco, CA 94102
  1100 Commerce, Dallas, TX 75201
  Part of the Wage & Labor Standards Administration.   Get Bureau
  Handbook and Publications List.   Established in 1920 by Congressional Act: Bureau in charge of a salaried woman appointed by
  the President with advice and consent of the Senate.   Duty: to
  formulate standards and policies which shall promote the welfare
  of wage-earning women, improve their working conditions, increase their efficiency, and advance their opportunities for profit-
  able employment.   Director: Elizabeth Duncan Koontz.

U. S. Equal Employment Opportunity Commission
1800 G Street NW
 Washington, DC 20506.   And local offices.
  Set up under Civil Rights Act of 1964 and charged with investi-
  gating complaints of discrimination and seeking to conciliate them.
  Obtain from local EEOC or national office the "Guidelines on

testing." Get copies of pamphlet, "Towards job equality for women" (1969) and distribute at meetings.

U.S. Library of Congress
Washington, DC 20540
    Susan B. Anthony, Carrie Chapman Catt, and National American
    Woman Suffrage Association Collections. Congressional Refer-
    ence Service prepares excellent selective bibliographies (reading
    lists) on women.

U.S. Supt. of Documents
Government Printing Office
Washington, DC 20402

United Women's Contingent
1029 Vermont Ave., N.W., 8th floor
Washington, DC 20005

Universal/16
155 Universal City Plaza
Universal City, CA 91608
    Part of Universal Education and Visual Arts, a division of
    Universal City Studios, Inc. Offices throughout the U.S.

University Microfilms, a Xerox Company
300 North Zeeb Road
Ann Arbor, MI 48106
    For reprints of out-of-print books.

University Women's Assoc. (UWA)
6031 South Kimbark Ave.
Chicago, IL 60637
    i.e. University of Chicago. Has WL materials--pamphlets, UWA
    News, buttons, etc. Jo Freeman compiling anthology of the new
    research, analysis and thinking re women. General reader for
    courses on women and the wider public.

Urban Research Corp.
5464 South Shore Drive
Chicago, IL 60615
    The Spokeswoman edited and printed by women.

Vassar--The College Club
718 27 Ave.
San Francisco, CA 94121

Vanderbilt University
Television News Archive
Nashville, TN 37203
    Began in 1968, a permanent collection of videotapes of the daily
    news programs broadcast over the 3 national TV networks; housed
    in the general library building of The Joint University Libraries.

WBAI-FM
30 East 39
New York, NY 10016
  Tapes of women's programs.   99.5 FM.   "Womankind" and
  "Electra Rewired."

WEAL. See Women's Equity Action League.

WISE: Women for the Inclusion of Sexual Expression
PO Box 558, Cathedral Station
New York, NY 10025

WLF Publications Collective
301 Jefferson Blvd.
Iowa City, IA 52240
  Ain't I A Woman? newspaper.

WLM Basement Press
PO Box 6323
Albany, CA 94706

Westbeth Playwrights.
Dolores Walker, Pat Horan, co-chairmen.
463 West, 402D
New York, NY 10014
  Feminist collective.

Widows Consultation Center
136 East 57
New York, NY 10022
  See McCalls':45, Feb. 1971. Mrs. David Sher (social worker)
  and Mrs. Joseph Druss (lawyer) have a grant from the Prudential Insurance Co. of America for a 3-year pilot program
  which might become a model: classes on managing money,
  finding a job, eventual placement as a volunteer, "where she
  can feel the rewards of contributing."

Wisconsin Committee to Legalize Abortion
1153 East Sylvan Ave.
Milwaukee, WI 53217
  For help: 414-962-5259

Wolper Productions
555 Madison Ave.
New York, NY 10022

Woman's Medical College of Pennsylvania. See Women's Medical
  College....

A Woman's Place
29 1/2 Cornelia
New York, NY 10014
  Gay women's bookstore.

Women Against Daddy Warbucks
339 Lafayette
New York, NY 10012
    Consumerism.

Women Artists in Revolution (WAR)
    New York-based spin-off of the Art Workers Coalition, spawned
    by the women members discontent with their second class status
    in this group.   Contact Pat Mainardi c/o Art News (444 Madison
    Ave., New York, NY 10022); also Louise Nelson re women stu-
    dent artists.

Women at AT&T
1601 41 Ave.
Seattle, WA 98102
    Traffic Jam newsletter.

Women for Equal Justice Under Law
753 Warner Building, 13th & "E" N.W.
Washington, DC 20004

Women for President and Other Public Office, Inc.
110 East 42
New York, NY 10017

Women in City Government United
c/o Susan Harmon, 52 Chambers
New York, NY 10007
    Newsletter (defunct?), 346 Broadway, 10013.

Women in Public Office
107 East 41
New York, NY 10017

Women in Publishing
c/o Women's Center, 36 West 22
New York, NY 10011
    Some People's Paper newsletter, first issue May 25, 1970.

Women in Struggle
Box 324
Winneconne, WI 54986

Women in The Arts, A Co-op.
185 School
Acton, MA 01720

Women on Words and Images
Box 2163
Princeton, NJ 08540
    "Sex stereotypes in school readers" ($1.50).

Women Strike for Peace
2140 P N. W.
Washington, DC 20032
    Memo. Outlets in major cities.

Women Theologians United
Andover Newton Seminary, Box 138
Newton Center, MA 02159

Women United
PO Box 300
Washington, DC 20044

Women's Abortion Clinic
5 Carmine
New York, NY 10014

Women's Abortion Coalition
130 10
San Francisco, CA 94103

Women's Abortion Project
Abortion Project of Women's Liberation
c/o Women's Center, 36 West 22, New York, NY 10011
    "network of some 400 women's liberationists dedicated to the
    right of every woman who wants an abortion to have one. In
    addition to making referrals to all the standard facilities plus
    its own doctors outside the city, the Abortion Project will find
    women places to stay and do just about anything else necessary
    to help someone having an abortion. ..." (New York Times Maga-
    zine:42, April 11, 1971.)

Women's Action Alliance, Inc.
200 Park Avenue, Room 1520
New York, NY 10017
    Clearinghouse on "local action projects."

Women's Ad-Hoc Abortion Coalition
PO Box 6083
San Francisco, CA 94101

Women's Archives. See Radcliffe College

Women's Assistance Bureau/Tour
212-245-2569
    Assistance in arranging abortion abroad-out of town. See
    Moneysworth, October 19, 1970.

Women's Bureau. See U.S. Dept. of Labor. Women's Bureau.

Women's Caucus for Political Science
3223 Brodhead Road
Bethlehem Township, PA 18017

Women's Caucus.   Union Theological Seminar
Broadway at 120
New York, NY 10027
   Founded spring 1969.   Formed permanent Assembly committee on
   women, several consciousness-raising groups, seminar.   Primarily
   a political organization, having as its aim the statement and solution of the problems of women's oppression, both in the seminary
   and outside of it.

Women's Center for Occupational & Educational Development
167 East 67
New York, NY 10021

Women's Equalization Committee
Los Angeles, CA
   Placed an advertisement asking husbands to send $1. for a
   legal form giving their wives an equal voice in managing family
   property.   (Time Dec. 20, 1971.)

Women's Equity Action League   (WEAL)
1254 4 SW
Washington, DC 20024
   Supports Equal Rights Amendment.   Has court actions against
   more than 100 colleges and universities in behalf of women employed by them.   National organization composed of men and
   women.   Files sex-discrimination cases.   Weal Word Watcher.
   Membership includes Bernice Sandler, Caroline Bird, Martha W.
   Griffiths.   For information, send SASE to: Elizabeth Boyer,
   7657 Dines Road, Novelty, OH 44072.   Washington Report.

Women's Film Crew
451 Courtland
San Francisco, CA 94110
   Making 50-minute film.

Women's Free Press.   See Know, Inc.

Women's Graphic Collective
   Part of Liberation News Service.

Women's Heritage Series, Inc.
Box 3236
Santa Monica, CA 90403
   Communications consultants.   Graphics: calendar, imprinted
   sweatshirts, posters, pendants.   By mail.

Women's History Research Center, Inc.
2325 Oak
Berkeley, CA 94708
   Small tax-exempt privately-operating foundation housing the
   International Archive of the present Women's Movement and a
   "Topical Research Library" of material by and about women
   everywhere and always.   For inquiries about microfilming,

catalogs, directories and Herstory, send tax-deductible donation and **SASE.** Open to members; call 415-524-7772 for appointment.

Women's Information Center
University of California at Los Angeles Extension
10966 LeConte Ave., Room 20
Los Angeles, CA 90024

Women's International League for Peace and Freedom
2006 Walnut
Philadelphia, PA 19103
    Four Lights.

Women's Joint Legislative Committee for Equal Rights
1207 Greycourt Ave.
Richmond, VA 23227
    Represents national organizations working towards passage of
    the Equal Rights Amendment.

Women's Legal Defense Fund, Inc.
3619 T N.W.
Washington, DC 20007

Women's Medical Center
80 Irving Place
New York, NY 10003

Women's Medical College of Pennsylvania
3300 Henry Ave.
Philadelphia, PA 19129
    In addition to the resource which the institution is itself, the
    Library includes a collection gathered over a period of years by
    a number of women physicians and presented to the American
    Medical Women's Assoc., which, in turn, presented it to the
    College.

Women's Medical Group. See Women's Services.

Women's Medical News Service
3 West 57
New York, NY 10019

Women's National Abortion Action Coalition
150 5 Ave.
New York, NY 10011
    Has newsletter, research committee, literature; participated in
    Women's National Abortion Conference, July 1971, New York
    City.

Women's National Book Assoc.
1180 6 Ave.
New York, NY 10036
    Founded 1917; not a WL group.

Women's News Service.   See Pussycat.

Women's Rock Band
c/o Jennifer Abod, 23 Beers
New Haven, CT 06511

Women's Services Clinic
133 East 73
New York, NY 10021

Women's Unit--New York State
Executive Chamber
Albany, NY 12224
    Also: 22 West 55, New York, NY 10019
    WU News.   July 1970 issue contained insert advertising Rocke-
    feller legislation, including 8 photographs of him, "Kitty's
    Calendar" column no relationship to women.

World Council of Churches
439 Riverside Dr., Room 439
New York, NY 10027
    Departments of Faith & Order and Cooperation of Men and Wo-
    men: "Concerning the Ordination of Women," 1964 pamphlet.

X, Laura.   See Women's History Research Center.

Yale Medical School
New Haven, CT 06510
    Philip Sarrel, M.D., Yale College Health Program Director,
    administers what SIECUS and others consider a "good program."

Young Women's Christian Association (YWCA)   USA: 600 Lexington
    Ave., New York, NY 10022
    Resource Center on Women.   Helen Southard.   Establishing
       women's resource center to launch action and training for
       branches.
    National Board Library.   Not an historical collection, but covers
       women in the contemporary world--their social, psychological,
       political development; primarily women in the U.S.A.
    Bureau of Communications (of National Board).   Has "Directory
       of YWCA's of the U.S.A." (latest edition) which includes com-
       munity and accredited YW's; student YW's; registered YW
       groups, USO-YW's and other world, national, Headquarters and
       regional offices.   Residence/transient accommodations indi-
       cated.   Student YW's are mostly on college campuses.   Also
       available: "World YWCA Directory" and "Pack for Europe."
    See also: Local phone directory.   Note: "Christianity" not
       necessary.

Zero Population Growth
267 State
Los Altos, CA 94022

Stickers and labels, posters, bumper stickers, literature.
Also: 30 Charles, New York, NY 10014; Box 147 Old Mystic,
CT 06372

WOMEN'S LIBERATION GROUPS AND CENTERS. Included here are
more or less unspecialized, non-professional groups. Arrangement
is alphabetical by country; within country, alphabetical by state or
province; within state, alphabetical by city or other community;
within community, alphabetical by names of organizations. See also
National Organization for Women.

Argentina
WLM c/o Gabriella Cristeller
Olleros 1969 4° 3
Buenos Aires

Australia
The Glebe Group
67 Glebe Point Road. Glebe
2037
Sydney, New South Wales
Mejane. Women's Libera-
tion Newsletter.

WL Group
22 Nicholson
Balmain, Sydney

Working Women's Group
c/o Sydney Trade Union Club

Canada
Calgary WL
2440 14 S.W., c/o Sharon Hunt
Calgary, Alberta

Edmonton WL
10-10168 100
Edmonton, Alberta

Vancouver Women's Caucus
511 Carroll
Vancouver, British Columbia
The Pedestal, 307 West
Broadway, Room 6; litera-
ture list.

Vancouver WL
1775 Alberta

Vancouver 5, British Columbia
Vancouver WL News.

WLM 1029 Coroydon
c/o Joyce Arnold
Winnipeg 1, Manitoba

Fredericton WL
748 Forest Hill Road
c/o Carol H. Smith
Fredericton, New Brunswick

Halifax Women's Caucus
Rosa Luxemburg Co-op
c/o C. Walker
6409 Quinpool Road
Halifax, Nova Scotia

WL
10 Water, apt. 205
Guelph, Ontario

Hamilton District WL
297 Wentworth North
Hamilton District, Ontario

Ottawa WL
360 Frank
c/o Valerie Angus
Ottawa 4, Ontario
WL Newsletter

WL Thunderbay
12 Lyle c/o Joan Baril
Thunderbay, Ontario

New Feminists
PO Box 597, Station A

Toronto 116, Ontario
  The New Feminist

Toronto WL
325 Church   c/o Ryerson Student Union
Toronto, Ontario

WL League
52 Elgin   c/o Peggy Morton
Toronto, Ontario

Women in the Labor Force
84 Follis, apt. 2
Toronto, Ontario

McGill Students' Society
3480 McTavish
Montreal, Quebec

Montreal WL
c/o Marlene Dixon, Sociology
  Dept., McGill University
Montreal, Quebec
    Newsletter: 3794 Ste.
    Famille

Regina Women's Caucus
3630 Argyle Road
c/o Doris Rand
Regina, Saskatchewan

Saskatook Women's Caucus
127 Lake Crescent
c/o S. Hamhood
Saskatoon, Saskatchewan

Denmark
Dansk Kvinnessamfund
Niels Henminggensgade 8-10
Copenhagen

WL Group, Denmark
c/o Biblioteket Dronningensgade 14
1420 Copenhagen K

England
Bristol Militant Group
8 Clifton Park
Bristol 8
    Enough Is Enough journal

Bristol WL
47 Princess Victoria
c/o Monica Sjoo
Bristol 8

WL Workshop
12/13 Little Newport
London, WC 2
    Shrew journal.

Women's National Coordinating
  Committee
3 Rona Road
London, NW 3
    Women's Struggle bulletin.

Socialist Women's Group
40 Inverness Road
c/o Ms. Leonara Lloyd
Southall, Middlesex

Nottingham WL Group
85 Rivermead, Wilford Lane
West Bridgeford, Nottingham
    Women Now! newspaper.

Socialist Women
16 Ella Road
West Bridgeford, Nottingham
    Socialist Women journal.

Finland
Democratic League of Finnish
  Women
Kotkankatu 9
Helsinki

France
Nicole Buffault (52, Bis Vaneau,
  Paris VII) has started a
  small group.
French WL can be contacted
  c/o LNS, 160 Claremont
  Ave., New York, NY 10027.

Italy
Contact Maria Pia Cantamessa,
  Piazza di Sant' Egidio, 14,
  Roma.   Rivolta Feminile.
Contact Annette Harrison and
  Marina Giovanella, RR#1, St.
  Croix Cove, Hudson, WI

54016; they will send information to and entertain women of Rome.
Italian groups include:
Il colletivo per la lotta feminista; La federazione Italiana per la lotta feminista; La fronte Italiana per la liberazione della donna; Il movimento per la liberazione della donna; Rivolta feminista.

Mexico
Federation of Mexican Women
Marta Tamayo, Bartolache
1931, Colonia del Valle
Mexico 12, DF
  Sra. Tamayo does not speak English.

Netherlands
Mad Minas ("Dolle Minas") of Amsterdam; named after Wilhelmina ("Mina") Drucker, 19th century women's emancipation leader in Holland.
Pake, POB nr6 Amsterdam

Sweden
Lindberg, Mona
Markgaten 31A
70355 Orebro

Hild-Gnugli, Sylvia
Korsbarsvagen 918F
Stockholm

Union of South Africa
The Women's Group
97 4 Ave.
Linden, Johannesburg
  WL Magazine

U. S. S. R.
Soviet Woman's Committee and Central Council of Trade Unions
22 Kuznetsky Most
Moscow
  Publish Soviet Woman (above address is editorial office)

U. S. A.
Alabama
Women for Equality (WE)
1849 Windsor Blvd.
Birmingham 35209

Arizona
WL
4204 North 38 c/o Debbie Coyne
Phoenix 85018

California
WL: Humboldt State College
132 13 c/o Barbara LaBotz
Arcata 95521

Bay Area WL
PO Box 4137
Berkeley 94704
  Tooth and Nail, 1800 Prince, 94703

East Bay Feminists
c/o Women's Center, Box 4399
Berkeley 94714
  Newsletter (defunct?)

Berkeley WL
2398 Bancroft
Berkeley 94704
  Newsletter (defunct?)

Gay WL
2828 Benvenue Ave.
Berkeley 94705

Sisters in Struggle
2713 Ellsworth
Berkeley 94704

University of California Women's Caucus. 94720:
  School of Social Work, Haviland Hall. Political Science Dept., 210 Barrows Hall, B. 4511 Tolman Hall.

Women of the Free Future
c/o Women's Center, PO Box 4399
Berkeley 94714

WL Center
1126 Addison (PO Box 4399)
Berkeley 94702

Dana Point WLM
33372 Palo Alto
Dana Point 92629

WL Center
University of California: Davis
Davis 95616
  Women's Forum.

Isla Vista Women's Center
6504 Pardall
Goleta 93017
  Restless Eagle.

Hayward United
25400 Hillary c/o Jill Spitzer
Hayward 94542

Verano Women's Center
Irvine Recreation Center
Irvine 94538

University Park WL
622 Bluebird Canyon
Laguna Beach 92651

Long Beach WL
848 Molino
Long Beach 90804

California. University. WL
Student Union Building UCLA
405 Hilgard
Los Angeles 90024

Sisters In Struggles
2111 Hillsboro Ave.
c/o Paule Litt
Los Angeles 90034

West Los Angeles Women
3215 Selby Ave. c/o Patsy
  Ostroy
Los Angeles, CA 90034

Women's Center
1027 South Crenshaw Blvd.
Los Angeles 90019
  Classes (men attend some);

counseling, including abortion
referral; Los Angeles WL
Newsletter.

Women's Gay Liberation
577 1/2 North Vermont
Los Angeles 90004

WL Mill Valley
c/o Gloria Sparrow
Mill Valley 94941

WLF
6313 Vicland Place
c/o Denise Warren
North Hollywood 91606

WL One: San Fernando Valley
5530 Corttina Place
c/o Marilee Grazis
North Hollywood 91342

WL
452 60
Oakland 94609

Off the Pedestal
376 Addison
Palo Alto 94301

WL
2492 Carlton Place
c/o Bobbie Wood
Riverside 92507

WLF
PO Box 1507
Riverside 92502

Sacramento WL
2009 N
Sacramento 94704

Sacramento Area WL
1420 22 c/o Christina Saed
Sacramento 95816

San Diego State College
5492 Collete Ave.
San Diego 92115
  WL Organization Center
  Center for Women's Studies
  & Services

Women's Center
120 Brookes Ave.
San Diego 92103

Breakaway
1785 Sutter
San Francisco 94115

California. University. Medical Center. Women's Caucus
c/o 415 Carl, apt. 1
San Francisco 94117

Mother Lode Collective
334 Winfield
San Francisco 94110
    Mother Lode.

WL
3740 25, room 101
San Francisco 94110

WL Orientation Meetings
330 Ellis, at Taylor
San Francisco 94102

WL of San Francisco
1380 Howard   c/o Ellen Ivans
San Francisco 94103
    Newsletter, 333 Chattanooga
    94114

Revolutionary Women's Union
686 South 7
c/o Judy Forrester
San Jose 94113

San Jose WL
22 South 7
c/o Trish Beverly
San Jose 95112

Sherwood Forest Women's
  Collective
210 West 3
Santa Ana 92701

Associated Students, University
  of California: Santa Barbara
c/o Joanne Frankfurt
Santa Barbara 93106
    Beyond the Looking Glass

WL & Peace
PO Box 14308, University of
  California: Santa Barbara
Santa Barbara 93107
    Wildflowers.

Santa Cruz WL
202 Lincoln
Santa Cruz 95080

WL Santa Rosa
740 Mendocino #2
c/o Barbara Hammer
Santa Rosa 95401

Vallejo WL
1821 Magazine   c/o Marilyn
  Herzog
Vallejo 94590

Venice WL
2229 Glencoe   c/o Sheri Cohen
Venice 90291

Colorado
WL of Denver
1151 Boston   c/o Margaret
  Trebbe
Aurora 80010

WL of Boulder
UMC   163 G
Boulder 80302

WLM
1453 Pennsylvania, Suite 17
Denver 80203

Connecticut
WL
148 Orange: Information Center
New Haven 06510

WL
PO Box 18
Storrs 06268

Delaware
WL
500 North Clayton
Wilmington 19804

District of Columbia
D. C. Women's Liberation
Box 13098
T Street Station
Washington, DC 20009
    Literation list.   Office at
    1840 Biltmore N. W.
    #10. 20009.   Women's
    Liberation Health Project.
    Media.

Florida
Gainesville WL
PO Box 13248, University Sta-
tion
Gainesville 32601
    Literature Packet.

WL
PO Box 1313, University Sta-
tion
Gainesville 32601

WL Umbrella
Box 12859, University Station
Gainesville 32601
    8 groups in this area.

FLIRT (Female Liberationists
    for International Rights and
    Territories)
2231 N. E. 34 Court
c/o Ms. Samantha Potter
Lighthouse Point 33064

Tallahassee WL
Box U 6800
Tallahassee 32306
    Has good list of materials.
    Sisters.   Free and Proud.
    Florida State University.

Georgia
Atlanta WL
Box 5432, Station E
Atlanta 30307
    Literature packet.

Great Speckled Bird
PO Box 7946
Atlanta 30309

Women's Center
72 Edgwood Ave.
Atlanta 30303

WL Atlanta
Box 21146, Emory University
c/o Dana Greene
Atlanta 30322

Hawaii
Hawaii WL
PO Box 11042
Honolulu 96814
    Akamai Sister.

Illinois
Chicago WL Center
5406 South Dorchester Ave.
Chicago 60619

Chicago WL Union
2875 West Cermak Road
Chicago 60623
    Has "Everywoman, " a play;
    graphics, literature list,
    Womankind newspaper (7730
    Paulina, 60636).

Grimke-Brown Coalition
40 North Ashland Ave.
Chicago 60607

La Dolores
2150 North Halstead
c/o Northside WL Center
Chicago 60614

University Women's Association,
    Chicago.   See "U" section.

Equal Rights Alliance
5256 Fairmount Ave.
Downers Grove 60515

WL Metro-East
Box 114   c/o Kay Stephens
Edwardsville 62025

Black Maria Collective
Box 230
River Forest 60305

WL Champaign-Urbana
502 West Main
c/o Judy Duchar
Urbana 61801

Indiana
Bloomington WL
414 North Park
Bloomington 47401
   Front Page.

Indianapolis WL
PO Box 88365
Indianapolis 46208

WL
c/o Penny Eastman
Richmond 47394

South Bend WL
1036 North Niles Ave.
South Bend 46617

Iowa
Grinnell WLF
Grinnell College, Box 784
Grinnell 50112

Kansas
Pot Pourri
5503 East Kellogg
Wichita 67218

Witchataw WL
Wichita State University
1845 Fairmont
Wichita 67208

Kentucky
Louisville Women's Liberation
1131 South Brook, apt. 1
Louisville 40203
   Newsletter; Women's Libera-
   tion Library

Louisiana
WL Coalition
Box 4026
New Orleans 70118
   Her Own Right; also 1608
   Milan, apt. 6

New Orleans Women's Center
1024 Jackson Ave., Room 3-4
New Orleans 70130

Maryland
Wildcat Women
PO Box 4729
Baltimore 21211

Women's Center
3028 Greenmount Ave.
Baltimore 21218

WL Maryland
2011 Guilford Ave.
Baltimore 21218
   Women.

Massachusetts
Boston Women United
Box 278
Allston 02134

WL
207 Hampshire House
Amherst 01002
   Connecticut Valley News-
   letter.   University of Mass.
   WL.

Boston Women United
Box 278
Boston 01432
   The Digging Stick newsletter.

Boston WLM
43 Grove
c/o Lillian Robinson
Boxton 02114

Female Liberation
Box 303, Kenore Square P.O.
Boston 02215
   Numerous publications include weekly Newsletter, "No
   More Fun and Games," Second Wave magazine. An
   organization which encompasses all aspects of the
   feminist struggle, including
   education and consciousness-
   raising activities, and action

around such basic demands of
the movement as child care,
abortion, and equal pay. Work
committees are constituted
around various projects. No
woman is excluded.

Cell 16
May be reached at 16 Lexington
Ave.
Cambridge 02138
"a fiercely clannish outpost
of what is nominally called
Female Liberation." (At-
lantic:91 March 1970.)

Harvard Women Organizing
Harvard University
Cambridge 02138

WL Massachusetts
Box 116
Cambridge 02138
Bread and Roses. 20th
century writers who write
about women.

Valley Women's Center
200 Main
Northampton 01060
The Woman's Journal.

Female Liberation
371 Somerville Ave.
Somerville 02143
Female Liberation Journal.

Springfield WLM Group
29 Broad
Springfield 01105
Also 37 Warriner Ave.,
01108.

Woods Hole WL Group
Millfield Street
c/o Nancy Ryan
Woods Hole 02543

Michigan
WL: University of Michigan
Student Activities Building
Ann Arbor 48104
Purple Star journal.

Detroit WL
415 Brainard
Detroit 48201
News & Letters.

WL Coalition of Michigan
2230 Witherell, Room 516
Detroit 48201
Detroit--Ann Arbor--Lansing
area groups.

WL Group
Michigan State University
East Lansing 48823

East Lansing Women
1404 East Oakland
Lansing 48906

WL
Oakland University
Rochester 48063

WL
7 West Ainsworth
c/o Meeropol
Ypsilanti 48197

Minnesota
WL of Duluth
412 North 8 Ave. East
Duluth 55805

Twin Cities Female Liberation
Group
12 Ave. & 4 S.E.
PO Box 1406
University Station
Minneapolis 55414

WL
2418 26 Ave. South
c/o Julie Morse
Minneapolis 55406

Women for Action
c/o Dottie Stumps
Minnetonka 56264

Missouri
WL: Stephens College
Hillcrest Dormitory
Columbia 65201

WL
4934 Forest
Kansas City 54110
    Also 721 West 16, 64108.

WL Union
3800 McGee
Kansas City 64132
    WL Newsletter. Ecstatic
    Umbrella covers Kansas;
    literature packet.

McPherson Community House WL
4487 McPherson
St. Louis 63108

Nameless Group
4155 Magnolia
c/o Liz Frazer
St. Louis 63110

Underground Women
2505 St. Louis Ave.
c/o Kathy Frederick
St. Louis 63106

Women's Center
1411 Locust
St. Louis 63103
    Real Women; a WL News-
    letter.

WL Washington University
6408 Cates   c/o Peggy Hoffman
St. Louis 63130

Montana
WL Discussion Groups
325 East Front #6
c/o Stephanie Henkin
Missoula 59801

Nebraska
Contact Dottie Cohen
1158 Howard
Omaha 68102
    Communal Library.

New Mexico
Southwestern Female Liberation
  Collective
804 Vassar N. E.
Albuquerque 87106
    Also 136 Girard N. E.

New York (State)
Albany and SUNY WL (SUNY =
State University of New York)
c/o SUNY at ALBANY
1400 Washington Ave.
Albany 12203

Bronx High School of Science
  WL Club
75 West 205
Bronx 10468

WL 1
243 Baltic
Brooklyn 11201
    Feelings journal.

Buffalo WL
538 Edward Ave.
Buffalo 14201

Queens Women's Center
153-11 61 Road
Flushing 11367

Women's Center, Cornell Uni-
versity
Willard Straight Hall, Room 25
Ithaca 14850

Alternate U WL Workshop
530 5 Ave.   c/o Lynn Laredo
New York 10036

Barnard College WL
106 McIntosh Student Center
New York 10027

Black Women's Alliance
c/o St. Peter's Church
346 West 20
New York 10011

Columbia (University) WL
Earl Hall
New York 10027

High School WL Coalition
711 Amsterdam Ave.
New York 10025

Lower East Side WL Collective.
    See New York City WL.

The New Woman
245 East Broadway
c/o Marilyn Lorone
New York 10002

New York City WL
509 East 5
New York 10009
   A Feminist Journal.

New York City WL Groups
2700 Broadway at 103, Room 7
New York 10025

New York Radical Feminists.
   See "N" Section

New York Radical Women
799 Broadway, Room 412
New York 10003

New York University Law Students' WL
c/o School of Law, Vanderbilt
   Hall
New York 10017

Older Women's Liberation (OWL)
c/o Women's Center, 36 West
   22
New York 10010
   Founded in 1969, segregating
   "itself on the basis of age
   with the goal of trying to contribute to the movement long
   experience in dealing with the
   likes of marriage, motherhood,
   divorce, spinsterhood and
   homemaking vs paid work.
   Providing a new sense of
   self worth and a new image
   are key objectives" (NOW
   Acts:10, July 1970).

Radical Feminists (or Radical
   Feminism)
PO Box AA, Old Chelsea Station
New York 10011
   "Notes from the First Year
   (1968); "Notes from the Sec-
   ond Year" (1969); "Notes
   from the Third Year" soon.
   A yearly journal.

Radical Lesbians
c/o Women's Center, 36 West 22
New York 10011

Red Women's Detachment
700 East 9
c/o Catherine Henry
New York 10009

Restockings
PO Box 748, Stuyvesant Station
New York 10009
   "Manifesto."

Revolutionary Women's Convention. c/o Women's Liberation Center of New York.

Uptown Women's Center
627 Amsterdam Ave.
New York 10024

WITCH
New York Coven: Box 694,
   Stuyvesant Station
New York 10009
   Covens throughout the world.

Women Health Pac
17 Murray
New York 10007
   Health Pac Bulletin.   Collective.

Women's Action Committee
PO Box 694
New York 10009

WL
PO Box 748, Stuyvesant Station
New York 10009

Women's Liberation Center of
   New York
36 West 22
New York 10010
   Functioning since April 1970
   as a meeting place for all
   women, a clearing house for
   information concerning issues
   vital to women--health, day
   care, abortion, self defense,
   divorce.   Literature col-

lective.   Abortion Project.
Media source.

Women's Liberation 55
40 West 83   c/o Klaus
New York 10024

WL Information Center
Old Westbury 11771

Skidmore WL
Skidmore College
Saratoga Springs 12866

Caucus on Women's Rights at
SUNY (CWRS)
50 Willowbrook c/o Dr. Ann
 Scott
Williamsville 14221
    Women from SUNY's 69
    campuses (largest university
    in the world) adopted above
    official title at first state-
    wide conference, at Syracuse,
    June 1970.

North Carolina
Female Liberation Center
Box 954
Chapel Hill 27514
    Durham--Chapel Hill--
    Raleigh area.

Charlotte Women's Center
1615 Lyndhurst Ave.
Charlotte 28203
    To, For, By and About
    Women newsletter.

Durham Women's Assoc.
1001 Carolina
c/o Liz Conroy
Durham 27705
    Durham North Carolina
    Newsletter.

WL
PO Box 7378, College Station
Durham 28208

High Point Women's Union
610 East Green
High Point 27260
    Newsletter (Box 84).

North Dakota
Minot Women's Collective
PO Box 235
Minot 58701
    North Dakota Women's Lib-
    eration Newsletter.

Ohio
WL
1281 Orlando Ave.   c/o Linda
Hart
Akron 44320

WL
PO Box 20017
Cincinnati 45220

The Outpost
13947 Euclid Ave.
Cleveland 44112
    Cleveland WL; abortion
    counseling.

OSU WL
Ohio State University
Columbus 43210
    OSU WL Newsletter.

WL
1721 Burroughs Dr.
Dayton 45406
    Newsletter.

WL Groups
Ohio Wesleyan University:
Smith Hall
Delaware 43015

Kent State WL
c/o Sociology Department
Kent 44240

WL
Tank Co-op
Oberlin 44074

Black Women United
Box 421
Wilberforde 45384

Women's Center
Antioch Union
Yellow Springs 45387
    Dayton--Cincinnati also.

Oregon
Portland WL
2940 South East Woodward
Portland 97202

Pennsylvania
High School Women
75 High
Philadelphia 19144

Women's Liberation Center
928 Chestnut, 4 floor
Philadelphia 19107
    Newsletter for WL of the area.
    Philadelphia Organization of
    Women for Employment Rights
    (POWER) c/o The Center.
    Awake and Move newspaper;
    also from Box 93, Penllyn
    19422.

Carnegie-Mellon University WL
c/o YWCA, Skibo Hall
Pittsburgh 15213

Pittsburgh Radical Women's
    Union
3107 Kennet Square c/o RISC
Pittsburgh 15213

University of Pittsburgh WL
201 Crump Building, 5 and
    Bigelow
Pittsburgh 15238

Pittsburgh WL
c/o Dept. of Philosophy,
University of Pittsburgh
Pittsburgh 15213

Slippery Rock WL
c/o Dept. of English,
Slippery Rock State College
Slippery Rock 16057

Rhode Island
WL (Umbrella)
50 Olive
Providence 02906
    Providence--Kingston--New-
    port.

Tennessee
Female Liberation of Nashville
Box 12333
Nashville 37312

Texas
WL
Box 7491, University Station
Austin 78712
    Also Box 8011.

Dallas Area WL
3601 Glacier
Garland 75040

Houston Liberation
3723 Quenby Road
c/o Jo Nelson
Houston 77005

University of Houston WL
4136 Anita   c/o Debby Bustin
Houston 77004

WL
2420 15
Lubbock 79401

WL
PO Box 32184
San Antonio 78216

Virginia
Charlottesville WL
508 16 N.W.
c/o Diane Mathiowetz
Charlottesville 23903

Washington (State)
Northwest Feminists
c/o Ann Katherine
Stehekin 98852

Seattle Radical Women
2940 36 South c/o Windoffer
Seattle 98144

WL Seattle Commune
5224 19 N.E.
Seattle 98105
    Abortion pamphlet.

Women's Majority Union
2021 East Lynn
Seattle 98102
   Lilith magazine, Box 1895,
   98111.

Wisconsin
Women's Action Group
306 North Brooks, University
   YWCA
Madison 93715
   Umbrella group

Kaleidoscope
Box 5457
Milwaukee 53711
   Milwaukee Owl.   Witch.

Westside Women's Center
2110 West Wells
Milwaukee 53233

Viet Nam
Viet Nam Women's Union
39 Hang-Chuoi
Hanoi
   Women of Viet Nam journal.

WOMEN'S STUDIES.   A great variety of women's studies programs,
courses, and related activities and services exists.   For information about the concept and some of the programs, contact the institutions themselves and refer to "The Education Index" and "The New
York Times Index."   Articles have appeared in issues of the Chronicle of Higher Education.   The following are some of the institutions
which have recognized this need in one way or another and to vary-
ing degrees.

Barnard College, New York, NY 10027.   212-280-2021.
   Annette Baxter, professor of history/chairman of the subcom-
   mittee on curriculum of the Barnard Committee on Women's
   Studies.
Bryn Mawr College, Bryn Mawr, PA 19010.
   Lila Karp and Kate Millett offered courses in 1971.
California:
   University of California: Irvine.   Irvine 92664.
      Dept. of Comparative Culture.
   University of California Extension: Irvine.
      Programs, lectures, discussion workshops, symposia.
   San Diego State College, College of Arts & Letters, San Diego
   92115.
      Women's Studies Program.   714-286-6524
   San Jose State College, New College, San Jose 95114.
      Margie Bernard.   408-294-6414.
Chicago.   University.   Chicago 60637.
   No program but courses have been offered by Paul Foster (soci-
   ology), Judith Long Laws (psychology), and Jo Freeman (political
   science).
Cornell University.   Female Studies Program, 120 East Rand
   Hall, Ithaca 14850.   607-256-3937.   Jennie Farley, Academic
   coordinator, Female Studies Program.
Goucher College, Baltimore, MD 21204.
   Dr. Alice Rossi (sociology), Ms. Florence Howe (English).

Manhattan College, Manhattan College Parkway & West 242; New
    York Theological Seminary, 235 East 49, New York, NY 10017;
    Union Theological Seminary, Broadway at 120, New York, NY
    10027.
        Dr. Letty M. Russell, 99 Claremont Ave., New York, NY
        10027, #423.   212-662-9785.
Radcliffe Seminars, 3 James, Cambridge, MA 02138.   617-495-8211.
    "Woman's changing role," Janet Giele (1970-1).
St. Catherine College, St. Paul, MN 55105.   612-698-5571.
Sarah Laurence College, Bronxville, NY 10798
    Dr. Gerda Lerner.   Women's Studies program.
Wesleyan University, Middletown, CT 06457
    Dr. Sheila Tobias.

For course lists, contact KNOW.

Part VI

APPENDICES

1. TITLES CONSIDERED IN PART II
(Documentation for Human Equality)

Alternative press index, 1969- .
Quarterly. Alternative press
center. (Bag Service 2500,
Postal Station E, Toronto.)

Alternatives in print; an index
and listing of some movement
publications reflecting today's
social change activities, compiled by the SRRT Task Force
on ABIP (of the American
Library Association). c1971.
(From Office of Educational
Services, Ohio State University libraries, Columbus
43210). 2ed/1972

American men of science, ed.
by the Jaques Cattell Press,
11th ed. 1965-8. R. R.
Bowker Co.

Annual register of grant support. 1969. Academic
media.

Bibliographic index, March
1938- . H. W. Wilson Co.

Biography index; a cumulative
index to biographical ma-
terial in books and maga-
zines, Sept. 1946- . H. W.
Wilson Co.

Book of the states, 1935- .
Biennial. Council of state
governments.

Book review digest, 1905- .
H. W. Wilson Co.

Book review index, 1965- .
Gale research Co.

Books in print, 1948- . R. R.
Bowker Co.

Consumer reports. Monthly.
Consumers' Union of U. S. ,
Inc.

Consumer bulletin. Monthly.
Consumers' research inc.

Cumulative book index; a world
list of books in the English
language. H. W. Wilson Co.

Current biography, 1940- .
H. W. Wilson Co.

Dictionary of American biogra-
phy. 1928-58, 20 vols. ,
Index and Suppl. 1 and 2.
Scribner.

Dictionary of American slang,
by Harold Wentworth and
Stuart B. Flexner. 1960 and
1967 with Suppl. Crowell.

Dictionary of national biography,
edited by Leslie Stephen and
Sidney Lee. Smith, Elder,
1885-1901. 63 vols. and
suppl. in 3 vols. Reissued
1908-9 and since 1922 by
Oxford University Press.

Directory of American scholars,
5th ed. 1969. R. R. Bowker
Co.

Directory of medical specialists, vol. 14/c1970 = "1970-1." Marquis Co.

Document and reference text; an index to minority group employment information. Prepared by the Research Division of the Institute of Labor and Industrial Relations, University of Michigan-- Wayne State University. Produced under contract with the Equal Employment Opportunity Commission. 1967 and 1971 suppl.

Encyclopedia Americana. Encyclopedia Americana Corp.

Encyclopedia of associations, 6th ed. /1970. Gale Research Co.

Familiar quotations, by John Bartlett, 14th ed. rev. and enl., 1968. 13th ed. = Centennial edition/1955. Little. See also " Guide to the use of...."

Foundation directory, 3rd ed., prepared by the Foundation Library Center. 1967. Russell Sage Foundation.

Guide to the use of "Bartlett's Familiar Quotations," by Joseph Mersand. 1962. Little.

Handbook on women workers. 1969 handbook. Bulletin 294. 1969-399-458. Biennial. U.S. Dept. of Labor. Women's Bureau.

How to keep in touch with U.S. Government publications. GPO 1968 0-297-613.

How to use "The Readers' Guide to Periodical Litera-

ture" and other indexes. H. W. Wilson Co.

Index to women, compiled by Norma Olin Ireland. 1970. Faxon Co.

International encyclopedia of the social sciences. c1967. David L. Sills, ed. Macmillan and Free Press.

Libros en venta. 1964 and 2 suppl. --'64-6, 67-8, Ed. by Mary C. Turner. R. R. Bowker Co.

Monthly labor review, vol. 1, July 1915- . Monthly Bureau of Labor Statistics.

Motion pictures and filmstrips. U.S. Library of Congress. (Published as part of the National Union Catalog.) Also: Music and phonorecordings.

National union catalog; a cumulative author list representing Library of Congress printed cards and titles reported by Other American Libraries Monthly with quarterly, annual and quinquennial cumulations. Library of Congress, 1958- .

New York Times Index, Sept. 1851- . New York Times, since 1913.

Official Congressional directory, 1809- . GPO.

Price lists (series). U.S. Supt. of documents.

Publishers' trade list annual, 1873- . R. R. Bowker Co.

Readers' guide to periodical literature, 1900- . H. W.

Wilson Co., since 1905.
See also "How to use 'The
Readers' Guide to Periodical
Literature' and other indexes."

Selected United States Government publications, July 11,
1928- . U.S. Supt. of
documents.

Statistical abstract of the United
States, 1879- . U.S. Bur-
eau of the census. 91st ed./
1970.

Subject guide to "Books in Print"
1957- . R.R. Bowker Co.

United States Government organization manual, 1935- .
U.S. national archives and
records service.

Who's who in America; a biographical dictionary of notable living men and women.
1899/1900- . Marquis Co.

Who's who of American women;
a biographical dictionary of
notable living American women, 6th ed., 1970/71.
Marquis Co.

World almanac & book of facts,
1868- . Annual. New York
World-Telegram.

World bibliography of bibliographies, 4th ed., 1965-6.
Comp. by Theodore Bester-
man. Societas bibliographica.

3. RELEVANT OUT-OF-PRINT TITLES

Source material of the Woman's Movement and historical studies by and about women are often out of print ("OP"). In addition, there are many recent relevant titles which publishers have apparently had to allow to go out of print, and still others which have not been made available in the United States. Reprint publishers are now an active part of the American publishing industry; when titles have not been reprinted, however, University Microfilms can sometimes provide a copy. As a final resort, a needed OP book can usually be obtained on an inter-library loan for you by your librarian. All titles listed are in the Library of Congress unless otherwise indicated.

American woman's association.
Women workers through the depression, a study of white collar employment..., Lorine Pruette, ed. Macmillan, 1934.

Anthony, Rey (pseud.)
The housewife's handbook for promiscuity. Tucson: Seymour Press, 1960. (Not in LC; in Univ. of Oregon.)

Aristophanes.
Lysistrata; an English version by Dudley Fitts. Harcourt, 1954.

Beauvoir, Simone de
Force of circumstance. Putnam, c1965.

Berry, Jane, et al.
Counseling girls and women; awareness, analysis, action. University of Missouri at Kansas City Press. Prepared for Missouri Dept. of Labor and Industrial Relations, March 1966. L7. 2:C83/4 0-264-469. (ERIC #=Ed 018-558.)

Benedek, Therese Friedmann, 1892-
Psychosexual functions in women. Ronald Press, c1952.

Blake, Judith
Family structure in Jamaica; the social context of reproduction. Free Press, c1961.

Blanshard, Paul
The right to read; the battle against censorship. Beacon Press, c1955.

Borgese, Elizabeth Mann
Ascent of woman. Braziller, 1963.

Brittain, Vera Mary
Lady into woman; a history of women from Victoria to Elizabeth II. Macmillan, c1953.

Calverton, Victor Francis, 1900-1940.
Sex in civilization. Macaulay, c1929. (University Microfilms OP 19813.)

Chesser, Eustace, 1902-
Live and let live; the moral of the Wolfenden Report. Foreword by Sir John Wolfenden.

Philosophical Library, 1958.

Esquire (magazine)
All about women, ed. by
Saul Maloff. Harper & Row,
c1963.

Furness, Clifton Joseph, ed.
The genteel female; an anthology. Knopf, 1931. (University Microfilms OP 19473.)

Glasgow, Ellen Anderson
Gholson, 1874-1945.
They stooped to folly; a
comedy of morals. Doubleday,
c1929.

Greene, Gael
Sex and the college girl.
Dial, c1964.

Himelhock, Herome and Sylvia
Fleis Fava, eds.
Sexual behavior in American
society; an appraisal of the first
two Kinsey reports. Norton,
c1955.

Irwin, Inez Haynes (or Hayes)
Angels and Amazons; a
hundred years of American women. Doubleday, 1933.

――――――.
Up hill with banners flying--
the story of the Woman's Party.
National Woman's Party, 1964.
Also Traversity Press (Penob-
scot, Me.).

Johnson, Nora (Mrs. Leonard
Siwek)
A step beyond innocence.
Little Brown, c1961.

Kendall, Elaine.
The upper hand; the truth
about American men. Little,
Brown, 1965.

Klein, Viola
The feminine character; his-

tory of an ideology. London:
Paul Kegan, c1948.

Komarovsky, Mirra (Mrs. Mar-
cus Heyman)
Women in the modern world;
their education and their dilemmas. Little, Brown, c1953.

Kronhausen, Phyllis, 1929-
Sex histories of American college men. Ballantine books,
1960.

Levine, Lena, M.D. and David
Loth
The emotional sex; why wo-
men are the way they are today.
Morrow, c1964.

Lewis, Joseph, 1889-
The bible unmasked. Free-
thought Pub. Co., c1926.
(1940 = 16th ed.?)

Lundberg, Ferdinand, 1902- ,
and Marynia L. F. (Foor?)
Farnham, M.D.
... Modern woman: the lost
sex. Harper, c1947.

Manette, Jan, pseud.
The working girl in a man's
world; a guide to office politics.
Hawthorn, c1966.

Mason, Otis Tufton, 1838-1908.
Woman's share in primitive
culture. Appleton, 1894, 1924?
Anthropological series, ed. by
F. Starr, 1.

Merriam, Eve
After Nora slammed the
door; American women in the
1960's: the unfinished revolution. World, 1964.

――――――.
The double bed from the
feminine side. Marzani &
Munsell, c1958.

Meyer, Annie Nathan, 1867- ,
ed.
    Woman's work in America.
H. Holt, 1891.

Mortimer, Penelope
    The pumpkin eater. Mc-
Graw, c1962.

National American Woman Suffrage Assoc.
    Victory, how the women won
it; a centennial symposium,
1840-1940. H. W. Wilson, 1940.
(University Microfilms OP49496.)

Newcomer, Mabel, 1891-
    A century of higher educa-
tion for American women.
Harper, c1959.

O'Brien, Edna
    The country girls. New
American Library, 1965. (In
Kent State University Library.)

_____.
    The lonely girl. London:
J. Cape, 1962.

O'Neill, Eugene Gladstone,
1888-1953.
    Lost plays (contents: Abor-
tion, The movie man, The
sniper, Servitude, Wife for a
life). New Fathoms, c1950.

Parker, Dorothy Rothschild,
1893-1967, and Arnaud d'Usseau
    The ladies of the corridor;
a drama in two acts.... S.
French, c1952.

Perutz, Kathrin
    The garden. Atheneum, 1962.

Pruette, Lorine, 1896-
    Women and leisure; a study
of social waste. Dutton, c1924.

Roe, Dorothy
    The trouble with women is
men. Prentice-Hall, c1961.

Russell, Mrs. Dora Winifred
Black
    Hypathia; or, Woman and
knowledge. Dutton, c1925.

Scheinfeld, Amram, 1897-
    Women and men. Harcourt,
1944.

Schmalhausen, Samuel Daniel,
1896-
    Woman's coming of age; a
symposium. Liveright, c1931.

Sherman, Susan
    Give me myself. World,
1961.

Spencer, Anna Garlin, 1851-
1931.
    Woman's share in social cul-
ture, 2nd ed. Lippincott,
c1925.

Stern, Madeline Bettina
    We the women; career firsts
of nineteenth century America.
Schulte, c1962.

Stevens, Doris, 1892-
    Jailed for freedom. Boni
& Liveright, c1920.

Syrett, Netta
    Portrait of a rebel. Dodd,
Mead, 1930.

Wood, Ethel Mary Hogg
    Mainly for men. London:
V. Gollancz, 1943.

Young, Agnes Brooks, 1898-
    Women and the crisis; wo-
men of the North in the Civil
War, by Agatha Young (pseud.).
McDowell, Obolensky, 1959.

4. DICTIONARY USE

The use of slang to deal with women has been pointed out. It is also important to understand words in general American-English usage. A dictionary should be on every woman's desk--at home and at her place of employment. Currently-available abridged word-books include:

American college dictionary. Random.
Thorndike-Barnhart comprehensive desk dictionary, rev. ed. by Clarence L. Barnhart. Doubleday.
Webster's new world dictionary of the American language (various editions). World.
Webster's 7th new collegiate dictionary [based on Webster's 3rd new international dictionary]. Merriam.

For starters, test yourself on contemporary, and sometimes historical, usage of the following words and terms. Be sure you can distinguish between words listed in pairs as well as their interrelationships:

slang/jargon/taboo/colloquial-
  ism
bias/prejudice/indoctrination
alimony/child-support
subject-heading
policy
professional/amateur
parthenogenesis
obstetrics/gynecology
VD/gonorrhea/syphillis
frigidity/impotence
perjury
nag
psychologist/psychiatrist/
  counsellor
psychoanalysis/psychotherapy
feminist/suffragette
copyright/patent
profession/occupation
complement/supplement
rape/assault
tranquilizer/barbiturate
fertility/sterility
libel/slander
martyr
abortion/miscarriage

masochism/narcissism/sadism
anulment/divorce/separation
chauvinism/male chauvinism
concubine/mistress
gynacium
machismo
miscegenation
misogynist
obscenity/pornography
orgasm
prostitute/call girl
sequestration
suttee
vasectomy/hysterectomy
ego/id
paranoid/schizophrenic
neurosis/psychosis
out of print/in print
cumulation/accumulation
comprehensive/selective
paraprofessional/clerical
eunuch
transvestite
fornication/adultery/infidelity
bigamy/cohabitation/common
  law marriage

womb /uterus
gonad /pituitary
Lilith
agnation
androgynous
clitoroidectomy
defloration /hymen
heterosexual /homosexual
masturbation
desertion
mullah
onus
patriarchy /matriarchy
purdah
slavery /caste
vagina /cervix
mastectomy
birth control / Planned Parent-
    hood /contraception
sodomy /Sodom
emasculation /castration
necrology
retrospective /current
contingent /adjunct
chimera
gynolatry
misandrism
diaphragm
adopt
estrogen /progesterone
Eros

5. AUDIO-VISUAL RESOURCES: Late Additions

See main section, beginning on page 219, to which the following entries are last-minute additions. On that page appears also a key to abbreviations.

A to B (mo pic)
Nell Cox (50 W 87, New York, NY 10024).
1970 36min C
Adolescent in contemporary society: documentary of white middle-class girl.

Abortion: Public issue or private matter (mo pic)
NBC 1971 25min R$13/3 days

Anything you want to be (mo pic)
New Day Film (267 W 25, New York, NY 10001).
1971 7min Liane Brandon, film-maker
Society's subtle indoctrination of women.

As long as the rivers run (mo pic)
American Documentary 1972 60min C
S$650 R$60 Filmed by Carol Burns.
American Indian women strong central characters.

The black woman (mo pic)
NET 1971 52min
Indiana University R$12.25/1-5 days
Discussion and entertainment; poet Nikki Giovanni, singer Lena Horne, Bibi Amina Baraka and others discuss the role of black women in contemporary society and the problems they confront.

But first this message (mo pic)
Action for Children's TV C 15min R$25 S$100
Analysis of what's on commercial TV for children, reactions from children themselves. Kit accompanies.

Doll's House (mo pic)
Part 1: Destruction of Illusion 33min R$22
Part 2: Ibsen's Themes 28min R$21
1968 C Univ. of Calif. Extension Media Center, Berkeley. Prof. Norris Houghton of Vassar, comments. Scenes from one of Ibsen's

best known plays here set in a modern suburban home.

The encounter (mo pic)
Perennial   10min   1971
An "almost" boy-girl relationship.

The fat fighters (mo pic)
Brigham Young Univ. Dept. of Motion Picture
Prod. (Provo, Utah 84601) 1971 20min C

Help Wanted-Women need apply (slides)
61 slides with script.   From Jim Farron, Dallas Regional Ofc.,
Civil Service Commission Dallas, TX.   S$20.
Designed to be shown to high school and college classes and
women's clubs, shows women in a variety of jobs.

Hunger (mo pic)
Perennial 1972? 20min

I am somebody (mo pic)
McGraw 1970 28min C
Black women take on the establishment.

It happens to us (mo pic)
New Day (267 W 25, New York, NY 10001
1971   30min   C
Women discuss their abortion experiences.

Katie's lot (mo pic)
Univ. of Calif. Extension Media Center, Berkeley.   1961.
C 18min R$23
Tomboy Katie's world is shattered when she must shed her jeans
for a party dress.

Lamps in the work place (mo pic)
Dept. of Labor Wage & Hour Division Information Ofc.
C 28min
Case study approach to the Equal Pay Act.

Never underestimate the power of a woman (mo pic)
Norma Briggs with a Dept. of Labor grant.
Walter Mieves, Dept. of Photography & Cinema, 45 N. Charter,
Madison, Wisc. 53715.   1971 15min C R$12.50 S$125.
Discusses myths and facts about working women.   Designed for
adults, it shows women in a variety of non-stereotypical blue-
collar jobs.

Something different (mo pic)
Grove Press 1963 65min R$100 S$400 #405
By Vera Chytilova.   Czech with English subtitles.
The dilemma of modern woman.

Three grandmothers (mo pic)
Univ. of Calif. Extension Media Center, Berkeley.   1963   28min
R$14
A glimpse into the lives of 3 grandmothers--a Nigerian (Muslim),
a Canadian (Protestant), and a Brazilian (Catholic).

Try it--you'll like it! (record album)
Pat Harrison and Robin Tyler   LP   Dore label
First feminist comedy team LP.   Laughs with feminism, not at it.

What's the matter with Alice?
Civil Service Commission   1972   C   30min
Newsfilms, USA (21 W 46, New York, NY 10036)   S$225

A woman in that job? (slides)
Women's Bureau   1971   C   Slides with script.   30min
Directed toward employers, their affirmative action plans and
showing them how to reengineer positions to encourage women to
apply.

Woman is the nigger of the world (rec)
Written, recorded by John Lennon and Yoko Ono.
Apple Label.   Co-producer Phil Spector.

Women's Lib--From What? For What? (mo pic)
Association--Sterling Films (866 3 Ave., New York, NY 10022)
30min   R$10   S$130
Prepared as a TV program with panelists Marya Mannes, Jac-
queline Grennan Wexler, Pauli Murray, Charlotte Bunch-Weeks and
Helen Southard, under auspices of the YWCA, deals with entrenched
discrimination, the media, child care, the black woman.

Women's Liberation (tapes)
San Francisco Women's Media Group   5 WL tapes running from 15-
30min $4 each
Topics include abortion, male chauvinism, small groups, sexism.

The X-Factor: Women as people (video tape)
ETV Center, Cornell University (Van Renesselaer Hall, Ithaca, NY
14850)   1" video tape, 30min   R$15.
Two half-hour programs on the status and image of women, developed for a course at Cornell.